FASCINATION

F A S C I N A T I O N

Faulkner's Fiction, 1919-1936

M I C H E L   G R E S S E T

Adapted from the French by Thomas West

Duke University Press   Durham and London   1989

© 1989 Duke University Press
All rights reserved
Printed in the United States of America
on acid-free paper ∞
Library of Congress Cataloging-in-Publication Data
appear on the last printed page of this book.

Had-One-Brother:

Claude Richard

1934–1988

CONTENTS

Part Five   The Absolute Relationship

ABBREVIATIONS

AA	*Absalom, Absalom!* (1936)
AA, CT	*Absalom, Absalom!,* the corrected text, ed. Noel Polk (1987)
Achievement	*The Achievement of William Faulkner,* Michael Millgate (1965)
AGB	*A Green Bough* (1933)
AILD	*As I Lay Dying* (1930)
AILD, CT	*As I Lay Dying: The Corrected Text,* ed. Noel Polk (1987)
AL	Alderman Library, University of Virginia
Appendix	Appendix "1699–1945. The Compsons," *Portable*
B&N	*Being and Nothingness,* Jean-Paul Sartre (1943)
Career	*The Literary Career of William Faulkner,* James B. Meriwether (1961)
CS	*Collected Stories of William Faulkner* (1950)
DrM	*Doctor Marino and Other Stories* (1934)
Elmer	*William Faulkner: Elmer,* ed. James B. Meriwether (1981)
End	*The End of American Innocence,* Henry F. May (1964)
EP&P	*William Faulkner: Early Prose and Poetry,* ed. Carvel Collins (1962)
ESPL	*William Faulkner: Essays, Speeches and Public Letters,* ed. James B. Meriwether (1966)
FA	*William Faulkner: Father Abraham,* ed. James B. Meriwether (1983)
FAB	*Faulkner: A Biography,* Joseph Blotner (1974)

FAB (1984)	*Faulkner: A Biography*, Joseph Blotner, one-volume edition, revised, updated, condensed (1984)
Fable	*A Fable* (1954)
FACCE	*William Faulkner: A Collection of Critical Essays*, ed. Robert Penn Warren (1966)
FFCP	*The Four Fundamental Concepts of Psycho-Analysis*, Jacques Lacan (1973)
File	*The Faulkner-Cowley File*, Malcolm Cowley (1966)
FITU	*Faulkner in the University*, eds. Joseph Blotner and Frederick Gwynn (1965)
Flags	*William Faulkner: Flags in the Dust*, ed. Douglas Day (1973)
GDM	*Go Down, Moses* (1942)
HAM	*The Hamlet* (1940)
Intertexuality	*Intertexuality in Faulkner*, eds. Michel Gresset and Noel Polk (1985)
LIA	*Light in August* (1932)
LIA, CT	*Light in August: The Corrected Text*, ed. Noel Polk (1987)
LITG	*Lion in the Garden: Interviews with Faulkner, 1926–1962*, eds. James B. Meriwether and Michael Millgate (1968)
MAR	*William Faulkner: The Marionettes*, ed. Noel Polk (1977)
MFS	*Modern Fiction Studies*
Miscellany	*A Faulkner Miscellany*, ed. James B. Meriwether (1974)
MOS	*Mosquitoes* (1927)
MQ	*The Mississippi Quarterly*
NOS	*William Faulkner: New Orleans Sketches*, ed. Carvel Collins (1958, new ed. 1968)
Novels	*The Novels of William Faulkner*, Olga W. Vickery (1959, new ed. 1964)
Novels 30–35	*William Faulkner, Novels 1930–1935*, Library of America, eds. Joseph Blotner and Noel Polk (1985)
Portable	*The Portable Faulkner*, ed. Malcolm Cowley (1946, new ed. 1967)

PYL	*Pylon* (1935)
PYL, CT	*Pylon: The Corrected Text*, ed. Noel Polk (1987)
REQ	*Requiem for a Nun* (1951)
SAN	*Sanctuary* (1931)
SAN, CT	*Sanctuary: The Corrected Text*, ed. Noel Polk (1987)
SAR	*Sartoris* (1929)
SL	*Selected Letters of William Faulkner*, ed. Joseph Blotner (1977)
SP	*Soldiers' Pay* (1926)
STOT	*William Faulkner, Sanctuary: The Original Text*, ed. Noel Polk (1981)
TMF	*The Marble Faun* (1924)
3 Decades	*William Faulkner: Three Decades of Criticism*, ed. F. J. Hoffman and O. W. Vickery (1960)
TSATF	*The Sound and the Fury* (1929)
TSATF (ML)	*The Sound and the Fury*, Modern Library edition (1946)
TSATF, CT	*The Sound and the Fury: The Corrected Text*, ed. Noel Polk (1987)
TI3	*These Thirteen* (1931)
TOWN	*The Town* (1957)
TWP	*The Wild Palms* (1939)
UNV	*The Unvanquished* (1938)
US	*Uncollected Stories of William Faulkner*, ed. Joseph Blotner (1979)
Vocabulaire	*Vocabulaire de la psychanalyse*, Jean Laplanche and Jean-Bertrand Pontalis (1968)
Yoknapatawpha	*William Faulkner: The Yoknapatawpha Country*, Cleanth Brooks (1963)

ACKNOWLEDGMENTS

Early drafts of Part I of this book have appeared in *The Southern Literary Journal, Sud,* and *Le Magazine littéraire.* Under somewhat different form chapter 11 was published in *Tropismes,* chapter 13 partly in *RANAM* and partly in *Etudes anglaises,* and chapter 14 in both *Faulkner and Idealism* and *L'Arc.*

I wish to express my gratitude to Professor Thomas West for the elegance with which he has performed the painstaking labor of translation and to Professor Patrick Samway, S. J., for his remarkably scrupulous reading of the manuscript.

Beyond that, my thanks are due to all those, persons and institutions, who over the years have facilitated my access to the Faulkner materials: the Harkness Foundation, the American Council of Learned Societies, the Franco-American Commission for Cultural and Educational Exchanges, and the staff of the Alderman Library at the University of Virginia (particularly Anne Freudenberg and Joan St. C. Crane). Above all, I wish to express my gratitude to William Faulkner's daughter, Mrs. Paul D. Summers, Jr.

My thanks are also due to all those who, for a quarter of a century, in the United States and elsewhere (in France, in England, in Spain, in Germany, in Italy, or in Japan) have been keen on sharing their views with me and shown a real interest in the French Face of Faulkner.

Fascination is a book that demonstrates the strange way in which literature arises out of the action of imagination and emotion on experience. Michel Gresset approaches the subtle and perverse psychology of creation with resourcefulness and without dogmatism. His portrait of William Faulkner, the man, enhances our understanding of his work in the same way as the account of the oeuvre sheds light on the behavior of the homo faber, the penitent and impotent brother of homo sapiens or Everyman.

Literary criticism seems to oscillate periodically between the cults of personality and of production, between positivistic deflation (and Romantic magnification) of the man and disinterested, Olympian scrutiny of the text. Few scholars have succeeded in bridging these two extremes, because to do this it is necessary to write with an equal respect for life and for letters and to push literature into the bigger—psychological and existential—picture. What one takes away from reading *Fascination* (from reading the whole book, it must be stressed) is the fruit of the middle way. In everyday life, after all, literature is a minor activity. And yet, as a symptom, it is universal insofar as it answers the pang or the urge that every human feels and must cope with. Professor Gresset's book moves critical debate away from the recent enthusiasm for structure and type (and the naive textual interpretations this generated) back in the direction of biography. Not, of course, the biography of dates and laundry tickets, but the biography of the psyche which, as he argues, is better thought of in terms of space and emotion than of time.

Fascination is constructed with the logic of intuition. As sometimes in reading Carl Jung, one feels in this book that the world has been turned upside down or is being surveyed from a strange new perspective. The book's curiously nonobjective (or nonconventional) approach was what set

Faulkner ou la fascination apart when it was published in 1982. In clarifying Faulkner's work and work process Professor Gresset made his mythopoeic transformations more palpable. There was no tearing away of the veil. Nonetheless, the temple was unlocked.

This English version is both more and less than a translation. It is an extensive revision (always carried out by the author) and a simplification of a manner of thinking and of imagining which, carried over literally, would have done no justice at all to the original. The style of the French was, in fact, very much a part of a deeply subjective imaginary construction. In opting for chasteness the translation aims merely to pass unperceived. Much of the personality and suggestiveness of the original has, however, been lost, and the reader should bear this in mind.

Thomas West
Paris, Autumn 1987

The Original Gaze

The Origins of the Gaze

There never was any forbidden fruit. Only temptation is
divine.—*André Breton, L'Amour fou*

"In order to seduce Eve the devil used the sexual *organs* of the serpent."
This is Samuel de Saci's gloss of the third chapter of Genesis.[1] The French
Hellenist Bailly defines the Greek word *organon,* a cognate of the word
ergon, thus: "I: An instrument, particularly: 1 an instrument used at work,
a tool. 2 an engine of war. 3 a musical instrument. 4 a bodily organ. 5 a
material one works on. 6 in the plural, linguistic forms, special aspects of
style. II: A work, an *oeuvre.*"[2]

The word *organ* reveals a wealth of meanings, which may reflect the
ambiguity of language and of linguistic forms in general. Where does this
suggestive word lead us? Directly to an intriguing relationship between the
notion of work, or even that of function, and the notion of appearance. The
association may conjure up a kind of decorativeness that is often referred to
as the baroque. Insofar as it is a periodic phenomenon and a recurrent mode
in art, the idea of the baroque is a particularly serviceable one for describing
the relationship between work and appearance.

Since an organ is "adapted for the performance of some specific function,"[3] what can the raison d'être, the etiology, of the organ be? Is it not,
precisely, to transform being into appearance? And does this function or
"performance" not involve a displaying of desire—in the sense that the
organ is desire itself? Is not the organ fundamentally that which transforms
a mute, bare world into its own image? It is no coincidence that the word
organ is most often used in association with sight and speech, because both
the eye and the mouth are the favorite media not only of sexual desire (itself,

of course, the master of the ultimate organ), but also of a kind of aesthetic desire associated with the exhibitionism of the baroque.[4]

In order to seduce it is in my interest that my eye or my voice display desire and that this display be registered or acknowledged. Otherwise, my desire is confined to its own impulse (as in the case of the voyeur or may erupt brutally (as in rape, or theft, its cousin). In both cases a transgression is committed against a normal, healthy relationship with the object which, though forbidden, nonetheless tantalizes the eye. But in terms of perverted (or sublimated) sexual desire it is precisely this transgression that gratifies. The eye is the favorite organ for beckoning, for inviting, for connivance. Each language has its treasury of words that refer to this subtle activity, and English, with its peeps and winks and stolen glances, is no exception. The eye, however, is not really an organ of gratification, but rather one of substitution. It is a vicarious organ, at best portentous, at worst frustrating. Always a proxy, its true principal master is desire.

The internalization of moral values, typical of Christian theology and, more generally, of the Judeo-Christian tradition, has generated a *psychology of the gaze*. If the devil manipulates the organ of the serpent, or manipulates the serpent as an organ, in order to seduce Eve, it is because he is aware of the corrupting power of the reptile's eye and of the sense of expectation that it nurtures in Eve. The devil knows, of course, that nakedness in itself is more a form of austerity than of eroticism—unless it is peeped at, preferably out of the corner of the eye. This is precisely what he arranges for Adam to do to Eve. Before the Fall, Adam was innocent and Eve was naked but did not know it. Paradise was beautiful, but it was not alluring.

If in theological terms the Fall results from temptation, in phenomenological terms it proceeds from perception, from sight (the Fall enthroned the eye as the ruling sensual organ).[5] After the Fall, unmediated, flagrant desire is replaced by self-conscious looking: a knowing gaze, a desirous, calculating glance. One may imagine that, without such a gaze, the world that God created would exist—an unknown, unlooked at world. There is no space since no glance exists to covet it. There is no history, unless it be a history of happiness, which, from my point of view, is no history at all.

Before the Fall, Adam and Eve "were both naked, the man and his wife, and were not ashamed."[6] Indeed, why should they be ashamed, since their organs had not yet begun to function? The serpent informed Eve clearly of the consequences of active organs when he predicted to her that "your eyes shall be opened, and ye shall be as gods, knowing good and evil" (Gen. 3:5). Then "the woman saw that the tree was good for food, and that it was pleasant to the eyes, and a tree to be desired to make one wise" (3:6). Eve, looking at the apple, ushered in the era of desire: "she took the fruit thereof, and did eat, and gave also unto her husband with her; and he did eat" (3:6). Desire begins and ends in the transition from glance to action, just as consummation reflects a transition from action to communion.

"And the eyes of them both were opened, and they knew they were naked" (3:7). This is hardly surprising since now, at last, they *saw* each other. But how sad it must have been for them to cover their loins with fig leaves! The reason for their shame was, of course, that their gratification was being coveted all along by the jealous eye of the ubiquitous Voyeur, Who in the following outburst—the turning point of the whole story— makes Himself known: "And they heard the voice of the Lord God walking in the garden in the cool of day: and Adam and his wife hid themselves. . . . And he said, Who told thee that thou wast naked?" (3:8–11).

If Paradise before the Fall was glorious with both happiness and ennui, it was because there was no playacting or playgoing—save for what God Himself was disposed to see. God was the only spectator and His was the only mise en scène. Everything changed with the Fall.

A glance leads to the sin of lust just as eating leads to the sin of gluttony. On the one hand, man is seduced away from the Good, *seductio* being "the act of placing apart, separation." On the other hand, man is tempted by Evil, *temptatio* being "an attack or a suffering due to sickness."[7] The opposite of seduction is repugnance. The opposite of temptation ("a drive that leads towards sin and evil in awakening desire"[8]) is plain indifference. Like health, goodness might be thought of simply as the normal working or activity of the organs. The fact remains nonetheless that the gaze leads to sin, to what André Breton calls "that vile Christian notion of sin."[9] In *L'Amour fou* Breton tried to reclaim man's natural right to look, to gaze, in defiance of the way in which "God's staggering stare" had destroyed the autonomy of man's senses.

Thus the very mission that the organs were created to accomplish led directly to censure, expulsion, and then to cosmic punishment. Man came into his own as a result of an act—the paradigm of all acts, the sexual act: "And Adam knew Eve his wife; and she conceived, and bare Cain" (4:1). History began.

History began, and history will end. Christianity has its Book of Origins, Genesis, just as it has its Book of Endings. Revelation is the last reckoning, the disclosure, the final uncovering of truth, the reestablishment of the sovereignty of the divine gaze and, along with it, the end of the rule of appearances, of baroque surfaces. In the meantime—our time here below—the reign of "ontological separation" continues.[10] The divine gaze, having abandoned the world to human glances, abides somewhere far away from the anarchy in which appearances continue to seduce the organs.

From such a perspective Christian teleology sends us back ultimately to an etiology. The secrets of all things, of all appearances, have some relationship with the Fall and Revelation—at least for writers who, like Faulkner, never stop writing glosses on Genesis.

The Back Country

"Mississippi Hills: My Epitaph," "Carcassonne"

It is my aim, and every effort bent, that the sum and history
of my life, which in the same sentence is my obit and my
epitaph too, shall be them both: He made the books and he
died.—*William Faulkner to Malcolm Cowley*

It is over twenty years now since I discovered the 2,000 or so manuscript
pages, together with six times as many typewritten pages, in the Faulkner
collection of the Alderman Library at the University of Virginia. Later, I
went on to study the smaller, though in some ways equally valuable,
collection of the University of Texas at Austin. Recently, the acquisition of
the "Rowan Oak papers" has put Oxford, Mississippi, on the map of
scholarly staging posts for whoever wants to understand the making of a
writer who, with disarming self-regard, wrote in August 1953: "Damn it, I
did have genius, Saxe [Commins]. It took me 55 years to find out. I suppose
I was too busy working to notice it before."[1] After reading the 148 sheets of
the autograph manuscript of *The Sound and the Fury*, as James B. Meriwether,[2] Michael Millgate,[3] and very few others had done before me, I
became convinced that nothing could be known with certainty about the
mystery of Faulkner's literary creation unless one became acquainted with
the nearly hieroglyphic calligraphy of the early manuscripts. I wrote at the
time, and still believe today, that the true Faulkner is to be found, if
anywhere, in his manuscripts.

By "Faulkner" I meant a man known—to me—only through texts, a
mysterious, somewhat transcendent persona who added a "u" to his name
and whom, in France at any rate, fame had even deprived of a Christian
name, as if the division (he so insisted on) between the man and his work
had not been enough: the anonymous author of nineteen novels—several of

which are among this century's greatest literary achievements—of a hundred or so short stories, of numerous poems and letters, of a few speeches and a few essays.

In a first attempt to understand "Faulkner," which now seems to me oddly antiquated as well as ambitious in a naive sort of way, I made a point of looking for everything that—in the writer's youth, in the sociocultural background, and more generally in what is called the zeitgeist—could cause him to become what he became. I had only begun my research and had no idea of the dimensions it would assume. In other words, I had no other aim than to cover the ground of Faulkner's works in general: no more, no less. My only "program" consisted in debunking what I felt was an all too French image of Faulkner, as *écrivain maudit,* perhaps too hastily drawn under the powerful influence of such great and familiar heralds as André Malraux, Jean-Paul Sartre, and Albert Camus.[4]

Paradoxically, however, I had no leads to pursue, since I began by scrutinizing a period (prior to 1919, when Faulkner published his first literary piece) during which Faulkner wrote nothing that could justify any interest in him as a writer: he was only a future writer. Although traditional, this approach soon turned out to be more absurd than innocent. In particular it assumed two falsehoods since it consisted in viewing the career in reverse, forcing me to end where the writer, by virtue of some innate urge to write, had started; it also consisted in supposing the individual and his culture to be like communicating vessels: as one empties, the other must fill. Although most critical schools, especially when they are blatantly ideological, assume that a writer must be a reflection of something—be it society in general, a single class, a crucial period in history, a family situation, or yet a psychological case—it is nevertheless true, and of paramount importance, that "writing entails above all an exorbitant self-interest."[5] The key word here is not "self-interest," but "exorbitant."

To a certain extent it is now possible to say that the writer in question became, retrospectively and, as it were, apologetically (that is, as if he felt, somehow, that he had to make up for this exorbitant self-interest) conscious of this when he wrote the following, well-known rejoinder to Malcolm Cowley: "It is my ambition to be, as a private individual, abolished and voided from history, leaving it markless, no refuse save the printed books; I wish I had had enough sense to see ahead thirty years ago and, like some of the Elizabethans, not signed them. It is my aim, and every effort bent, that the sum and history of my life, which in the same sentence is my obit and my epitaph too, shall be them both: He made the books and he died" (SL, 285). Thus, in a way, I found myself with a conclusion all the more negative as it is a mere truism to say that there is nothing to discover in a writer before he has written.

I had made a few discoveries, however—for example, from reading the local press of the time in the Oxford courthouse—such as the unbelievable state of innocence in which Faulkner lived for the first twenty years of his life, an innocence from which he and his fellow Southerners (like most Americans) awoke only with the advent of the First World War: "War Has Been Declared/America's Sweet Liberty is Now at Stake."[6]

There was "the cardboard placard hanging above the stove in her kitchen . . . on which she [Faulkner's mother] had written in red paint in her neat, clear brush strokes, 'Don't Complain—Don't Explain.'"[7] Should one put a high value on this double prohibition? Should one speak of trauma and trace its roots back into the puritanism that critics have often assumed to be in Faulkner? I, for one, would rather begin by dismissing such an assumption about Faulkner's puritanism as an unhelpful cliché. I would distinguish, on the one hand, between an extreme kind of idealism in which one can see the original impulse behind the desire to write at all and, on the other, a certain stoicism that soon became associated with a key value in Faulkner's books.

Methodologically, however, was it sound or even responsible to assume that either quality (idealism and stoicism) could come out of the kitchen, as it were, in a straight line? Not that the kitchen is a contemptible place, far from it; but in the case of a writer of this magnitude it seemed to me that such influences deserved only modest regard. This is so true that in the beginning, as Faulkner well knew, a writer's first duty is to get rid of all influences so as to allow oneself to grow unhindered.[8] As for the possible influence of the state of innocence in which the prewar Deep South lay even more completely than did the rest of America, it may well be that Faulkner's idealism, instead of being a product of the culture, in fact ran counter to the pragmatic goals of his age.

One should not forget that the writer spent the first twenty years of his life in the quiet backwater of a country where the spirit of the nineteenth century ran unchecked well into the twentieth. On the one hand, one finds the widespread optimism of what Henry F. May has called "the prewar mixture of exuberant innovation, cheerful mysticism, insistent spontaneity, and certainty that everything was turning out superbly."[9] On the other hand, there is, as always in a budding writer, the self-delusion (self-absorption or its extreme, solipsism) that seems to flaunt the fact that the ego does not exist, let alone develop, outside of history.

Indeed, through his now well-known poses (bohemian and dandy, later airman and hunter, then "farmer")[10] the young Faulkner contrived to deny reality so obstinately as to make important choices not just with reference to the ideal, but in total subservience to it. I shall cite only a few examples of such poses that later shaped his ideal self. One is the fact that Faulkner always liked to see himself as a vagabond.[11] This pose can be traced back to his own brief *Wanderjahr* and to his postwar preference for not settling down; but how can one fail to establish a relationship between this tendency and the presence of so many "tieless," footloose, wandering figures among his literary characters?

The second example is even more revealing: it consists in the possibility that Faulkner saw (at least unconsciously) the falcon his very name refers to as an adumbration not only of the airmen he wrote about, but of the pilot he eventually became himself. This "objective correlative" of the ideal self, especially if it is related to the problem of Faulkner's small stature, is no doubt what Roland Barthes would have called a "biographemes"—a private inscription (not a "reflection") hidden within the fabric of the work.[12]

By far the most important fact of Faulkner's early life, however, is the choice, or series of choices, he made after his visits to New Haven and Toronto (1918), New York City (1921), New Orleans (1924–25), and finally Paris (1925), where he took the essential, though characteristically negative, decision not to linger in the company of the lost generation. The choice was therefore to go back and live in his native country in order to do two things. One was spiritual: to prepare, as Addie Bundren's father would later say, "to stay dead a long time."[13] The other was material: there is no underestimating how dramatic the decision was which led him to a self-imposed exile of twenty-five years of writing.[14]

In the absence of anything like a conventional autobiography in the body of Faulkner's writings, it seems to me that the relevance of Faulkner's biography to the study of his works by a critic lies first and foremost in what he himself considered to be important. This assumption runs against an older critical instinct, characterized for instance by Hippolyte Taine's "*la race, le milieu, le moment.*" Thus, for example, only because the writer made the notion of home assume dramatic, even tragic proportions in his works can we understand it as a real or literal value in the man's life. The same holds true for the voyeur motif in his novels and the relationship to the dogged, stubborn, almost neurotic emphasis he placed on privacy in his life. Indeed, there is a perfect articulation between the two: for what is home if not a sanctum of privacy?

As one works backward from the texts to the life of the writer, it is tempting to consider the former as a mere record of a compensation. One may be tempted, like a New Critic or a Structuralist, to ignore these frustrations as irrelevant to the study of the texts per se, but it is important to review them briefly, to look, as it were, at the negative from which the picture was developed.

First, there was the frustration of action and glory, since the war ended just as Faulkner had almost finished training as a pilot in the Royal Air Force; thus, if we choose the rather melodramatic tone of his own early writings, we may say that Faulkner missed the camino real into the new century. Second, there was the quest for love, and the repeated failure to win the hand of the fair maiden (which is now fairly well documented).[15] If there is something remarkable about Faulkner's case, it is probably not his feeling of deep bitterness in 1919—which after all was common to most of the writers of his generation—but the conflictual nature of the relationship between this bitterness and the high dreams which his falcon-ego pursued. Indeed, after this double or even triple failure (the social humiliation of professional failure plagued him too), what else but writing (or some other kind of artistic expression) could allow him to say what he could not make life "say" for him? This all seems so prototypical (and, given Faulkner's youth, so well "acted-out") that one senses here the rite of passage of any young writer.

As could be expected, this reconstruction is neither confirmed nor denied by Joseph Blotner. As we read his biography of Faulkner, we find ourselves in the "works and days," not in the Work, nor even, in spite of many quotations, in the texts. And yet, to how many flaws in the fabric of Faulkner's life does Blotner call our attention! To so many indeed that one can easily lose all sense of the literary monument which, after all, is the only justification for such a painstaking and praiseworthy enterprise. In other words, by necessity Blotner gives us answers to questions we would not have asked; conversely, he cannot (or chooses not to, at least in the first edition of his book) answer the questions we would like to ask. It is for this reason that David Minter found it easy to take issue with Blotner, for instance, by emphasizing the record of the parents' quarreling, thus constructing a triangle among parents and eldest son where Blotner, probably out of reserve as well as respect for the living Mrs. Faulkner, only showed us each of two sides: William Falkner's relationship with his mother and his relationship with his father. Whether a happy childhood (which is more or less the impression left by Blotner) or an unhappy one (Minter), wasn't Sartre right when he wrote, in *Les Mots*, that neurotic children can grow out of either?[16]

However, the publication of Blotner's biography in 1974 followed the successive publication, in 1972 and 1973, of the two versions of Faulkner's introductions to the (unpublished) 1933 Random House edition of *The Sound and the Fury*. The impact of these publications in the Faulkner field can best be described in the terms used by Faulkner to express the effect of the writing of the novel on himself: "It taught me what I had already read, because on completing it I discovered, in a series of repercussions like summer thunder, the Flauberts and Conrads and Turguenievs which as much as ten years before I had consumed whole and without assimilating at all."[17] The closest approximation to an autobiography that we shall probably ever see, these two versions of Faulkner's introduction to *The Sound and the Fury* deserve being called the most important event in Faulkner's now twenty-five-year-long posthumous career. Their effect has never ceased to grow upon us—indeed, "in a series of repercussions like summer thunder."

Even to those who had read the typescript of the shorter version with one page maddeningly missing, there was a surprise: Faulkner was indeed unveiling himself as a writer, so much so in fact that he had replaced autobiography with a confession: "that ecstasy, that eager and joyous faith and anticipation of surprise which the yet unmarred sheets beneath my hand held inviolate and unfailing." (*Miscellany*, 160). To a generation of scholars and critics raised in the heyday of the New Criticism and Structuralism, this came as a shock. So *The Sound and the Fury* was autobiographical after all!

But then it soon became clear that the shock could only be one of recognition. What else, what less could have been expected of one whose writing was incandescent when at its best and haunting even when not? "I did not realize then that I was trying to manufacture the sister which I did not have and the daughter which I was to lose, though the former might have been apparent from the fact that Caddy had three brothers almost before I wrote her name on paper" (*Miscellany*, 159). Here was the private justification of the statement so often made publicly about Caddy, beginning with the very first class conference at the University of Virginia: "To me she was the beautiful one, she was my heart's darling" (FITU, 6). Without the overwhelming revelation of the 1933 introduction, none of us could have known how literally true was Faulkner's statement almost twenty-five years later; none of us would have dared conceive of such a private quality in the writing of *The Sound and the Fury*, nor of such an extraordinary persistence of Faulkner's fantasies.

According to H. E. Richardson, "When I asked Phil Stone what happened to Faulkner between *Mosquitoes* and *The Sound and the Fury*, his reply was surprisingly simple: 'He was writing all the time.'"[18] Indeed, in three years, from the beginning of 1927 to the beginning of 1930, Faulkner wrote *Sartoris* (or rather *Flags in the Dust*), *The Sound and the Fury*, the first version of *Sanctuary*, and *As I Lay Dying*. But this was not all. In 1930 alone (as shown by the short story sending schedule he kept for a while), he sent no less than thirty-two stories to magazines. "At the end of 1929," writes James B. Meriwether,

> Faulkner had published four novels and written two more (the first version of *Sanctuary* and *As I Lay Dying*), but had made little money from them. He had published no stories. But at the same time, barring the luck of a real commercial success, the best way of making a living from his writing would be the sale of short stories to magazines. (It is likely that Faulkner received more, on an average, from the sale of each of the four stories accepted by *The Saturday Evening Post*, during the period covered by this schedule, than he did from any of his first five novels.) The luck of a commercial success, of course, came with the sixth novel, the revised *Sanctuary*. (*Career*, 167)

However, imperious financial needs, soon to be increased by his marriage with his childhood sweetheart, Estelle Oldham (1929), and by his acquisition of Rowan Oak (1930), do not suffice to explain a literary activity so intense as to be prodigious. The observer of such an outburst of literary creation can only note the coincidence of this activity with Faulkner's inward retreat into himself and his hometown, a retreat which has much in common with exile.

Indeed, the prospect of a retreat cannot have been very exciting to someone who had always dreamed of action, and perhaps of glory. However provincial, Faulkner had already experienced the refinements of more than one cultural metropolis. He probably knew better than anybody that he could expect everything except a audience from his "little postage stamp of native soil."[19] Therefore, what could he hope to gain from staying in Oxford, apart from the obvious opportunity to write at little cost?

As we know, once settled, nothing but the most pressing need for money, at least until the notoriety of the Nobel Prize for Literature in 1950, could draw him out. Between 1930 and 1950 he did everything he could to hide behind the public image aroused by his novels and stories. Invited in October 1931 to participate in the Southern Writers' Conference at the University of Virginia, he characteristically illustrated the relationship he had with his locale in words full of both accuracy and humor: "You have seen a country wagon come into town, with a hound dog under the wagon. It stops on the Square and the folks get out, but that hound never gets very far from that wagon. He might be cajoled or scared out for a short distance, but first thing you know he has scuttled back under the wagon; maybe he growls at you a little. Well, that's me" (SL, 51). Fifteen years later, in one of his very few self-portraits in fiction, Faulkner described himself as "almost violently sedentary"—a phrase to be found twice in the sketch entitled "Afternoon of a Cow."[20] Where did this immovable violence come from?

At the age of thirty, when he inscribed the title "Twilight" at the top of the first page of the manuscript that was to become *The Sound and the Fury,* action was still an unaccomplished dream. To return to his hometown jobless—with the social difficulties this involved, particularly with his future in-laws—was to begin adult life without status or even identity. When in the spring of 1928 he did begin the novel that he later said he "did not believe anyone [would] publish" (SL, 41), but which he knew was a "real sonofabitch" (FAB, 590), what else was he, at thirty-one, but a young man still frustrated by unrealized dreams, including the new one of making a name for himself out of his ill-fated *Flags in the Dust?*[21] And yet, his lovely letters to his mother from Paris show just how ambitious the young man was (SL, 10–28).

A careful reading of Faulkner's first novels reveals a striking polarity in the lives of most of his young characters. It is as if acts and words excluded each other. The active ones are silent, the talkative ones passive.[22] And yet, the implicit value attached to action does not prevent the verbal characters from being agents of seduction. In other words, everything seems to function according to a double law: one lures with words, but one can only conquer through action.

Where does literature stand in relation to this neat dichotomy? In *Mosquitoes* the "little black man" named "Faulkner" is perfectly silent.[23] We know too well how uncommunicative Faulkner was in person not to think that there was a big difference, for him, between speech and the written word. It may well be that literature was, from the very beginning, a means of coming to terms with (if not of solving) the irreducible conflict between Word and Act, perhaps even of transcending it, by converting it into some idealistic concept of Word-as-Act.[24] In other words, writing meant three things at the same time: a compensation within the "economy" of his own fantasies, a bitter way of paying homage to an unaccomplished dream, and a hope that failure would thus be transcended. In more Freudian terms writing had all the symbolical meaning of an acting-out, the actualization by the subject of his desires and of his unconscious fantasies.

Robert Penn Warren explains the structure of Faulkner's work as a whole in terms that are different but perfectly compatible: "We can, in fact, think of the poles of Faulkner's work as *history-as-action* and *history-as-ritual*. We may even see this polarity as related to another which he was so fond of—and so indefinite in the formulation of—the polarity of fact and truth. We may see it, too, in the drama of his outraged Platonism—outraged by the world and the flesh."[25] It is worth noting here how suggestive and how accurate the last sentence is. Faulkner made decisive choices during two periods of equal duration. The first period, from 1919 to 1924, was marked by hesitation, indecision, wavering, and waiting. There was uncertainty as to a profession. This led, for instance, to Faulkner being urged into an ill-fitting job at the University of Mississippi. There were hesitations as to where he should live—which were finally resolved by the return to the native land. Last, there were uncertainties of a psychological and social order. These were years of contradictory behavior. Faulkner was both bohemian and dandy: both roles were part of the same inability, or refusal, to choose. This inability in turn appears to have rested on some deep, prescient confidence in some hidden capacity. Faulkner was biding his time.

The second half of the decade, after the publication of the first volume of poems, *The Marble Faun* (15 December 1924), on the contrary, was clearly marked by a conviction of the aptness of the choice soon to be made. This conviction found literary expression in two small pieces which have a privileged status because of the way Faulkner later valued them. Significantly, like codas or final statements, he placed them at the end of two of his collections, one of poems (*A Green Bough*), the other of short stories, (*These 13*). Neither was published until the early 1930s, but their composition goes back to the years 1924–26 (or 1927 at the latest), which is to say to the brief and quite unromantic period of Faulkner's *Wanderjahr*. In the poem "This Earth" and in the story "Carcassonne," Faulkner found one solution to his problems—in the dual sense of the word, that is, resolution and disintegration. Both works are dominated by a tone of determination rather than of resignation.

One of the first complete versions of the poem that was to close the collection entitled *A Green Bough* was dated "17th October 1924."

Mississippi Hills: My Epitaph

Far blue hills, where I pleasured me
Where on silver feet in dogwood cover
Spring follows, singing close the bluebird's "Lover!"
When to the road I trod an end I see;

Let this soft mouth, shaped to the rain
Be but golden grief for grieving's sake,
And these green woods be dreaming here to wake
Within my heart when I return again.

Return I will! Where is there the death
While in these blue hills slumbrous overhead
I'm rooted like a tree? Though I be dead
This soil which holds me fast will find me breath.

The stricken tree has no young green to weep
The golden years we spend to buy regret.
So let this be my doom, if I forget
That there's still Spring to shake and break my sleep.[26]

Although it disappeared, partially or completely, from some of the versions published later, the title should not be overlooked. The exclamation "Return I will!" sets the tone. The poem is an oath of allegiance to the poet's birthplace. It is also used as an exorcism of winter, of time, and even of death. In the sense once given to the words *"arrière-pays"* by the French poet Yves Bonnefoy,[27] and to the word "back country" by Gary Snyder,[28] the poem could well be entitled "Elegy to the Back Country."

The same poem appeared on the last page of *A Green Bough* in a shorter, modified form, and without a title:

XLIV

If there be grief, then let it be but rain,
And this but silver grief for grieving's sake,
If these green woods be dreaming here to wake
Within my heart, if I should rouse again.

But I shall sleep, for where is any death
While in these blue hills slumbrous overhead
I'm rooted like a tree? Though I be dead,
This earth which holds me fast will find me breath.[29]

In this later version there are no nostalgic overtones, no recollections of spring or of a love song. Fall, death, and mourning alone remain. And yet there is more than hope, there is a subtle wager in the hypothesis of the first stanza—a wager that the second stanza associates with an inalienable faith in the nurturing capacity of the sleepy, innocent back country. Thus Faulkner's second (and last) collection of poems, which generally told of a self divided between the contradictory calls of Eros and Thanatos, found a logical ending in these eight lines, which were obviously dear to the author.

Deep-rootedness appeared as the solution to the antagonism between life and death. Though just over thirty years old, the writer had chosen to die at home and stay in his native land in order to be able to live. One of Faulkner's best-known fictional characters did the same in a moving piece of prose: no doubt Addie Bundren's monologue in *As I Lay Dying* could be subtitled either "My Epitaph" or "This Earth."

The other piece one might consider in this respect is "Carcassonne," a short story of six or seven pages which Faulkner also published twice, both times as portentous codas to collections of stories, *These 13* and *Collected Stories*. A young man lives in a loft lent or rented to him by the Standard Oil Company in Rincon (Rincon de Romos in Mexico? Or simply Spanish for a small plot of land?) All the reader knows of him is this: He has a dream, or a vision, the first and last image of which is: *"me on a buckskin poney with eyes like blue electricity and a mane like tangled fire"*—a mount on which he imagines himself *"galloping up the hill and right off into the high heaven of the world."*[30] Just before the repetition of this sonorous movement (which, thanks to the use of the italics, appears as unmediated vision), the young man expresses his vital wish in a triad of adjectives that is all the more striking since it recurs variously but unmistakably in several works written in Faulkner's youth: "I want to perform something bold and tragical and austere" (T13, 358; CS, 899).

The first typescript of the story is a little more enlightening than the published version, not only because the young man's landlady's name is Mrs. Maurier—a character familiar to the readers of *Mosquitoes,* where she appears as a rich, idle woman fascinated by artists, preferably young ones—but also because of the young man's name, David. The story is centered on the poet-king mounted on his imaginary Pegasus, while the text stages a conversation between matter (the "skeleton") and spirit (the "I"). The "I" asserts the predominance of vision over the wordly wisdom which the skeleton would like to impose upon him with words reminiscent of "My Epitaph" or of Addie Bundren's father's message: "I know that the end of life is lying still." The high-spirited charger that carries him to heaven can be interpreted as a sexual symbol, which, sublimated (the ascending movement), tears him away from matter and from the desolation of his situation, allowing him access to the ideal (*"the high heaven of the world"*). But the fire itself, the *"tangled fire"* of the horse's mane, constitutes the poetic core of the story: an effulgent flight from the restraints of space, time, and the flesh—all equally unbearable to the idealist artist. Therefore, there is no need to look for exterior proof in order to assume that in this text Faulkner expresses his own vision of himself as poet. However, that proof can be supplied.

First, David is the name that Sherwood Anderson chose in drawing a portrait of Faulkner in the short story entitled "A Meeting South" in which, in 1925, he told of his discovery of a "Southern poet" who drank because he had been injured in the leg and was left disabled. The same name David can be found in a short story significantly entitled "The Leg" in *Doctor Martino and Other Stories* (1934). Second, the hero's wish that he perform "something bold and tragical and austere" not only recalls the end of Faulkner's early critical piece entitled "Verse Old and Nascent: A Pilgrimage" (EP&P, 118), but also calls forth the innermost dream of the generic hero: Bayard Sartoris and Quentin Compson, in particular, who can both be said to be heroes of an intransigent idealism and who both walk the same path to their deaths.[31] Then again, if David's horse makes one think of Jewel's in *As I Lay Dying*, the young man's vision also evokes Darl—another persona of the visionary poet. If one rereads the allusion to the "King of Kings," *"where fell where I was King of Kings but the woman with the woman with the dog's eyes to knock my bones together and together,"* one finds a clear allusion to Clytemnestra, the "bitch" of the *Odyssey* who, in the passage which gave Faulkner the title of *As I Lay Dying*, refuses to close Agamemnon's eyes. The bones knocking together are one of the images which haunt Quentin's mind in *The Sound and the Fury*.

In "My Epitaph" the living man is concerned not with resignation, but with a solution to his existential predicament in the form of an acceptance of that eternal rest which awaits him in his native hills. In "Carcassonne" the other self—the dreamer, the poet—asserts the everlasting greatness of the work of art in comparison with his own perishable skeleton. On one side, we find the diachronic, syntagmatic vision of a lasting, stimulating relationship between native land and living man; on the other, the synchronic, paradigmatic vision of the poet dedicated to his ideal.

Each work implicitly incorporates the other's main theme as a subdominant, or opposing, dimension. In "My Epitaph," the "blue hills slumbrous overhead" bring a sense of transcendence to the lowly theme of a return to the earth. Even more striking is the *Durch-komposition* in the final paragraph of the story:[32] "Still galloping, the horse soars outward; still galloping, it thunders up *the long blue hill of heaven,* its tossing mane in golden swirls like fire. Steed and rider thunder on, thunder punily diminishing: a dying star upon the immensity of darkness and of silence within which, steadfast, fading, deepbreasted and grave of flank, muses the dark and tragic figure of the Earth, his mother" (T13, 358; CS, 899–900). Apart from the near repetition of a line from the poem, which I have underlined, what is striking here is that the flight toward the ideal seems also to establish the mythic principle of the physical world or Earth-Mother, which Faulkner always depicts as a *Mater Dolorosa*.

It is remarkable that the first three novels, *Soldiers' Pay, Mosquitoes,* and *Sartoris* or *Flags in the Dust* should be novels in which the protagonists have no mother, or only the whining caricature of a mother to be found in *The Sound and the Fury,* the fourth novel. In *Sanctuary* the mother figure is split into two substitutes: Miss Reba, the fat, asthmatic, and alcoholic madame, acts as a surrogate mother for Temple, who has only a father and four brothers; Ruby Lamar, who has only been capable of producing one puny, sickly child, is perhaps the only character not to be associated with the "Waste Land" doom of the novel. Faulkner's mothers seem to be doomed to this dichotomy. Lena Grove in *Light in August* may well be the only example of a good mother in Faulkner's world.[33] In *The Sound and the Fury* Dilsey embodies the part of the nurturing mother; in *As I Lay Dying* Addie comes close to being the archetypal overbearing, castrating mother. As a consequence, it seems that the great mythical figure behind the back country, the Earth-Mother, is the only reliable feminine presence in Faulkner's world. This is his metaphor of the ideal mother in absentia.

In the poems and prose pieces of the 1920s the father figure emerges most often as a *Pater Irae*. Symbolized allegorically, he is the omnipresent, sarcastic, sinister figure of Death itself: "Forgotten his father, Death" (AGB, X).

In the dual setting of the Mississippi back country, the young idealist's sublimated mental landscape (the idealist's makeup), and of a literary background (mostly symbolist), art appears as the only path worth treading. It occupies a third dimension. Neither life (mother) nor death (father), it partakes of both principles. Essentially, the artist draws sustenance from the real (or, to use Faulkner's own words, "breath" from "this earth") even while aspiring to its absence: the ideal. Just as Faulkner describes himself as "violently sedentary" in "Afternoon of a Cow," art can best be described with an oxymoron, too: it begins in a movement away from a place of intolerable tensions and stresses, and it tends toward its opposite, a space utterly inconceivable though not quite unimaginable ("Carcassonne").

These are the conditions in which, structurally and textually, Faulkner's use of the supreme romantic trope, metaphor, develops. The following statement, his only known comment on "Carcassonne," can almost be quoted as a paraphrase of the word "metaphor": "I—it seemed to me that fantasy was the best way to tell that story. To have told it in terms of simple realism would have lost something, in my opinion. To use fantasy was the best, and that's a piece that I have always liked, because there was the poet again. I wanted to be a poet, and I think of myself now as a failed poet, not as a novelist at all but a failed poet who had to take up what he could do" (FITU, 22). Again, the ideal and the real, the poet and the novelist. The working, organic link between the two is called "fantasy," but the story itself invites us to interpret fantasy as a metaphor of imagination. As such, fantasy is the only way to the absolute. Indeed, this statement seems to me to be one of Faulkner's most revealing. It implies that his work, perhaps his whole career, consisted in compensating for his inability to realize his dream of being a poet. Only in this light can one speak of "progress" in Faulkner's work—and, even this, provided one does not consider progress as a linear, forward movement, as neopositivists would, but as a spiral—as Jorge Luis Borges rightly prefers to do.

It should be clear by now that the biographical approach cannot help us understand the author of "This Earth" and "Carcassonne," quite simply because these pieces represent the substitution of fiction for autobiography. In both, the metaphoric triumphs over the literal.

The writer who in the late 1920s stood on his own feet and saw with his own eyes had protected himself against the greatest and most urgent danger. He had chosen to live in his self-appointed back country in order to write. He had thus exorcised the temptations of suicide and of what Robert Frost, in another context, called "aberrationism." He now needed to give himself the right implements in order to mount, or stage, the inner drama that called urgently for expression. A careful reading of the precious critical piece, "Verse Old and Nascent: A Pilgrimage," shows, in fact, that as early as 1925 he knew where his best tools lay. They lay in curbing or controlling his tendency to narcissism, aestheticism, sterile self-contemplation, and formal and verbal acrobatics. These were most opposed to what he had already recognized as values: soundness, fortitude, endurance.

The aesthetic tendencies, however, would leave their mark. Nothing is ever lost in the imaginative economy of a writer, least of all the obstacles that have been overcome. Perhaps this is the outstanding characteristic of

Faulkner's development as a writer: the difference within repetition. This is the reason why, in the following chapters, I deal with his publications roughly in chronological order, without, however, forgoing the possibility of looking forward and backward since, as suggested above, the most adequate spatial representation of Faulkner's work as a whole seems to be the spiral.

PART ONE

The Theatre of Eros

chapter one

Cold Pastoral

Early Prose and Poetry

With Faulkner, the incredible mediocrity of the poetry becomes
a major problem.—*Karl Shapiro*

Taken together, the critical prose writings demonstrate a
remarkable progression over a very few years.—*Henri Thomas*

I. Portrait of the Artist as *Pierrot lunaire*

"L'Après-Midi d'un faune,"[1] the title of the first literary work published by
William Faulkner establishes an overt relationship with Mallarmé's well-
known masterpiece, especially since the young author repeated the original
title as he had also done with three of the four poems he translated from
Verlaine.[2] The titles themselves must have been like magic labels for him. In
the case of Mallarmé he may have been impressed by the title alone, which
by 1919 he could have heard mentioned by his well-read friend Phil Stone.[3]
Indeed, it is quite possible that the notoriety of Debussy's music, inspired by
Mallarmé's eclogue (and first performed in New York in 1912, a year before
both *The Rite of Spring* and the Armory Show), was enough to attract
Faulkner to the subject. In all events, however slight they may be, and
however unlikely the intellectual affinity between the self-taught young
Mississippian and the highly sophisticated Parisian, certain echoes are
undeniably present in Faulkner's poem, even though it is considerably less
refined than its model. Faulkner was clearly attracted from the outset by a
kind of poem that dwells as obviously on eroticism as the one he published
next, under the title "Cathay," dwells on the solicitation of some distant,
golden land. One can imagine the young aesthete, long on ambition and
short on technique, being tempted by a glossy patina of words or by the

sulky timbre of French titles borrowed from the Symbolists or from Villon—and only later discovering the difficulty of giving them an emotional integument and a body. Faulkner's predilections, moreover, surely reflect a need to be associated with some recognized master.

The theme, if not the subject itself, of Mallarmé's poem concerns the ambiguity of a vision that refuses to be subjugated by the question: Is this a dream, or is this reality? (*"Aimai-je un rêve?"*: "Have I been in love with a dream?") By contrast, Faulkner's poem never poses the problem of the reality of the desire that is dramatized, even if his faun, once the nymph has fallen asleep, is carried away by a dream. It is notable that this dream is far more sentimental than the truly erotic meditation of Mallarmé's faun. The dream that closes the first section, and which a heavy hand underscores on three occasions with the use of the word itself, turns out to be a waking dream—not even a daydream. The meditation has, in other words, virtually nothing oneiric about it. In the alternation of long, palatal assonances ("lascivious dreaming knees / Like gleaming water from some place / Of sleeping streams . . .") and hushed and tripping alliterations ("She whirls and dances through the trees / That lift and sway like arms and fleck / Her with quick shadows . . ."), one is struck by signs of immaturity—or by the influence of Swinburne rather than Mallarmé.

A comparison of Faulkner's and Mallarmé's settings underscores again the former's inability to deal with nature in other than conventional, anthropomorphic terms—always a bit close to the pathetic fallacy so dear to Elizabethan sonneteers. By contrast, the masterly luxuriance of Mallarméan suggestion serves to show how ineffectually Faulkner's setting glimmers. It is made up naively of slapdash adjectives frozen into conventional poeticisms, such as "the singing trees . . . the sighing trees," "sleeping streams," "the green night in the silver west," and "where lonely streams whisper and flow / And sigh on sands blanched by the moon." On the other hand, the atmosphere of both poems is comparable: Faulkner's "autumn leaves / Slow shed through still, love-wearied air" echoes Mallarmé's "*l'immobile et lente pâmoison*" ("the motionless and lingering swoon"). And the climax of the faun's desire can be traced back to an identical burning glance which pierces through a veil of hair. The image of the voyeur is essential to both poems.

Despite the undeniable loss of creative and erotic potential that goes with Faulkner's decision not to use the second nymph that Mallarmé exploited superbly in his poem, the Woman figure, in both works, is characterized by her hair. The hair excites both aesthetic pleasure and sensual desire:

> Mallarmé: Et le splendide bain de cheveux disparaît
> Dans les clartés et les frissons, ô pierreries!

> Faulkner: She pauses: and as one who grieves
> Shakes down her blown and vagrant hair
> To veil her face, but not her eyes—
> A hot quick spark, each sudden glance, . . .
> (Lines 7–10)

Faulkner finds a voice only in the second part of the poem, in the moonlit meditation that quickly turns into a rather abstract vision of distant and chaste dancing nymphs that are associated with the posturing persona of the immature poet himself—that is, the person who refers to himself: "Now hand in hand with her I go" (line 18). This is as unlike Mallarmé as is the wispy, pale, and bloodless conclusion. If a model comes to mind, it would be Laforgue and his "anemic memorial."[4]

Having first encountered the explosive virtuosity of Mallarméan suggestiveness, the reader is bound to find Faulkner's imitation something of a watercolor. In terms of poetic value it bears no comparison with its model: Faulkner does not even allude to the musical motif that is inherent in all Pan-like characters or Panic scenes. What matters is the difference of artistic treatment, which seems to correspond closely to a considerable difference in maturity.[5] In comparison with the young Mallarmé, Faulkner appears unadventurous, embarrassed, and conventional. Clearly, both title and protagonist are alibis: unable to conceive his Mediterranean drama with any robustness, the poet slips mechanically into a narcissistic pose of self-discovery in which he meditates, beneath the moon, on some inaccessible world. Moreover, the poem lacks the haunting quality of those of Edgar Allan Poe. The only passage with a hint of originality clearly betrays the split between erotic desire and the subject's psychological makeup—his ability to gratify the desire:

> Or like the wild brown bee that flies
> Sweet winged, a sharp extravagance
> Of kisses on my limbs and neck.
> (Lines 11–13)

If the potentially dangerous verbal license is unengaging, the Coleridgean image of desire as a tantalized hornet is more attractive. The image is, however, undermined by the poet's timid, conformist temperament. His medium is not suited to the requirements of painting a faun on a sultry afternoon. Faulkner's picture belongs to an adolescent's flighty reverie.

Nonetheless, these observations about Opus 1 do reveal some qualities that proved to be more persistent than one might at first sight believe. The author's attitude at this period might be characterized as a precious, superficial kind of refugee-aestheticism (distinct from Keatsian aestheticism, which is a form of full involvement in the real). As a servile derivation of French Symbolism and English Decadence, Faulkner's expression of this attitude is far too hesitant and impersonal not to be portentous of excess and violence later on. The works that follow a few years later confirm these two directions. Paradoxically, however, at this early stage this coexistence was hardly a personal trait. Naturalism and aestheticism had their active spokesmen, though each seemed a little old-fashioned in the years before the war. How could a postwar poet (even allowing for all the cultural difference between New York City and Mississippi) still be pottering about at this particular crossroad? Perhaps because, according to Henry May, "one thing that happened after the war was the reemergence with new prestige of the two main nineteenth-century heresies, extreme naturalism and extreme aestheticism" (*End,* 396).

At this first stage, however, Faulkner's work derives entirely from late nineteenth-century aestheticism. His faun behaves like a Pierrot, which is not surprising if one reflects on how late the Symbolist vogue was in coming to America: "By 1913, in the midst of an American poetic renaissance, a few Americans were finally discovering the Symbolists" (*End,* 198). Even before the Symbolists, the first writer apparently to affect young Faulkner had been Swinburne. Later, at the age of twenty-eight he devoted a large part of "Verse Old and Nascent: A Pilgrimage" to the latter's work. This article—an essay, in fact—is so remarkable for the way in which the critical self asserts priority over the self that has been sidetracked by insincerity, and therefore so important for any appreciation of the budding writer, that it is worth quoting from at length:

> At the age of sixteen, I discovered Swinburne. Or rather, Swinburne discovered me, *springing from some tortured undergrowth*

of my adolescence, like a highwayman, making me his slave. My mental life at that period was so completely and so smoothly veneered with surface insincerity—obviously necessary to me at that time, to support intact my personal integrity—that I can not tell to this day exactly to what depth he stirred me, just how deeply the footprints of his passage are left in my mind. It seems to me now that I found him nothing but a flexible vessel into which I might put my own vague emotional shapes without breaking them. It was years later that I found in him much more than bright and bitter sound, more than a satisfying tinsel of blood and death and gold and the inevitable sea. True, I dipped into Shelley and Keats—who doesn't, at that age?—but they did not move me.

I do not think it was assurance so much, merely complacence and a youthful morbidity, which counteracted them and left me cold. I was not interested in verse for verse's sake then. I read and employed verse, firstly, for the purpose of furthering various philanderings in which I was engaged, secondly, to complete a youthful gesture I was then making, of being "different" in a small town. Later, my concupiscence waning, I turned inevitably to verse, finding therein an emotional counterpart far more satisfactory for two reasons: (1) No partner was required (2) It was so much simpler just to close a book, and take a walk. I do not mean by this that I ever found anything sexual in Swinburne: there is no sex in Swinburne. The mathematician, surely; and eroticism just as there is eroticism in form and color and movement wherever found. But not that tortured sex in—say—D. H. Lawrence. (EP&P, 114–15; my emphasis)

If Faulkner dwells at length on Swinburne, and if he does so by using a metaphor that we shall find again in a much more dramatic context, it is because the latter was a landmark in his juvenile reading. Not without humor, he blames his early aesthetic contretemps on the triad: adolescence/sexuality/Swinburne. In fact, Faulkner was, in psychological terms, settling an old score with this compromising master. He had already alluded to Swinburne in his very first critical article of 10 November 1920 with reference to the work of the young Mississippi poet, William Alexander Percy: "like Swinburne, he is a mixture of passionate adoration of beauty and as passionate a despair and disgust with its manifestations and accessories in the human race . . . like Swinburne, he obscures the whole mental horizon" (EP&P, 71, 73). This was a remarkably clear-sighted judgment for a poet, aged twenty-three, who was still himself more or less unable to identify what was "obscure" on his own "mental horizon." And the fact that he perfectly understood the necessity of clarifying it seems, in retrospect, to bode well for the personal and authentic voice that eventually came through in Faulkner's work. However, before concluding with this influence, whose sterility Faulkner quickly perceived, one ought to quote from the recollections of an American intellectual of the time, Arthur Mizener:

> The people who were in college when the first war broke out were still reading Swinburne almost as a contemporary; and even in the thirties, in one of the finest and most angry of the "Camera Eye" passages, Dos Passos was quoting from *Song in Time of Order* to support a revolutionary attitude. Like Swinburne, the writers who came to age in the period of the First World War committed themselves to both the esthetic attitude and the social conscience without—at least at first—any sense of conflict.[6]

To this may be added, finally, an observation made by Pierre Leyris, the French translator of *The Waste Land,* concerning T S. Eliot, that "Swinburne was still the authority one had to break away from."[7]

It would be natural that in order to progress further down the path already traveled by Swinburne, Faulkner should read next the French Symbolists and the English Aesthetes and Decadents of the 1890s. However, it is surprising to note how infrequently their names appear in Faulkner's critical writings (as well as in his later interviews). He knew Verlaine better than the others, of course, for having "translated" some of his poems. But he never seems to have quoted the most important French poet of the period, Baudelaire, with whom, it seems to me, he has more in common than with any other.[8] As for Rimbaud, besides a single allusion in the 1952 interview with Loïc Bouvard, during which he obviously made a special effort to speak of French writers (such as Bergson and Proust),[9] Malcolm Cowley has noted that Faulkner "obviously" knew his work, as well as that of Flaubert, Baudelaire, Verlaine, Eliot, and Joyce (*File,* 153). Nothing is less sure, however.

According to Arthur Symons, who played a key part as an ambassador of French poetry to the English-speaking world, "to Verlaine, happily, experience taught nothing; or rather, it taught him only to cling the more closely to those moods in whose succession lies the more intimate part of our spiritual life."[10] This rejection of the value of experience is one of the recurrent themes voiced by Faulkner's early protagonists, from Elmer to Horace Benbow. It should, however, be recalled that, as T. S. Eliot has shown, Symons turned Baudelaire through his translations into "a contemporary of Dowson and Wilde"[11]—just as Faulkner himself in his translations turned Verlaine into a kind of French William Alexander Percy.

Wilde and Beardsley are both mentioned in *Absalom, Absalom!*—in a description of a burial scene that could have been sketched by Faulkner himself, such is the visual likeness of the verbal description to his own drawings.[12] Beardsley seems to have impressed Faulkner far more than Wilde, as can be seen as early as 1926 in *Soldiers' Pay*.[13] Nonetheless, the influence remained mostly graphic. Faulkner never spoke of any other British prose writers or poets of the 1890s, including, surprisingly enough, W. B. Yeats. Nevertheless, Yeats is, not only in terms of his development as a writer but also in terms of his ultimate conception of art, one of the great contemporary writers who had much in common with Faulkner, one whose works Faulkner apparently knew so well as to be able to quote from memory and who, according to Joseph Blotner, was "one of his favorite poets" in the later years (FAB, 1772).

Through Yeats one comes to Joyce, to Pound, to Eliot, and to the beginnings of the great modernist revival of English and American literature at the start of the century. Adopting the French Symbolists' demanding standards in form and technique, their belief in the complex relationship between language and reality, and of course their urge to break with the sanctions of conventional poetics, including Romanticism, these writers rejected what they saw as fin de siècle posturing. Turning their backs once and for all on art for art's sake, they forged a new kind of poetry with a more contemporary feel, at once sophisticated and down to earth, arguably nearer to the spoken language. With one impulse encouraging the other, they reinvented or rediscovered mythopoesis, going beyond the French Symbolists in developing a kind of writing in which the symbol retains an organic or experiential quality even if it is sometimes put in a strongly ironic light. Their first mature works were published just before the United States entered the war. As Yeats wrote, perhaps sarcastically, "In the third year of the War came the most revolutionary man in poetry during my lifetime, though his revolution was stylistic alone—T. S. Eliot published his first book."[14]

But Faulkner was still working on something quite different at the time, which he hoped would be like "Omar to one's mistress as an accompaniment to consummation—a sort of stringed obligato among the sighs" (EP&P, 115). This was a small book of verse in handmade covers entitled "The Lilacs,"[15] dated 1 January 1920 and proudly signed "W. Faulkner." In the same period and in an even more Blakean cast, Faulkner was writing, copying, illustrating, and binding a small play entitled *The Marionettes*.[16] The source of the title becomes apparent when one reads the memoirs of Lucy Somerville Howorth, one of Faulkner's friends at the University of Mississippi in 1920–21:

> William Faulkner was definitely interested in the drama, this fact and Ben Wasson's prescience in sensing Faulkner's genius led to our casual association in the two years I spent at the University Law School. It was the third day of the 1920 fall term, as I recall, that Ben asked me to help organize a dramatic club. . . . Ben had a list of students who might be interested and almost the first named was Bill Falkner, a special student, son of the Secretary of the University. Bill wanted to write plays, Ben said, and his talent and deep interest in the theater would mean much even though Bill was reserved, shy and wouldn't attend meetings or hold office. . . . I have read that Bill was a "charter member," we were not that formal, but from the start he was a member. Ben was elected President and on his suggestion the name "The Marionettes" was selected. Shortly after this name was selected I read a review of *A Book of Marionettes* by Helen Haiman Joseph (B. W. Huebsch, publisher) and ordered it. On the fly leaf of the copy which turned up in a box of books not long ago is written my name and the date "October, 1920" so by then the Club was a going concern. This book was circulated among the members, including Bill, whether he read it I do not know; I do know that puppets can be scratched off any list of his interests. Bill was planning to write a play, he was reading plays and he was interested in the drama as an art form

and in all the phases of the theater. As of that date he was not thinking of a play as primarily a way to make money. Having a play successfully produced in 1920 did not mean instant wealth as it does in 1965. It did mean recognition and this was important to him.[17]

The Marionettes was never staged, but the play, or rather the dramatic sketch, is of interest because it associates a number of elements (decor, poses, action, images) that the poems had figured forth feebly. Here is the beginning of the stage directions, particularly remarkable for their graphic detail: "The sky is a thin transparent blue, a very light blue merging into white with stars in regular order, and a full moon. At the back center is a marble colonnade, small in distance, against a regular black band of trees; on either side of it is the slim graceful silhouette of a single poplar tree. Both wings are closed by sections of wall covered with roses, motionless on the left wall is a peacock silhouetted against the moon" (MAR, 1). The setting is palpably fin de siècle, and its symmetry draws on a specific cultural mode (one thinks of Wilde's *Salome* illustrated by Beardsley, a copy of which was in Faulkner's library), which is rehearsed by the tragic love of the story. After a descriptive and lifeless dialogue between two figures (the characters may have been inspired by the spirits of Shelley's *Prometheus Unbound*), Marietta appears, unable to sleep, because of the warm night. Overcoming her natural reticence, she bathes in the pool. Then Pierrot arrives. We learn that he was "born one morning in Paris." With responses from the chorus he draws our attention to his lunar origins. He then discovers Marietta, whom he seduces despite her initial dread. They move off together as Pierrot appeals to the power of love. Then two figures herald the coming of autumn, whose spirit recounts in a long monologue the joys of being loved and the sadness of being jilted. After another dialogue between the figures, Marietta returns alone and is amazed by her transformation. While the figures tell of her beauty, she already evokes death, which is alone more beautiful than herself when she is in love. Meanwhile Pierrot has disappeared. The last time that he was seen he stood upright, against the moon, peering at Marietta: "And so he stops, half turned toward her and for a fleeting second *he is the utter master of his soul: Fate and the gods stand aloof, watching him,* his destiny waits wordless on either hand. Will he turn back where she awaits him in her rose bower, or will he go on? Ah, he goes on, his young eyes ever before him, looking into the implacable future" (MAR, 34; my emphasis). This is the only passage which cuts through the varnish of exquisite insincerity: here, the author expresses an emotion which, two years later in "The Hill," became part of an important symbolic setting and moment: the "moment of the choice"—when questions about real experience had to be answered.

A stylistic study of *The Marionettes* would demonstrate how much the vocabulary and the imagery have been borrowed from the Symbolist store-house. In fact the fragile backbone of the whole little book is based upon the elementary opposition of feminine water and erotic fire, while the play of colors, dominated as in Laforgue, Verlaine, and Mallarmé (in *Hérodias* in particular) by the moon, yields a generally golden hue, for instance in the hair of the young woman transfigured by love. All this represented a decent bit of writing for a twenty-four-year-old poet. Yet Faulkner clearly had not found a style to help him steer away from his own narcissism, a style or tone which would help him out of adolescence and into literary manhood. The universe of *The Marionettes* is cold, symmetrical, and frozen. It is, iron-ically enough, a faithful mirror of the imaginative palsy brought about by the domineering influences that one feels throughout. One could almost apply to the Faulkner of this period Faulkner's own description of Joseph Hergesheimer in 1922: "he is like an emasculate priest surrounded by the puppets he has carved and clothed and painted—a terrific world without motion or meaning" (EP&P, 103).

Did Faulkner read what Arthur Symons wrote in 1925 about the charac-ter aptly called the "metaphysical Pierrot" by Laurette Veza?[18]

> Pierrot is one of the types we live, or of the moment, perhaps, out of which we are just passing. Pierrot is passionate; but he does not believe in great passions. He feels himself to be sickening with a fever, or else perilously convalescent; for love is a disease, which he is too weak to resist or endure. He has worn his heart on his sleeve so long, that it has hardened in the cold air. He knows that his face is powdered, and, if he sobs, it is without tears; and it is hard to distinguish, under the chalk, if the grimace which twists his mouth awry is more laughter or mockery. He knows that he is condemned to be always in public, that emotion would be su-premely out of keeping with his costume, that he must remember

to be fantastic if he would not be merely ridiculous. And so he becomes exquisitely false, dreading above all things that "one touch of nature" which would ruffle his disguise, and leave him defenceless. Simplicity, in him, being the most laughable thing in the world, he becomes learned, perverse, intellectualising his pleasures, brutalising his intellect; his mournful contemplation of things becoming a kind of grotesque joy, which he expresses in the only symbols at his command, tracing his Giotto's O with the elegance of his pirouette.[19]

A beautiful and touching passage indeed—largely because the superficial subject or pretext fades away before a real concern. This confession by a member of the fin de siècle generation would no doubt have interested Jean Starobinski in his *Portrait of the Artist as an Acrobat*.[20]

Did Faulkner really believe that he had been born too late, that he had missed "the moment out of which we have just come"? Certain disappointment at not being accepted for military service in 1917 and a number of statements such as "Mr. Percy—like alas! how many of us—suffered the misfortune of having been born out of his time" (EP&P, 71) suggest strongly that he did. The same feeling of frustration is uttered by a number of Faulkner's fictional characters: by Dr. Blount in "Rose of Lebanon," "A Return," and "Dull Tale";[21] by Gail Hightower and Percy Grimm in *Light in August,* and by Rosa Coldfield in *Absalom, Absalom!,* to name only a few. Indeed in *Absalom,* Quentin Compson exclaims: "I am older at twenty than a lot of people who have died" (AA, 323)—a bitter remark that seems to be addressed at those who jeered at the war veteran in *A Green Bough:*

> They bend their heads toward me as one head.
> —Old man—they say—How did you die?
>
> I—I am not dead.
>
> I hear their voices as from a great distance—Not dead
> He's not dead, poor chap; he didn't die.
> (AGB, 11)

Finally, Cass McCaslin seems to be sorry for his cousin Ike for having "been born too late in the old time and too soon in the new."[22] The recurrence of this kind of remark, by virtue of which a number of quite different characters can be associated, seems to indicate that for Faulkner, birth, or the first manifestation of what he has one character call "the stupid mischancing of human affairs"[23] may well be responsible for an unsatisfactory relationship with one's own time—indeed, with reality at large. In this way one might understand more clearly the motivation of the young poet who interiorized a cultural moment all too dutifully, only to discover that history had judged it to coincide with "the end of American innocence."

Behind the mask of the faun the literary persona that Faulkner thus constructed for himself was that of the artist as *Pierrot lunaire*.[24] This figure was an avatar of an earlier pose—which was to cultivate the *mal du siècle*—and which blighted the first part of his career. Faulkner was quite simply looking for his own voice in poetry, just as a man deprived of his primary vocation seeks fulfillment in a secondary one:

> When the co-ordinated chaos of the war was replaced by the uncoordinated chaos of peace I took seriously to reading verse. With no background whatever I joined the pack belling loudly after contemporary poets. I could not always tell what it was all about but "This is the stuff," I told myself, believing, like so many, that if one cried loudly enough to be heard above the din, and so convinced others that one was "in the know," one would be automatically accoladed. I joined an emotional B.P.O.E.
>
> The beauty—spiritual and physical—of the South lies in the fact that God has done so much for it and man so little. I have this for which to thank whatever gods may be: that having fixed my roots in this soil all contact, saving by the printed word, with contemporary poets is impossible.
>
> That page is closed to me forever. I read Robinson and Frost with pleasure, and Aldington; Conrad Aiken's minor music still echoes in my heart; but beyond these, that period might have never been. I no longer try to read the others at all.
>
> It was "The Shropshire Lad" which closed the period. I found a paperbound copy in a bookshop and when I opened it I discovered there the secret after which the moderns course howling like curs on a cold trail in a dark wood, giving off, it is true, an occasional note clear with beauty, but curs just the same. Here was reason for being born into a fantastic world: discovering the

splendor of fortitude, the beauty of being of the soil like a tree about which fools might howl and which winds of disillusion and death and despair might strip, leaving it bleak, without bitterness; beautiful in sadness. (EP&P, 116–17)

In this passage Faulkner seems to be certain and proud of his solitary itinerary; it occurs in his 1925 "Pilgrimage." At the end of this critical piece he calls for an exemplary kind of literature—a model for which he had already created in 1922 in "The Hill." One must, nonetheless, wait for the writing of *Sartoris* to see Faulkner return to this much more "natural" art and then for *Go Down, Moses* to read a masterly orchestration of what is only asserted in the sentence about the beauty of the South, God, and history. Between 1929 and 1942 ("the major years")[25] the writer who was convinced of the rightness of the choice he tells us about in the next sentence ("I have this for which to thank") saw nothing on the horizon but literature and the necessity of finding a form that would correspond to the ethics of that choice.

At this point (that is, immediately after the war) Phil Stone's influence began to manifest itself, especially in Faulkner's poetry: "I gave him books to read: Swinburne, Keats and a number of the moderns, such as Conrad Aiken and the Imagists in verse and Sherwood Anderson in prose" (*File*, 153). It may well be that Stone was not responsible for the discovery of Housman, the poet to whom Faulkner attributed his rediscovery of a more vital and simple style in literature. Housman's influence is evident above all in the second collection of verse, *A Green Bough*, which it affects quite differently from the first volume, *The Marble Faun*, since it clearly vindicates Faulkner's choice. Yet *The Marble Faun* was by far the most ambitious piece of writing he had embarked upon before his departure for New Orleans in November 1924—and the beginning of his career as a novelist.

II. The Faun's Despair

In a review of the joint edition of *The Marble Faun* and *A Green Bough* in 1965, Karl Shapiro wrote that "with Faulkner, the incredible mediocrity of the poetry becomes a major problem."[26] I tend to agree with this observation, not only in opposition to the many critics who dispatch these two very different anthologies summarily into the limbo of adolescent romanticism, but also to the rare readers who feel that the poems alone would have assured Faulkner's notoriety.

The Marble Faun was dated by Faulkner "April, May, June 1919," but, as James B. Meriwether has shown, it is likely that the author continued to revise his poems during the years preceding their appearance in print on 15 December 1924 (*Career*, 10). Indeed, he wrote many other poems during that period, as can be seen in the posthumous publication of *Helen: A Courtship and Mississippi Poems*[27] and of *Vision in Spring*.[28]

The Marble Faun in fact contains no trace of a poem written in haste. It is a pastoral sequence of nineteen poems including a prologue and an epilogue which span the four seasons of the year. The structure is fastidious and clearly meant to avoid monotony. If the fact that ten of the poems take place in a spring setting is revealing, it is equally revealing that each of the ten should be centered upon a different moment of day, or a different atmospheric mood: rain, May, moonlight, woods at sunset, and night. Within the sequence there are therefore a number of variations on a pictorial theme (VI, VII) or a musical one (XII, XVII). The general tone is elegaic; sounds are generally languorous, muffled, or dampened: sadness is the dominant note.

The faun in fact suffers from being imprisoned from within:

> Why am I sad? I?
> Why am I not content? The sky
> Warms me and yet I cannot break
> My marble bonds. That quick green snake
> Is free to come and go, while I
> Am prisoner to dream and sigh
> For things I know, yet cannot know,
> 'Twixt sky above and earth below.
> The spreading earth calls to my feet
> Of orchards bright with fruit to eat,
> Of hills and streams on either hand;
> Of sleep at night on moon-blanched sand:
> The whole world breathes and calls to me
> Who marble-bound must ever be.
>
> (P. 12)

Thus, it is as a voyeur fixed to his plinth (the verb "to watch" or its equivalent occurs seventeen times in the course of the whole cycle) that the faun follows the slow unfolding of the seasons, hears the wheedling call of Pan, contemplates the disturbing grace of the frail, feminine poplars, experiences the cold of night, the explosion of spring, the din of nocturnal dances and the inaudible music of setting suns, until at last, with the return of spring, he finds himself the "sad prisoner" whose "heart knows only winter snow":

> Ah, how this calls to me
> Who marble-bound must ever be
> While turn unchangingly the years.
> My heart is full, yet sheds no tears
> To cool my burning carven eyes
> Bent to the unchanging skies:
> I would be sad with changing year,
> Instead, a sad, bound prisoner,
> For though about me seasons go
> My heart knows only winter snow.
> (Pp. 50–51)

Both the subject of the poem and the character who serves as the poet's persona are revealing. The self, we learn, is destined to be forever cut off from the main stream of experience. The frequency of images that refer to an attenuated, stifled, distant world testifies to this. Although the sun does prevail over the moon (as distinct from the Symbolists), and despite the sway of spring, coldness prevails over warmth, silence over sounds, and slumber hovers over all. The colors are subdued, repetitive, and dull: gold, then silver and white, finally green and blue—the palette of *The Marionettes* contains little else. Bursts of spring are counterbalanced by motionlessness, and the dominant verbs are "to dream, to sigh, to die." Since the landscape is conventional and so bears little relation to anything Faulkner could have actually known, it does not really have the feel of a dream-scape. The world of the poem is sensually and ideally abstract and unreal. The poet is too conscious of his dreaming not to pose as a dreamer—instead of dreaming without self-regard—as he had already done in "L'Apres-Midi d'un Faune." In no sense does the world of *The Marble Faun* rely on experience; neither sensuous nor truly interiorized, the poem's qualities are confined to an entirely conventional code, the pastoral.

And yet *The Marble Faun* is a meditation upon experience. The poet has chosen to freeze in the face of experience and to allow life to unfold before him, rather than plunge into it (the verb to plunge is used, timidly, twice in the text). The fascination exerted upon the poet by the image of the faun is significant in that the objective choice of the topic of his poem conceals the "real," subjective need for freedom: "If I were free, then I would go" (p. 13). Yet by freezing the faun in marble Faulkner removes the possibility not only of action, but of choice and, therefore, of freedom. These values are more or less abstract subjects of a kind of aesthetic contemplation that excludes all hope of participation. The marble faun is a first, though definite, foreshadowing of the typical Faulknerian voyeur: a voyeur without vice or ugliness, more at home in purgatory than in hell, but a voyeur all the same, that is, a subject defined as living only through his frozen gaze at life outside. It is nonetheless difficult to submit imaginatively to the faun's plight, since, as the projection of a mental space, the faun conveys above all the feel of a period, just as a period piece in the decorative arts does. This was all part of Faulkner's "aesthetic phase."[29]

To my knowledge only two critics have looked at *The Marble Faun* closely enough to merit our consideration. One has looked at the poem from a strictly literary point of view, the other from a biographical one. George Garrett, himself a poet and a novelist, begins by asserting that *The Marble Faun* is "a highly complex literary exercise":

> The poems are, as Phil Stone says in his preface, "the poems of youth," but they are promising in more ways than it was possible to see then. The book fails, but the principal cause of failure is in the almost impossible task which the young poet set for himself. *The Marble Faun* is a cycle of nineteen poems, including a prologue and an epilogue, in the pastoral mode. . . . The effect gained by joining the evocative method of symbolist poetry with the highly developed patterns of the English pastoral is a unique conjunction. It could scarcely have been attempted by an unlettered, accidental poet. The structure of the book, separate poems joined together by common subject and both external and internal devices, indicates an early awareness of the problems of creating

structural unity. Concern with form has marked Faulkner's work from the beginning and throughout a career noted for variety and subtlety of structural experiment.

But Garrett also studies the content of the poem:

> The mood of the nineteen pieces is elegiac, though it is not death but a personal sense of loss that the poet laments. He speaks in the person of the marble faun, sometimes "marble-bound" physically in the space of "this gray old garden," more often the prisoner of interior powers which isolate him from the quick unthinking vitality of the idealized pastoral scene. His separation comes from knowledge, a sense of the identity and loss, the memory of the dreamy past and a sense of the recurrence and repetition of all things, good and evil. The burden of the separation is awareness; its anguish is increased by the contrast between the impotence of knowledge and the thoughtless vigor of natural life, everywhere personified, or, more exactly, made animal, everywhere swaying and moving to a dance he cannot share. But he can hear the tune and be moved by it.

Garrett's conclusion is that "concealed in the guise of this pastoral cycle is one of the dominant themes of our literature, the struggle to identity, in this case defined in symbolic terms."[30]

The second critic, H. Edward Richardson, writing several years later, uses this analysis to attempt an anecdotal identification of the writer with the faun. "In one sense," he writes, "Faulkner's war experience may have been one young man's desire for adventure—or again, regional escape— but I have tried to point out that it was also an attempt by young Faulkner to identify with the old Colonel." This attempt "aborted," he says, though it may have justified the "martial heroics" that Faulkner acted out: "Only by this fanciful means could he find a kinship with the past—the hope of measuring up to his sense of ancestral obligation." As a consequence, "the mirror images in *The Marble Faun* echo the poet's own introspection, and the faun's frequent sadness his own dejection." Richardson concludes that the poet who casts himself as faun is just a romantic poseur, an observation that is hardly debatable. However, the final interpretation is all too restrictive: "like the faun, bound and isolated in his knowledge of past, Faulkner seems to have sensed that he, too, was inescapably 'marble-bound' in the past of his own South" (*Journey,* 58–60).

Garrett had also noted that the "inner dialectic of the poem is stressed by the struggle of opposing images, fire and ice, dancing and immobility, silence and music, youth and age, spring and winter, night and day." He could have added sun and moon, Apollo and Dionysus, because the goal of this static drama (even more than *The Marionettes*) concerns the future of an idealized being, lunar and Apollonian, on the threshold of the world of solar or Dionysiac influences. In fact, the goal is sexual in nature: only an exacerbated frustration can cause the faun to view the moon as "mad," because he well knows that it is "old," of the same cosmic age as all outer space, whereas he is young in a way that only newly made flesh can be. But for the faun everything is frozen. Movement is outside, in "the dance he cannot share," as Garrett rightly puts it. Within, the reader senses only a feeble groping for something else. The poet is not part of movement and, thus, does not live in time. The paralysis is clearly of mental origin, but the romantic imagination of the poet confers on this predicament the gravity of Fate.

By immobilizing his faun Faulkner had found an easy way of dramatizing his own predicament. The image of the self is sincere, but the creative means are not. They constitute a transparent obstacle between the poet (or innocence) and the world (or experience). *The Marble Faun* is thus a monadlike work both as representation and as meaning. Dramatization is all the easier because the conclusion of the poem is impossible: to wish oneself a faun and to cast oneself in marble is obviously to live out an absolute contradiction. However, the collection can also be understood as a courageous and sophisticated discourse which sets in motion a process of liberation. Moreover, it is true that with Faulkner, progress included, as if engraved at the center of his artistic consciousness, the memory of this algolagnic stasis where the self proved so inadequate when faced with the world. Images of stasis and the word "hiatus" recur in his novels like the remnants of a near psychological extinction. Faulkner's passage from such aesthetic egocentrism to a more ethical kind of perspective could only occur by giving up the myth of a protected self. The creation of the petrified faun perhaps contributed to make this transparent, especially since, at the same time, Faulkner showed signs of a remarkable intellectual lucidity.

Reading the eight critical essays Faulkner wrote and published between 1920 and 1925, one is indeed struck by the degree to which he had set out quite independently. Henri Thomas, who translated *Early Prose and Poetry* into French, was surprised by the fact: "Taken together, the critical prose writings demonstrate a remarkable progression over a very few years. They may even explain why Faulkner never returned to the themes that preoccupied him in the poetry."[31] This is all the more true since this group of articles may well be considered as an index to Faulkner's intellectual growth. It appears that, at the very time when Faulkner was sinking into the formal impasse of *The Marble Faun,* he had, using his own readings, embarked upon the sort of willful and rigorous reflection which alone could free him to exercise his own judgment.

At the end of this period and on the eve of his departure for New Orleans, he seems to have attained two parallel results, results whose coexistence indeed seemed to engender the dynamic force of his future works. On the one hand, Faulkner, through a thoroughly conventional and constraining poetic route, had brought to a labored conclusion the process which I have successively called his literary error, his alibi, his pose, and his insincerity. On the other hand, following a parallel and invisible path, and using at the same time his well-read friends (Phil Stone, Stark Young, Sherwood Anderson), his trips (New Haven, New York, New Orleans), his readings,[32] and, of course, the expanding compass of his experience (particularly the social and sexual attitudes of a young artist in a small, deeply provincial community), Faulkner sharpened his judgment as he grew increasingly dissatisfied with aestheticism. He learned by himself how to judge other authors and, above all, how to judge himself in relation to those he read. And all this work shows up in the eight articles which record the intellectual and the creative progress of these formative years. The earliest works reflect an intellectual Bildung: "Poetry, criticism and even critical consciousness seem now to be joined in his mind." Henri Thomas could not have put it more aptly, for criticism served Faulkner as therapy for the problems he met in his poetry. Not by chance did Faulkner end one of his articles with this appeal: "Is there nowhere, among us, a Keats in embryo?" (EP&P, 118).

Indeed, besides Conrad Aiken (for whom his admiration did not endure) and Eugene O'Neill (of whom he says, as though about himself, "He is still developing" [EP&P, 88]), none of the contemporaries Faulkner wrote about really interested him. In the course of the articles he called upon literary values which reflect his personal taste so directly that we may profit by a brief examination of them.

What Faulkner praised in Aiken is his intelligence, the impersonal tone, the sincerity, and the fact that he had "developed steadily" (EP&P, 88). In Edna St. Vincent Millay, Faulkner admired "a lusty tenuous simplicity" and "a strong wrist" (85); in Eugene O'Neill, "good, healthy plays" (88), inspired by a man's experience. By and large the dominant epithets are "sane," "sound," "strong." By the same token, Faulkner condemned Joseph Hergesheimer for his lack of "masculinity," of "life," of "movement," of "meaning": "he is like an emasculate priest surrounded by the puppets he has carved and clothed and painted—a terrific world without motion or meaning" (103).

He wanted to see a "sound" American drama: the adjective appears three times in this article, which he introduces with a denunciation of "the deadly fruit of the grafting of Sigmund Freud upon the dynamic chaos of a hodge-podge of nationalities" (93). Yet "One rainbow we have on our dramatic horizon: language as it is spoken in America" (95). And he insisted: "In America, however, with our paucity of mental balance, language is our logical savior" (96). Why not read here psychological instead of simply "logical"? When Faulkner took aim at American critics who, unlike the English, he said, criticized the man and not the book, the criterion was again the notion of soundness: "Saneness, that is the word" (112).

It is easy to decode Faulkner's language: the basis of his criteria is entirely sexual. Despite what he may say, Faulkner's own critical comments were addressed at the authors, not at the books. Thus, William Alexander Percy was only a "little boy" (72). Aiken wrote "in the fog generated by the mental puberty of contemporary American versifiers" and is fighting against "the tide of esthetic sterility which is slowly engulfing us" (76). Even Edna St. Vincent Millay wrote in "this age of mental puberty" where authors give us only a "sterile clashing of ideas innocent of imagination" (85). As for Hergesheimer, "No one, since Poe, has allowed himself to be enslaved by words as has Hergesheimer. What was in Poe, however, a morbid but masculine emotional curiosity has degenerated with the age to a deliberate pandering to the emotions in Hergesheimer, like an attenuation of violins. A strange case of sex crucifixion turned backward upon itself" (101). Virtually all of Faulkner's "pilgrimage" argued for a masculine literature.

The model, now enthroned for the duration of the whole career, was John Keats:

> I read "Thou still unravished bride of quietness" and found a still water withal strong and potent, quiet with its own strength, and satisfying as bread. That beautiful awareness, so sure of its own power that it is not necessary to create the illusion of force by frenzy and motion. Take the odes to a nightingale, to [sic] a Grecian urn, "Music to hear," etc.; here is the spiritual beauty which the moderns strive vainly for with trickery, and yet beneath it one knows are entrails; masculinity. (117)

Thus Faulkner had located his ideal in Keats, whose work became both a reference and a vantage point. The "Ode on a Grecian Urn" in particular represented for him a true, pure artistic kernel. But it is also clear that Faulkner found Keats only by the detour of inauthentic aestheticism. His reference to Keats's work in 1925 shows that he had rid himself of his aggressiveness and had discovered harmony, even though the price may have been a certain amount of sentimentality. Clearly, Faulkner's exasperation was borne of a secret complicity between his own immaturity and the strident literary adolescence he perceived in the contemporaries he chose to criticize. Henceforth, who was Keats for Faulkner if not a father figure? In rereading his passage quoted above, one realizes that the evocation is really an invocation.

In this light we may find it illuminating to look again at "American Drama," subtitled as it is, "Inhibitions." He wrote: "We have, in America, an inexhaustible fund of dramatic material. Two sources occur to any one: the old Mississippi river days, and the romantic growth of railroads" (94). These were certainly two of the historical dimensions of "dramatic" America. They may have represented an alternative for Faulkner at the time even if now they would appear rather limited to us. However, there is hardly a doubt that the two "mines" of dramatic material he chose were taken straight from the life of the Old Colonel, Faulkner's great-grandfather.

In a poem entitled "Once by the Pacific," Robert Frost wrote several lines of a remarkable robustness:

> You could not tell, and it looked as if
> The shore was lucky in being backed by cliff
> The cliff in being backed by continent.[33]

In 1925 Faulkner was strong, stronger in all events for having discovered two complementary ramparts: the historical, American archetype of ancestor as pioneer (not as writer), and a vocation for a kind of art which springs from the struggle of the artist with the paradox of arrested movement, of life that has become an object of contemplation. For him, Keats would always embody the ethical face of aestheticism, indeed an ethical vision capable of shining through aestheticism.

In other words, Faulkner, the writer, had discovered both the end and the means of his art. For a young writer already dedicated to literature (in part because of his failure to succeed as a man of action), this was of capital importance. After retracing his steps over a mistaken path, he had found at last a direction. As it happened, this direction was neither straight nor easy—though Faulkner virtually never deviated from it. He was not alone because he was accompanied by the American past as novelistic material and by aesthetic principles that he redeemed from inauthenticity and immobility by hard work. Faulkner was at last in motion.

chapter two

Locus Solus

"The Hill," *A Green Bough*, "Nympholepsy"

For a while he stood on one horizon and stared across at the
other, far above a world of endless toil and troubled slumber;
untouched, untouchable; forgetting, for a space, that he must
return.—*"The Hill"*

> Nymph and faun in this dusk might riot
>
> Beyond all oceaned Time's cold greenish bar
>
> To shrilling pipes, to cymbals' hissing
>
> Beneath a single icy star
>
> Where he, to his own compulsion
>
> —A terrific figure on an urn—
>
> Is caught between his two horizons,
>
> Forgetting that he cant return.—*A Green Bough, X*

I. Setting the Stage

How does one pass from a monadlike state, shut up in oneself, to an
awareness of a world beyond oneself? This is a question which Jean Laplanche and J.-B. Pontalis ask in their article on narcissism.[1] The same
question needs to be asked now about how a young idealist becomes a
realistic writer. In the case of the young Falkner, soon to become the writer
Faulkner, the solution lies in exposing the precious monologues and di-
alogues of the Faun and of Pierrot—the matrix of the would-be poetic
oeuvre—to the light of the sun, to objective reality. Most of Faulkner's
verse is set in locations dominated by some lunar influence. This setting
derives largely from imagery that is recurrent in much late nineteenth-

century poetry. Just as a negative is turned into a glossy photograph or a dark celluloid is projected onto a silver screen, so the old setting, once lit by experience, takes on a new life. The landscape and its frozen protagonist (the marble faun) are suddenly animated by living beings. Indeed, Faulkner's new prototype is a character who by definition is constantly in movement.

This character could be called a generic "other" figure, at once a brother and a stranger. He is introduced on the visible stage, the stage set by the published text. This stage conceals another one and is rather like a palimpsest on which Faulkner has rewritten, and perhaps even censured, the staging of the initial idea. It is a remarkable event when the posthumous publication of a text suddenly illuminates a mysterious and apparently incomplete version of the same text. This is, however, precisely what has happened in the case of "The Hill." Looking at its earlier (or later) version entitled "Nympholepsy" is like witnessing the changes on a palimpsest.

"The Hill" is a short prose poem, five paragraphs long, which first appeared on 10 March 1922 in *The Mississippian,* and was later reprinted by Carvel Collins in *William Faulkner: Early Prose and Poetry* (pp. 90–92). It was signed only "W. F.", but its authorship was easily established by a comparison with the tenth poem of *A Green Bough.* "The Hill" may indeed be considered the true, if diminutive, gateway to the novelist's oeuvre.

A man is walking to the summit of a hill, which stands out against the sky. Yet because the man is observed by someone, he seems obliged to walk with the "futile" gait of a puppet, "as though his body had been mesmerized by a whimsical God . . . while time and life terrifically passed him and left him behind." Then his shadow reaches the summit and disappears over it (end of the first paragraph).

The valley is surveyed in a slow, dreamlike pan shot. It has a beauty that lacks masculinity ("peach and apple trees in an extravagance of pink and white"). Once the man's shadow springs out and falls across it, "quiet and enormous," the valley appears in a less aesthetic, "agrarian-idyllic" mode: "The hamlet slept, wrapped in peace and quiet beneath the evening sun, as it had slept for a century: waiting, invisibly honeycombed with joys and sorrows, hopes and despairs, for the end of time" (end of second paragraph).

We go into the valley next, "a motionless mosaic of tree and house." The description becomes microscopic, even though the point of view is still located on the top of the hill. The language of the description suggests the relation between the summit and the valley, but the author tells the reader above all about things the man does not see: "There was no suggestion of striving, of whipped vanities, of ambition and lusts, of the drying spittle of religious controversy: he could not see that the sensuous simplicity of the court house columns was discolored and stained with casual tobacco."

Then we find ourselves again with the man, right next to him, since we can see on his face the effect produced by what he has seen—which is far from being what we have seen: "The slow featureless mediocrity of his face twisted to an internal impulse: the terrific groping of his mind." Only now do we learn who—or rather what—he is: "before him lay the hamlet which was home to him, *the tieless casual*; and beyond it lay waiting another day of toil to gain bread and clothing and a place to sleep" (my emphasis).

Finally the sun sinks and shadows invade the valley: "And as the sun released him, who lived and labored in the sun, his mind that troubled him for the first time, became quieted." Now, before the final, remarkably brief conclusion, the quintessential Faulknerian dream appears:

> Here, in the dusk, nymphs and fauns might riot to a shrilling of thin pipes, to a shivering and hissing of cymbals in a sharp volcanic abasement beneath a tall icy star. * * * Behind him was the motionless conflagration of sunset, before him was the opposite valley rim upon the changing sky. For a while he stood on one horizon and stared across at the other, far above a world of endless toil and troubled slumber; untouched, untouchable; forgetting, for a space, that he must return. * * * He slowly descended the hill.

The same time and place recur repeatedly in Faulkner's oeuvre. The author is clearly concerned with describing the fate of a man who is groping for a revelation (which never materializes). But the imaginative configuration here also has a private dimension: for the first time the reader is at the threshold of the real Faulknerian world.

Take Faulkner's character, first of all. He is suggestive of new vigor if only because he counteracts the typically marmoreal character/persona the author was burdened with at the time. This "tieless casual" is perhaps based on a real model that Faulkner may have encountered in Oxford. Yet the relationship between his status as a vagabond and the fact that he is described as feeling himself "at home" in the hamlet allows one to guess just how much a personal projection the character actually is. The remarkably scrupulous biographical sketch Faulkner sent to his first publisher on 9 September 1924 is relevant:

> Born in Mississippi in 1897. Great-grandson of Col. W. C. Faulkner, C.S.A., author of "The White Rose of Memphis," "Rapid Ramblings in Europe," etc. Boyhood and youth were spent in Mississippi, since then has been (1) undergraduate (2) house painter (3) tramp, day laborer, dishwasher in various New England cities (4) Clerk in Lord and Taylor's book shop in New York City (5) bank- and postal clerk. Served during the war in the British Royal Air Force. A member of Sigma Alpha Epsilon Fraternity. Present temporary address, Oxford, Miss. "The Marble Faun" was written in the spring of 1919. (SL, 7)

Since all the other details here are correct, there is no reason to doubt that Faulkner was once himself a "tramp, day laborer" at least for a time. Besides the detached tone of his biographical résumé, one is also struck by the insistence on the author's temporary address. As a matter of fact, even as late as 1956, Faulkner repeated: "By temperament, I'm a vagabond and a tramp" (LITG, 249).

"The Hill" gives voice to a fundamental if still unconscious decision. Two years later, in 1924 when he wrote the résumé, Faulkner continued to see himself as a vagabond. And yet, as we have seen, only one month later he wrote the revealing "Mississippi Hills: My Epitaph."

The day laborer of "The Hill" is therefore the first "other" on whom the writer, anxious to establish his own identity, casts a momentary glance. Most of all, this character possesses the reassuring quality of an objective presence. The "tieless casual" is a still anonymous prototype for the many poor whites of future works, also trapped by "the devastating unimportance of [their] destiny," that is, the geographical milieu (hill and valley) and the sociocultural context (the hamlet). They too are trapped by the "compulsions" of "bread, clothing, and a place to sleep." One could even say that a principal preoccupation in Faulkner's work is to assess how much liberty is actually available to characters caught in the determinism of such compulsions. The day laborer is an ancestor of the convict in *The Wild Palms* and of both the wandering and the sedentary Snopeses. But he is above all the father, or the big brother, of the Bundrens in *As I Lay Dying* and of Byron Bunch in *Light in August*. Furthermore, the color of his skin can be said to be "devastatingly unimportant," because he is also the brother of many a future Negro, Joe Christmas in particular. In short, this "tieless casual" is truly the male prototype in Faulkner's fiction, the homo faber of the novels, and the author's proto-fictional hero. He is an unprivileged person whom Faulkner sets apart from all others and to whom he accords the paradoxical privilege of being a protagonist. With his appearance in "The Hill" Faulkner had laid the first stone of his anthropological edifice. As much could certainly not be said of the poems.

Man has "two great primitive instincts: hunger and love, in other words, the instinct of preservation and the sexual instinct. Our life is essentially motivated by a double goal: to assure itself of the means of existence and, at the same time, to seek pleasure in this existence."[2] The very banality of this naturalistic assertion of inherited, impersonal structures of behavior in both human and animal species may cast some light on Faulkner's first fictional steps (I am discounting "Landing in Luck" for reasons that shall become apparent later). His very unheroic hero is presented as the plaything of life's crudest contingencies. By putting his character in such a situation, Faulkner not only turned his back on the narcissistic preoccupations of an ideal self living in the rarefied atmosphere of an aesthetic world, but he also moved toward a kind of fiction based not on psychology but on anthropology. His tieless casual puts one in mind of the Wordsworthian or the Frostian man.

But one also thinks of the Andersonian hero. The way in which Faulkner praised *Poor White* in the *Dallas Morning News*, 26 April 1925, is worth recalling at this juncture: "In this book he seems to get his fingers and toes again in the soil, as he did in "Winesburg." Here again is the old refulgent earth and people who answer the compulsions of labor and food and sleep, whose passions are uncerebral."[3]

Indeed, the tieless casual's aborted revelation is expressed in an almost physical way: "the slow featureless mediocrity of his face twisted to an internal impulse: the terrific groping of his mind." In an early story entitled "Love," Beth, the troubled young heroine is described thus: "She struggled with something internal momentarily."[4] It is easy to associate these two characters with the young heroes of *Winesburg, Ohio*, especially when they are described in the same terms that Faulkner used in his article: "Mr.

Anderson is tentative, self-effacing with his George Willards and Wash Williamses and banker White's daughters, as though he were thinking: 'Who am I, to pry into the soul of these people who, like myself, sprang from this same soil to suffer the same sorrows as I'" (NOS, 133). "To suffer the same sorrows as I": this was the sesame to the path that later led to "the communal anonymity of brotherhood" in *Go Down, Moses* (257) and, still later, to the grotesque and sublime "*Amis Myriades et Anonymes à la France de Tout le Monde*" in *A Fable* (146). In fact, only this identification with an avatar of the ordinary man, which drew the narcissistic self away from the sterility of self-contemplation, allowed the poet to escape from his pose. By admitting his interdependence with other human beings, Faulkner saved himself from the solipsism that had loomed so near. In other words, the aesthetic impasse was closely associated with a personal neurosis that the anthropological perspective helped to heal. In the works to come, particularly in *Sartoris*, many fragmented repetitions of the scene described in "The Hill" are found.

The setting of "The Hill" was soon to become the locus solus, the central dramatic location in Faulkner's work: at the top of a hill overlooking a valley in which a hamlet nestles in a rural setting, not unlike that commended by Phil Stone:

> We both feel that Oxford and the country around it have done enough for a man when they permit him to live here. From any part of Oxford it is only a little walk to numerous places where one can find the unspoiled golden peace of legendary days and where the sound of mankind's so-called progress comes only dreamlike and from afar. There are dim and shadowy groves of silver-white beeches where springs gurgle out from the foot of the hill and sunlight spills dimly through the trees and there is no company but the birds. There are soft carpeted pine hills white with dogwood in the spring. There are rows on serried rows of far hills, blue and purple and lavender and lilac in the sun, hills upon which you can look day after day and year after year and never find light and shadow and color exactly the same.[5]

This is nothing less than an eclogue. Yet Faulkner did not pause here for long: he went on to appropriate the hill both literally, as a stage setting, and metaphorically, as a symbolic site.

From the point of view of the writer's creative development the most interesting of the long unpublished early short stories is "Adolescence." Its denouement takes place on a hill at the summit of which the young heroine is accompanied by the revelation of "change and death and division. She rose at last and slowly descended the hill toward the creek" (US, 471). At the end of the story the same hill even becomes a metaphor: "The last echo of the horn slid immaculately away from her down some smooth immeasurable hill of autumn quiet, like a rumor of far despair" (US, 473).

In *Soldiers' Pay,* Faulkner's first published novel, not only does the romantic epiphany of Emmy and Donald take place amid the hills, but Emmy's revelation about her cosmic role and the "devastating unimportance" of her destiny is also set in a location almost identical to that of "The Hill":

> Before her descending, the hill crossed with fireflies. At its foot among dark trees was unseen water and Emmy walked slowly on, feeling the tall wet grass sopping her to the knees, draggling her skirt.
>
> She walked on and soon was among trees as she moved, moved overhead like dark ships parting the star-filled river of the sky, letting the parted waters join again behind them with never a ripple. The pool lay darkly in the dark: sky and trees above it, trees and sky beneath it. She sat down on the wet earth, seeing through the trees the moon becoming steadily brighter in the darkening sky. A dog saw it also and bayed: a mellow, long sound that slid immaculately down a hill of silence, yet at the same time seemed to linger about her like a rumor of a far despair. (SP, 300)

In *Mosquitoes,* immediately after Gordon spanks Patricia Robyn, familiar imagery is used to exteriorize the erotic sublimation of his dream: "*It is dawn, in the high cold hills, dawn is like a wind in the clean hills*" (MOS, 272). *Sartoris* is likewise punctuated by the apparition of hills, notably during young Bayard's mad sorties in his car. The first hill is only a hill; but it grows in significance, becoming a "final hill" (SAR, 211), then "the ultimate hills" (280), and lastly the "blue changeless hills beyond" (375).

In *The Sound and the Fury,* Luster and Benjy never seem to stop walking up and down the hill next to the Compson house. As he travels back from Cambridge, Quentin remembers home by associating the hill at home with the hills of Virginia, where the train stopped and where he enjoyed talking with a Negro—who is none other than a new, static avatar of the day laborer:

> The train was stopped when I waked and I raised the shade and looked out. The car was blocking a road crossing, where two white fences came down a hill and then sprayed outward and downward like part of the skeleton of a horn, and there was a nigger on a mule in the middle of the stiff ruts, waiting for the train to move. How long he had been there I didn't know, but he sat straddle of the mule, his head wrapped in a piece of blanket, as if they had been built there with the fence and the road, or with the hill, carved out of the hill itself, like a sign put there saying You are home again.[6]

The Bundren house in *As I Lay Dying* is at the top of a hill. There, Jewel ends his only monologue by wishing that "It would just be me and her [his mother Addie] on a high hill and me rolling the rocks down the hill at their faces, picking them up and throwing them down the hill . . ." (AILD, 12; CT, 14). In *Sanctuary* the old Frenchman place is also located on the edge of a hill. Horace Benbow, who loathes the flat land of the Delta, wishes he "just had a hill to lie on for a while": "It was that country. Flat and rich and foul, so that the very winds seem to engender money out of it. Like you wouldn't be surprised to find that you could turn in the leaves off the trees, into the banks for cash. That Delta. Five thousand square miles, without any hill save the bumps of dirt the Indians made to stand on when the River over-flowed."[7] This passage invites a psychoanalytical reading, which would no doubt focus on the state of impotence which is typical both of this character and many other Faulknerian idealists.[8]

The special effect of the hill in the first chapter of *Light in August* is well-known. But here, the focus in these famous pages is transferred from the Wordsworthian character to the Keatsian scene, since, as in the "Ode on a Grecian Urn," Faulkner seeks to express the fascination experienced by the artist contemplating a movement even as he immobilizes or freezes it in his art. This important aspect of Faulkner's technique is discussed in chapter 10 but it should be noted at this point that (1) the description concentrates on the climbing of a hill beneath a vertical sun, (2) Lena Grove is accompanied by a man who has all the mental characteristics of the tieless casual, and (3) once on the top they see smoke spiraling up in the valley. The inevitable presence of smoke in Faulkner's valley has an ambiguous meaning; in *Light in August,* it is an omen of destruction and death, whereas in "The Hill" no dramatic irony is attached to it: "Here and there a thread of smoke balanced precariously upon a chimney." What is essential to the structure of the scene, however, is that, in order to perceive this sign of daily rural life, one must climb a hill. In an urban setting this is impossible: the setting of *Pylon* is as lamentably devoid of hills (a fact noted at the beginning of the novel)[9] as that of *The Hamlet* is entirely conditioned by them (it is "hill-cradled and remote").[10]

The valley always appears in connection with the hill. Together they form a total landscape which structures in both a genetic and a formal sense each work and the oeuvre in general. One could even borrow Piaget's terms in calling this landscape a "matricial structure."[11]

After crashing his car young Bayard in *Sartoris* lies "with his chest full of hot needles, stroking her [Narcissa's] dark head with his hard, awkward hand. Far above him now the peak among the black and savage stars, and about him the valleys of tranquillity and peace" (254). As a pilot Bayard is fascinated by height and verticality and does not rest (in "the valleys of tranquillity and peace") until he has met the same death—in an airplane—as his brother John.

In *As I Lay Dying,* upon reaching the last hilltop before Jefferson, Darl, the seer, thinks in the following, unmistakable terms:

> From the crest of a hill, as we get into the wagon again, we can see the smoke low and flat, seemingly unmoving in the unwinded afternoon.
>
> "Is that it, Darl?" Vardaman says. "Is that Jefferson?"
>
> . . . .
>
> Life was created in the valleys. It blew up onto the hills [, on the old terrors, the olds lusts, the old despairs].[12] That's why you must walk up the hills so you can ride down. (AILD, 218–19; CT, 209)

This is exactly the idea expressed nine years earlier in "The Hill," in which the inhabited valley, both the feminine cradle of life and the location "of striving, of whipped vanities, of ambition and lusts," appears as the polar opposite of the hilltop, which is associated both with sight and distance and with a clean, masculine ideal. Horace's wish in *Sanctuary* can be explained in this way, too. And the reverie of poor Byron in chapter 18 of *Light in August,* an echo of the initial scene of the novel, can also be read as a paraphrase of "The Hill"—except that the reader is now allowed into the tieless casual's mind:

> The mild red road goes on beneath the slanting and peaceful afternoon, mounting a hill. 'Well, I can bear a hill,' he thinks. 'I can bear a hill, a man can.' . . .
>
> The hill rises, cresting. He has never seen the sea, and so he thinks. 'It is like the edge of nothing. Like once I passed it I would just ride right off into nothing. Where trees would look like and be called by something else except trees.' . . .
>
> But then from beyond the hill crest there begins to rise that which he knows is there: the trees which are trees, the terrific and tedious distance which, being moved by blood, he must compass forever and ever between two inescapable horizons of the implacable earth. Steadily they rise, not portentous, not threatful. . . . 'Well,' he thinks, 'if that's all it is, I reckon I might as well have the pleasure of not being able to bear looking back too.' He halts the mule and turns in the saddle.
>
> . . . From here he cannot even see the scars of the fire; he could not even tell where it used to stand if it were not for oaks and the position of the ruined stable and the cabin beyond, the cabin toward which he is looking. It stands full and quiet in the afternoon sun, almost toylike; like a toy the deputy sits on the step.[13]

Despite its having a manifestly sexual significance (the hill is phallic and the sea, so rare in Faulkner's work,[14] is feminine—a very simple but remarkably well integrated symbolism, since Byron Bunch, who is probably still a virgin, has "never seen" Lena), this passage cannot but be seen as yet another development of "The Hill": to climb a hill is to take the risk of encountering a revelation.

However, this symbolic and even mythic locus does not possess its full significance unless it is associated with a special moment. Evening, especially at sunset, is the moment of revelation, because it lifts man out of time, giving him the illusion of being able to see right into his dreams. In "The Hill," in addition to the tieless casual, evening is the only other agent that determines what happens (or what might happen). It is not the hill alone, but the combination of the hill, the valley, and the sunset which structures the meaning.

The manuscript of the tenth poem of *A Green Bough* was originally entitled "Twilight"—the same title which appears on the first page of the manuscript of *The Sound and the Fury*. In the novel Quentin's monologue is literally absorbed by evening and night. All of Hightower's solitary meditations in *Light in August* take place at night, just as do most of the haunting reveries of Rosa Coldfield in *Absalom, Absalom!* For Faulkner, as for Baudelaire, evening is a time of metamorphoses. In Baudelaire's "Harmonie du soir," the line "*Le ciel est triste et beau comme un grand reposoir*" (The sky is sad and beautiful like a great altar of repose) makes the end of the poem possible: "*Ton souvenir en moi luit comme un ostensoir*" (Like a monstrance inside me your memory glows). Joyce also dwells on this transitional moment in the second poem of *Chamber Music*. But Faulkner's joining together of a moment and a special place is personal, and original, in two ways: first, dramatically, because climbing a hill in the evening becomes in his work the objective correlative of a striving for clarity and self-control; secondly, reflexively, because the scene symbolizes and even literally acts out the gaining of the distance and the perspective which are so important for a novelist.

In point of fact, in "The Hill" the revelation does not descend upon the tieless casual ("for a moment he had almost grasped something alien to him, but it eluded him"), yet the possibility is clearly in the author's mind and is conveyed to the reader obliquely through the entirely negative third paragraph as well as the end of the fourth: "In this way he worked out the devastating *un*importance of his destiny, with a mind heretofore *un*troubled by moral quibbles and principles, shaken at last by the faint resist*less* force of spring in a valley at sunset" (emphases mine). This revelation, which could well be called an epiphany manqué, consists in perceiving one's place in the universe, or measuring oneself in the landscape of the real. Then the ideal self, like the shadow of the man, topples: it is absorbed or snatched up by the valley, that is, by everyday destiny.

However, there is another, Freudian, reading of the text which is more complementary than contradictory to the one above. If the hamlet, the smoke, and the "extravagance of fragile pink and white" of the peach and apple trees in the valley are feminine, then the climbing of a hill represents an assertion of virility (compare Byron Bunch's "I can bear a hill, a man can"). The illusion of power described in the first paragraph can even be considered as a fantasy erection, suggested by familiar symbols: the crest, the wind, the man's feet. Then the long legs of the shadow fall, and they appear ludicrous: the man is overcome by guilt. Repression appears (the "whimsical God"): it is the image of the father, which shows itself to be the source of frustration and sexual deprivation. Virility disappears at the very moment when the dream of femininity looms up in the second paragraph, with its graceful evocation of the landscape. But the valley is dominated by the sun, as much a symbol of masculinity as the shadow is the symbol of repression (the latter constitutes one of the main motifs of Quentin's monologue in *The Sound and the Fury*). Repression becomes "enormous" in the second paragraph and "monstrous" in the fourth. The second paragraph represents the configuration of the family (father-sun assaulting mother-valley) upon which the young man (the son) projects both his desire and the repression of his desire. The importance of the third paragraph is crucial, for the fact that he can see none of the shabby details confirms the idea that, because of the burden of repression, he continues to idealize his libido. He only sees beauty in sexual life. The fourth paragraph analyzes the conflict between conscious and unconscious—the same conflict that is Freud's definition of neurosis. The subject, however, cannot see clearly into the conflict. The latent barrier remains. This is why he wisely reconciles himself with the principle of reality. In other words, he has been on the brink of grasping the existence of the id, but the father betrays him at this point: "the sun plunged silently into the liquid green of the west and the valley was abruptly in shadow. And as the sun released him, who lived and labored in the sun, his mind that troubled him for the first time, became quieted." This is what transforms his desire into an adolescent's regressive vision of a beautiful, harmless sexuality, a dream of form in which dancing nymphs and fauns entertain an impossible relation with the real world.

Faulkner the novelist was born in "The Hill." For the first time the writing subject has identified himself with a character while experimenting fictionally with the distance between himself and the nonself or fictional persona. This distance is expressed, albeit summarily, in the play of negatives in the third paragraph and, with more subtlety, at the end of the fourth, once the man has been identified as what he is: the tieless casual—a type. By refusing to do this in poem X of *A Green Bough* (which treats the same topic and even the same topos as "The Hill"), Faulkner tries to acquire a universality for his theme which he pays for by losing a specific human feel and, with it, authenticity. It is not an accident if the final stanza calls to mind the "Ode on a Grecian Urn" and if the last line expresses an idea which is the very opposite of that expressed at the end of the prose sketch.

> Nymph and faun in this dusk might riot
> Beyond all oceaned Time's cold greenish bar
> To shrilling pipes, to cymbals' hissing
> Beneath a single icy star
>
> Where he, to his own compulsion
> —A terrific figure on an urn—
> Is caught between his two horizons
> Forgetting that he cant return.
> (AGB, 30)

Between the end of the sketch and the end of the poem Faulkner seems to voice once more his hesitation between the desire to escape into the ideal, free from the necessity of making any moral choices, and the imperious need for a home in the real. This is why "The Hill" is an adumbration of Faulkner's "choice." In it he asserts the necessity of a return that is a reconciliation with the principle of reality. For Faulkner reality is and will always be the earth—and his poetics shall be the poetics of a return to "this earth."[15]

II. Pavane for a Late Poet

In the course of Faulkner's career, the earth can be seen to acquire a number of meanings that gradually become superimposed, like the layers of a kind of semantic geology. In the final paragraph of the unfinished manuscript of *Father Abraham* (1925), for example, it is very clear what Faulkner's prose still owes to his poetry:

> But supper over, you emerged into a different world. A world of lilac peace, in which Varner's store and the blacksmith shop were like sunken derelicts in the motionless and forgotten caverns of the sea. No sound, no movement; no tide to knock their sleeping bones together. And yet it was not quite night. The west was green

and tall and without depth, like a pane of glass; through it a
substance that was not light seeped in sourceless diffusion, like the
sound of an organ.

Suratt's buckboard stood at the hitching rail[16]

But the orchestration of the earth's shaping influence on men and women
under the Southern sun in both "rural" novels, *As I Lay Dying* and *Light in
August,* is quite another matter. Eventually, the soil came to be less a motif
than a definite literary theme in Faulkner's fiction. It even grew into a
cosmic value in the two masterpieces of his maturity, *The Hamlet* and *Go
Down, Moses.* However, this evolution was already perceptible in *A Green
Bough.*

A Green Bough is a collection of forty-four poems, published on 20 April
1933, but written, if not completed, much earlier. As early as 1925 the New
Orleans *Double Dealer* had announced a volume of poems by the name of
A Greening Bough. Not only did Faulkner alter the title, which is somewhat
reminiscent of Sir James Frazer's monumental study of ancient myths, *The
Golden Bough* (1890), but he continued to work at the collection until he
had organized it into a kind of spiritual autobiography in five parts.

At the center is the figure of Orpheus, who "stands and sings" in poem
XX (last line). Although traditional, the emergence of an orphic figure
represents an advance over the pathetic posturing in *The Marble Faun,* of
which *A Green Bough* is in many ways a counterpart. The second volume
seeks to enrich but also to correct the impression left by the first. It sets in
motion the paralyzed vision of the earlier work. Faulkner clearly wished to
go beyond *The Marble Faun,* and one may guess that this was the reason
why he published it even after his first, great novels had been published, and
even though he had no illusion about its claim to immortality.[17]

The first sequence of poems could be entitled "After the War." We have
already touched upon the first poem, which reflects all too overtly the mood
of T. S. Eliot's "The Love Song of J. Alfred Prufrock" and which deals with
the feeling of guilt for not having died in battle. But the five poems of this
first part, the longest in the collection, also introduce its most forceful
motif, the opposition of Eros and Thanatos.

After a short transition (VI and VII), the second sequence (VIII to XIV) is
concerned with "The Return of the Native": these little vignettes include a
rhymed version of "The Hill" (X). Together, they make up a short rural

cycle influenced at times by Housman (XII, XIII), dealing with such subjects as the ploughman (VII), the harmony of the evening (IX), the young girl and her suitors (XII), the evening (IX), the mother and her son (XIV). Though quite sentimental, the tone of the poems can be situated halfway between the traditional pastoral mode and a Jean-François Millet-like "peasant" realism, which represents some kind of advance.

After a mediocre octave (XV)—about which William Rose Benét inquired, "Is this some Border Ballad abominably going Housman? The eminent English poet would presumably rather be murdered in his bed than commit all these 'bonnys',"[18]—there follows a sequence which might be called "The Poet and his Perspectives." Although the settings are sometimes identical to those of the second group (compare XVIII, X, and XI), the difference lies in the fact that we feel here a live poet, pondering the many possibilities that are available to him. (One is struck throughout this collection by the repetition of "between . . . and . . ."). The most recurrent possibility is erotic in nature. Poem XVII introduces the ideal image of the embrace of a couple of eagles and suggests that this is beauty in movement. The same image is used next (XVIII) in connection with the poet as seen upon "an adolescent hill": "Yet still upon this lonely hill the lad / Winged on past changing headlands . . ." Poem XX, which ends with the description of the same persona ("before the door / He stands and sings") begins with a key image: "Here he stands, while eternal evening falls / And it is like a dream between gray walls / Slowly falling, slowly falling. . . ." This hero would no doubt profit from turning his attention in the direction of experience. Still, one can understand why Faulkner placed this poem at the center of his collection. For him it represented a kind of Festschrift in honor of a defunct poet—namely himself in 1933.

When, in a review of *A Green Bough,* Eda Lou Walton wrote that she was pleased to find the poems "amazingly free of the obsessions so evident in his novels,"[19] she was sensitive to the care for form that is typical of Faulkner the poet. It is this care for form that lends a rather illusory (though less frigid) unity to the whole work, when compared with *The Marble Faun.* William Rose Benét was shrewder: "He does not truly know his way about. His hand is still prentice. He almost seems to be precocious, peculiarly enough, rather than accomplished. There are gleams. There should be. But where is the impressively original and the strikingly integrated personality? Not in this book."[20]

After sounding a blast of the horn at Roland, "Whose fame is fast in song and story" (XXI), the poet introduces the theme which, after the andante of the fourth cycle, becomes the subject matter of the final erotic scherzo. Beginning with the Mallarmean question "Was this the dream?"—which Faulkner did not ask in "L'Apres-Midi d'un Faune"—the poet stages the rest of poem XXV in a strikingly horizontal setting, "on quavering sands where kissing crept and slaked . . ." under the moon. But, as though out of desperation, the poem contains the following stanza, which, as we shall later see, is a crucial representation of the central phantasm in Faulkner's imaginary world,

> O I have seen
> The ultimate hawk unprop the ultimate skies,
> And with the curving image of his fall
> Locked beak to beak. And waked
>
> And waked.

As opposed to this ecstasy, the human flesh remains irremediably associated with the earth and with the "ludicrous postures" of which Januarius Jones, quoting from poem XVII of *A Green Bough* in *Soldiers' Pay,* is acutely aware: "Do you know how falcons make love? They embrace at a enormous height and fall locked, beak to beak, plunging: an unbearable ecstasy. While we have got to assume all sorts of ludicrous postures, knowing our own sweat" (SP, 227).

The fourth group of poems can be called "Intimations of Mortality," although its objective correlatives are quite superficial. It is the season of cold (XXVII, 2; XXIX, 3; XXXIV, 8; XXXV, 9), and the cold is associated with death, which is mentioned in almost all of the last poems of the collection. Death is sometimes clean and pure (XXVIII, 12), sometimes maternal (XXXIII, 5), always feminine (in spite of the English allegorical tradition). The earth is sad (XXX, 5) and bitter (XXXIII, 9), and it conceals its promise of fertility. Here, at last, the vision appears integral. By associating desire with time, pain, and death (as the allegorical figures in *Mayday*),[21] this group of poems presents the other, experiential side of the myth of love. The theme of disillusion prevails in poem XXX, but the poet also sings "one stubborn leaf that will not die" (XXXIII, 8); he even sings "Nativity" (the manuscript title of XXXIV), preparing the way for the return of hope. The renewal, trumpeted with an awkward fervor in poem XXXV, is opposed to the "courtesan," Autumn: "Spring will come! rejoice! But still is there / An old sorrow sharp as woodsmoke on the air."

In the last group (XXXVI to XLIII) Spring has returned and cannot chase away the consciousness of death present in each poem. Yet this very consciousness also asserts life—the triumph (a mitigated one, for sure) of Eros over Thanatos, or rather the triumph of "some leafed dilemma of desire" (XLII). Here, Faulkner has traveled a considerable distance down the path of experience since the pale spring and impotent voyeurism of *The Marble Faun*. At last there is participation in experience: poem LXIII is a joyous and mocking declaration of desire. The poem even ends with the depiction of a spanking and might, irreverently, be given the title of one of W. H. Auden's war poems, "The Naming of Parts." Besides this poem and poem LXI, however, most of the verse in the last group expresses an agon in the confrontation of desire, time, and death. Taken as a whole, the last poems repeat the effect achieved in the four earlier ones and serve to underscore the rather slender philosophical content of the book.

Nonetheless, the structure of *A Green Bough* is testimony of a real effort to adapt the dramatic tension of the forces that govern us emotionally to a lyrical mode: the call of glory, the peace of earth, flesh and time, love and death. However mixed the results, there was no lack of ambition in *A Green Bough*.

III. Acting-out

As he was putting his poems into a publishable form, Faulkner was occupied with the far more important task of shaping his own "self" into the subject of his prose fiction.

"Nympholepsy" was part of this concern. "The oddly-entitled 'Nympholepsy'," writes James B. Meriwether, "is an expansion of 'The Hill,' which Faulkner apparently wrote early in 1925, within the first month or two of his arrival in New Orleans" (*Miscellany*, 149). Only in a purely objective and rather superficial context does the title appear odd, however. In "Nympholepsy" we are taken to the region of the consciousness (not quite the Freudian unconscious) where fantasies originate and where self-consciousness does not censure the transcription of dreams onto the written page.

The best instance of this absence of censorship is the well-known scene at the branch between Caddy and Quentin in *The Sound and the Fury.*

Seen from the psychic rather than the aesthetic point of view, the title is in no way odd. It simply makes explicit what is left unsaid in "The Hill." Moreover, there is no conclusive proof that "Nympholepsy" was written later than "The Hill." On the contrary, one may well be reading a first, uncensored version of that highly polished prose poem. Whatever the truth of the matter may be, there are many reasons for considering the two texts as twins or for reading "Nympholepsy" as "The Hill" turned inside out and thus revealed.

"Nympholepsy" starts and ends like "The Hill." After a beginning even more sibilant than that of "The Hill," the scene unfolds in a similar way until the "tieless casual," reaching "the sharp line of the hill-crest," discovers the valley where "the town lay in lilac shadows." Here, "Nympholepsy" diverges from "The Hill" insofar as not only food and shelter, but also sex are conjured up by the sight displayed below: "Among the lilac shadows was the food he would eat and the sleep that waited him; perhaps a girl like defunctive music, moist with heat, in blue gingham, would cross his path fatefully" (*Miscellany,* 149–50). The man is described with more "realistic" detail: for instance, we see "the trickling dust from his inverted shoes" (150). There is the symbolic presence of the sun, which is hardly mentioned in "The Hill," except as a force which "releases" the man. First described as a "red descending furnace mouth," then as a "little silver flame moving across the trees," the sun finally is a "little flame that had somehow lost its candle and was looking for it" (150). However, since the central part of the text functions on the level of a dream—that is, as a "nympholepsy," or the bewitching of man by a nymph—most of the story takes place elsewhere—precisely where the three mysterious asterisks interrupt the text of "The Hill," immediately after the sunset has elicited the abbreviated version of what one might call the quintessential Faulknerian dream. It is, therefore, necessary to return to this point, especially as the references to the courthouse at sunset and then to the silo under the moon in "Nympholepsy" clearly allude to "a dream dreamed by Thucydides" (150), and to "a dream dreamed in Greece" (155). What is so remarkable about Greece in Faulkner's imagination, besides the obvious mythological and literary heritage? The question opens up not only the symbolist sources of the oeuvre, but also what could be called the great alibi of the author, because, here again, Faulkner the writer is not where he appears to be—that is, at center stage.

The stubbornness with which the poet set out to (re)write for himself the Greco-Latin pastoral can be explained, on the one hand, as part of his continuing reluctance, at this point, to use local, that is, rural, material for the setting of his fiction. One smiles when one realizes that Faulkner did not set his first novel, *Soldiers' Pay,* in Mississippi, but in Georgia. Read in this context, the well-known anecdote about Sherwood Anderson's advice to write about his "own little postage stamp of native soil" (LITG, 255) is a quite pertinent piece of advice; his passage from poetry to prose could be seen as reflecting his decision to accept Anderson's advice. Yet it is unlikely that the setting per se—that is, the setting as decor—was the most important thing for Faulkner. What was important, of course, was the agon or action or drama that he would stage in the setting. After all, the pastoral was only a framework that had sooner or later to be altered or discarded, just like "the more comfortable beliefs [that have] become outworn as a garment used everyday" ("Nympholepsy," 152). Moreover, ever since "L'Apres-Midi d'un Faune," the drama that Faulkner sets in an apparently pastoral setting has in fact very real, though only sometimes explicit, erotic implications. The pastoral is in this sense a useful cover for creating an aura of chastity or of harmlessness, if not of innocence. Using the pastoral setting was like casting out insistent evils.

One may ask why Faulkner invested so much effort in such an archaic and conventional genre. One answer would suggest that the genre offered him the alibi that his guilty conscience needed in order to dramatize or act out what it suppressed. Within the confines of the subtle game of equivocation that Faulkner was playing with his imaginary world, the pastoral was what sealed or covered up desire. The pastoral kept desire under control even while it acknowledged its existence as a latent, subliminal, desperately suppressed force.

One can further illuminate this question by posing another one, implied above: why did Faulkner shrink away for so long from using the rural material that was at hand? I have said that in "The Hill," as well as in some of the poems of *A Green Bough,* what Faulkner did was to let his newly found anthropological "other" enter upon the stage. But this anthropological other was also a psychological double: the alter ego, in short. He is an *alter* not just from a social point of view—even though for a petit bourgeois, even in a small provincial town, the transient farm worker is a person of almost a different race: in the South, he was precisely what Faulkner was not: a "poor white." He is an *alter* from an existential point of view—the *other* who exists as it were in spite of oneself, outside of one's own intimate sphere. Chances are that the representation of this other by Narcissus is all the more dramatic as the other is full of the glamour inherent in transient people.

However, this other or *alter* is also an *ego* since, in this case at least, he shares two features with the subject: (1) he lives close to the earth and yet (2) he is a migrant. In other words, he shares the subject's life in both real and imaginary senses. All that is necessary is to lift him up to the symbolic level—which is exactly what "The Hill" and "Nympholepsy" do, as long as they are read together, as it were stereoptically, or one against the other.

The task for the writer was to pass from one universe to the other, from the pastoral to the "real," to the back country, and to bestow upon the *homo pastoralis* (the faun) the attributes of the *homo ruralis* (the tieless casual). This is what was *not* done in "The Hill," and what was done without the least ambiguity—indeed, almost too overtly—in "Nympholepsy." Hence the title that lays the emphasis precisely on the weak point of "The Hill": on the man's sexual dream life and desire.

Thus, what took place between 1922 and 1925 was no less than crucial, since (1) the full fleshing out of the pastoral dream, that is, the novels' rural setting, took no less than fifteen years to accomplish, from the inception of *Father Abraham* in 1925 to the completion of *The Hamlet* in 1940; (2) Faulkner's first use of the "objective" hero, the humorous character named Suratt and later Ratliff, who is central in the later oeuvre, dates from this period; (3) the whole oeuvre is colored by a powerful urge to wander, a kind of wanderlust or urge to return to a state of things before life's main decisions were made. The title given by Joseph Blotner to Book 4 (1925) of his biography, "The Vagabond," could hardly be more apt.

At the sight of a woman in "Nympholepsy," desire and prohibition mix. The man has this curious intuition: "How he knew it was a woman or a girl at that distance he could not have told, but he did" (150). Guilt settles in immediately: "Then his once-clean instincts become swinish got him lurching into motion." Next follows a true *satyricon* in a rural scene with little residual pastoral grace. As could have been expected, an "immortal dance" is nonetheless revealed at sunset. Then there follows the inevitable cycle of desire, frustration, and sublimation. The Faulknerian correlatives of sun, stars, and moon correspond to these phases. At the end we have the spectacle of the tieless casual perched upon his hill again . . . like a Pierrot lunaire.

The first act consists of a confrontation between desire (or discourse) and fear (or silence). The sunset functions as a trigger: daytime scenes are reviewed, particularly one which would recur throughout the novels: "sucking cold water from a jug with another waiting his turn" (151). There are as well other vignettes of country life. In these, sweat comes as much from desire as from work. With the approach of night, however, three grinning witches materialize: silence, solitude, and fear. "For here was something that even the desire for a woman's body took no account of. Or, using that instinct for the purpose of seducing him from the avenues of safety, of security where others of his kind ate and slept, it had betrayed him. If I find her, I am safe he thought, not knowing whether it was copulation or companionship that he wanted" (*Miscellany,* 151). The analytical directness here is remarkable. So, when distinguishing between pastoral and rural, one was in fact taking account of the absence or presence of a woman—for the deceptively simple reason that she is the key to the reading of the landscape! Now it is clear why "Nympholepsy" is the exact reverse of the epiphany manqué in "The Hill": the starting point of "Nympholepsy" is this passage in "The Hill": "he had almost grasped something alien to him, but it eluded him; and being unaware that there was anything which had tried to break down the barriers of his mind and communicate with him, he was unaware that he had been eluded" (EP&P, 91–92). Grasp, break down, communicate, elude: the semantic chain is clear enough: but the real question concerns the status of desire, here and now.

It is worth exploring further this Faulknerian fairyland, where man is fauna and woman is flora: "whether it was copulation or companionship that he wanted. There was nothing here for him: hills, sloping down on either side, approaching yet forever severed by a small stream. The water ran brown under alders and willow, and without light, seemed dark and forbidding" (151–52). This is a landscape full of the images that Faulkner repeats and develops work after work, culminating in the unforgettable beginning of the final version of *Sanctuary.* Here, the trees are "calm and uncaring as God," gazing "on him impersonally, taking a slow revenge" (152). But what sparks this revenge, if not a transgression or an attempted transgression? Fear, silence, and solitude are indeed the antidotes of desire. The trees, however, are only small, ironic imps skulking beneath the sovereign, brooding glance of the great "god to whose compulsions he must answer long after the more comfortable beliefs had become out-worn as a garment used everyday" (152). This god cares very little for the identity of the trespasser, since it is only as a trespasser that the man is being watched, "where he had no business being" (152). Needless to say, the man runs very little chance of escaping. In terms of a poetic justice as simple as those in the lurid dramatic world of children's nightmares, he must die: "Crouching, he felt the sharp warm earth against his knees and his palms; and kneeling, he awaited abrupt and dreadful annihilation" (152). But who is keeping watch over him if not the good, healthy, masculine (though cold) star of the Faulknerian ideal? "Nothing happened, and he opened his eyes. Above the hill-crest, among tree trunks, he saw a single star. It was as though he had seen a man there" (152). Accompanied by this guardian and fraternal angel, the man now picks himself up and heads for town. But lo! "Here was the stream to cross." The text cannot be more explicit: "The delay of looking for a crossing place engendered again his fear. But he suppressed it by his will, thinking of food and a woman he hoped to find."

But the man slips, as could be expected, so that he again thinks he must die, "feeling that imminent Presence again about him" (153). Then everything seems to take on life in a typical moment of total metamorphosis: "For an arrested fragment of time he felt, through vision without intellect, the waiting dark water, the treacherous log, the tree trunks pulsing and breathing and the branches like an invocation of a dark and unseen god" (153). The man falls, and "in his fall was death, and a bleak derisive laughter." This contrasts wonderfully with what one reads in poem X of *A Green Bough:*

> But now, with night, this was forgotten:
> Phantoms of breath round man swim fast;
> Forgotten his father, Death; Derision
> His mother, forgotten by her at last.

Repeated twice, the phrase "Then the water took him" makes no attempt to conceal the sexual implication, since "here beneath his hand a startled thigh slid like a snake."[22] Then "among the bushes he felt a swift leg; and, sinking, the point of a breast scraped his back." Woman and Death are brought explicitly together as in *Mayday* and above all as in the Quentin section of *The Sound and the Fury:* "Amid a slow commotion of disturbed water he saw death like a woman shining and drowned and waiting, saw a flashing body tortured in water" (153). Though this text is basically allegorical, one wonders why, if death is a woman, it is impossible to pursue her: the pursuit does in fact begin, with the laborer/faun running after the woman/naiad, beneath the glance of the old madam, the moon.

Failing to catch her in water, the man now runs, crossing "the wheat slumbrous along the moony land." He has kicked off his mud-covered shoes like burdensome fragments of the real and climbs the inevitable hill on top of which a visual apotheosis awaits him: "There she was, in a wheat field under the rising harvest moon, like a ship on a silver sea" (154). But the woman is apparently protected by her natural milieu, the wheat field; she disappears. Like death, she has the status of a fantasy. When the man awakes, he falls a prey to the throbbing effects of his lingering dream:

> The moon swam up, the moon sailed up like a fat laden ship before an azure trade wind, staring at him in rotund complacency. He writhed, thinking of her body beneath his, of the dark wood, of the sunset and the dusty road, wishing he had never left it. But I touched her! he repeated to himself, trying to build from this an incontrovertible consummation. Yes, her swift frightened thigh and the tip of her breast; but to remember that she had fled him on impulse was worse than ever. I wouldn't have hurt you, he moaned, I wouldn't have hurt you at all. (154)

This passage, with its dramatization of the pang of frustration (expressed by the use of the verb "to writhe"), foreshadows Byron Snopes's inferno in *Flags in the Dust*. To Faulkner the hell of voyeurism and the hell of fantasies are the same. They represent the starting point of his fiction.

The ending of "Nympholepsy" is the well-known cycle of frustration and sublimation. Just as, in the beginning, the courthouse was "a dream dreamed by Thucydides," now it is a mere silo that is magnified into a "dream dreamed in Greece." The pastoral, in the ascendant again, helps to beautify the muggy and stifling night of ungratified desires. Under the ever present moon the man's attention is drawn to the real world through the dirt that is encrusted on his bare feet. Slowly he begins, as in "The Hill," to descend back into the valley—back to reality.

PART TWO

The Ballet of Desire

chapter three

La Ronde

Early stories, *Soldiers' Pay, Elmer,* "Portrait of Elmer"

In the young male there still lingers a trace of the old pagan
worship of the body, of beautiful physical articulation, which
the Roman was later to taint with an admiration for prowess,
for superiority. . . . A boy up to and through adolescence runs
the whole gamut of civilization, anyway, getting in brief
episodes the whole spiritual history of man.—*Elmer*

When, shortly after New Year's Day, 1925, Faulkner left Oxford, Mississippi, for New Orleans with the apparent intention of heading for Europe, apart from the poetry which he was still producing, he had finished only a few short stories, most of which were only published posthumously in 1979. Three of them can be dated before 1924. One is written in a prose style that contrives to be "tough," perhaps in imitation of the early Hemingway stories. The other two are about adolescent experiences along the lines of the stories about the young protagonists of *Winesburg, Ohio.*

Faulkner himself called "Moonlight"[1] "about the first story I ever wrote" (*Career,* 87). It is the story of two adolescents arriving at the *limen copulationis* and of the young man's last minute retreat from total consummation. At first stereotyped ("the courthouse among its elms and fronted by the marble Confederate soldier, was like a postcard"), the scenery gradually becomes associated with an intensely subjective vision, centered in the anxiety of the two young people who sense something imminent and grave: "The house was dark, as were other houses along the street, yet there was a definite sense of unoccupation about this one, as though the house itself were holding its breath and waiting for something." "She stopped. The street was deserted, dissolving in either direction into treacherous vistas, like camouflage, and she leaned her body against him." In a style cluttered with sexual symbolism, the young man is compared with "the hunter who finds the game suddenly and then discovers that he has never learned how to load a gun."

In "Love,"[2] the most pointlessly complicated of the three stories and, for the contemporary reader, the most dated, the main character resembles a figure from Faulkner's own drawings: hardened, cold (he is a major in the army), and a bit blasé, he has "bronze skin and silver temples and ice-colored eyes." The melodramatic plot has just one goal, which is to show the author manipulating various characters on the same stage: men of the "lost generation" (the major is a former pilot, unjustly suspected of never having flown), bored women drinking tea (there are clear Prufrockian undertones), and laconic and wise non-Westerners, embodied by the major's yellow servant. The title expresses bitterness, irony, and disillusion.

"Adolescence" is described by Michael Millgate as "a slightly sentimentalized treatment of a young girl's conflict with her stepmother and grandmother and of her gradual growth out of childhood" (*Achievement,* 11). Precisely because of this conflict, however, it is the most interesting of the three stories. It foreshadows the nighttime scene between Donald and Emmy in *Soldiers' Pay* as well as the sociocultural and linguistic background of *As I Lay Dying* (Juliet, the protagonist, is the daughter of Joe *Bunden,* and her boyfriend Lee is the son of *Lafe* Hollowell). As a character, Juliet clearly adumbrates Jo-Addie Hodge, the protagonist's sister in both *Elmer* and "Portrait of Elmer."

Like a literary naturalist, Faulkner conscientiously follows the child up to puberty, to a time when she is almost perfectly well-balanced in Faulknerian terms, that is, she is epicene, "an elfish creature, thin as a reed and brown as a berry" (US, 460). But, one day, in the company of her wild little boyfriend,

> She lay back again and closed her eyes. Bright sun spots danced before and behind her lids, madly and redly. But she was not satisfied: her feminine insistence was not to be placated so easily. As she was vaguely troubled and sad, like the changing year, with an intimation of mortality and mutability, learning that nothing is changeless save change. They were voluptuously silent in the strong refulgence of sunlight until a sound caused Juliet to open her eyes.

Ludicrously inverted above her stood her grandmother, a shape-
less hunched figure against the bland ineffable blue of the sky. The
old woman and the girl stared at each other for a space, then Juliet
closed her eyes again.

"Git up," said the old woman. (US, 464–65)

The youngsters are ruthlessly separated, Juliet to live with her grandmother "in a state resembling a corked champagne bottle" (US, 466). The
bottle explodes when the old woman decides to send Juliet back to her
father, whom she loathes. Then the girl directs her hatred at her guardian,
who answers back with an "evil" laugh and threatens her with a forced
marriage to another boy, one more respectable than "that triflin' Hollowell" (US, 468). Juliet dashes away on horseback. Once returned from her
escape, she learns that both her father and Lee's father are dead: both have
been killed by revenuers near a still. Her friend Lee and her stepmother have
gone away. "So she sat in the dark, watching her childhood leaving her . . .
change and death and division" (US, 471). Going out, she meets her youngest brother, who has come to look for her, but she refuses to go and live with
their grandmother:

He looked so small and lonely, kneeling in the dead leaves, and
the common bond of hatred drew them together. He raised his
streaked dirty face. "Oh, Jule," he said, putting his arms around
her legs and burrowing his face into her sharp little hip.

She watched the fitful interruptions of moonlight torturing the
bare boughs of trees. Above them the wind sucked with a far
sound, and across the moon slid a silent V of geese. The earth was
cold and still, waiting in dark quietude for spring and the south
wind. The moon stared through a cloud rift and she could see her
brother's tousled hair and the faded collar of his shirt, and her
racking infrequent tears rose and slid down the curve of her cheek.
At last she, too, was frankly crying because everything seemed so
transient and pointless, so futile; that every effort, every impulse
she had toward the attainment of happiness was thwarted by
blind circumstance, that even trying to break away from the
family she hated was frustrated by something from within herself.
Even dying couldn't help her: death being nothing but that state
those left behind are cast into. (US, 471–72)

I have quoted this passage not only because it is a kind of purple patch in Faulkner's early prose, but because it contains many motifs and phrases that were to become, as it were, the trademark of Faulkner's fiction. It begins like one of his poems, but it rises, awkwardly, as if groping for the kind of universal apostrophe that punctuates the narrative of *Winesburg, Ohio*.[3] Furthermore, the "silent V of geese," which one also reads as "a V of geese" in an unfinished early piece entitled "And Now What's To Do" (*Miscellany*, 147), clearly foreshadows "the cries of the geese out of the wild darkness in the old terrible nights" in *As I Lay Dying* (166).

Juliet stays on alone after giving her brother some money and food for his grand departure. In the last paragraph her portrait makes one think both of the attraction to the earth felt by Dewey Dell in *As I Lay Dying* (AILD, 61) and of all the "dying falls"[4] to come:

> Here at her feet lay the pool: shadows, then repeated motionless trees, the sky again; and she sat down and stared into the water in a sensuous smooth despair. This was the world, below her and above her head, eternal and empty and limitless. The horn sounded again all around her, in water and trees and sky; then died slowly away, draining from sky and trees and water into her body, leaving a warm salty taste in her mouth. She turned over suddenly and buried her face in her thin arms, feeling the sharp earth strike through her clothing against thighs and stomach and her hard little breasts. The last echo of the horn slid immaculately away from her down some smooth immeasurable hill of autumn quiet, like a rumor of far despair.
>
> Soon it, too, was gone. (US, 473)

Thus, Faulkner's first novelistic heroes are young people in a small town, no longer pastoral but rural in character. He focuses on the couple in a moment of crisis, dramatizing their feelings in the face of an eruption of sexuality, fate, and maturity—as in "And Now What's To Do?" These topics, as well as their sentimental and even slightly melodramatic treatment, recall Sherwood Anderson's "Book of the Grotesques": Faulkner seems to be using the style commended by the older writer in his preface to *Winesburg, Ohio*, a style growing out of a passionate interest, full of empathy, for the hidden life (mostly psychic and sexual) of the ordinary people in a small community, life caught in a moment of revelation, described without undue embellishment, with a kind of low-key audacity.

In April 1925 Faulkner published an article on Sherwood Anderson that is full of discerning praise. The article was the last in the series of eight critical essays discussed earlier. Of *Winesburg, Ohio* Faulkner wrote:

> The simplicity of this title! And the stories are as simply done: short, he tells the story and stops. His very inexperience, his urgent need not to waste time or paper taught him one of the first attributes of genius. As a rule first books show more bravado than anything else, unless it be tediousness. But there is neither of these qualities in "Winesburg." Mr. Anderson is tentative, self-effacing with his George Willards and Wash Williamses and banker White's daughters, as though he were thinking: "Who am I, to pry into the souls of these people who, like myself, sprang from this same soil to suffer the same sorrows as I?" The only indication of the writer's individuality which I find in "Winesburg" is his sympathy for them, a sympathy which, had the book been done as a full-length novel, would have become mawkish. Again the gods looked out for him. These people live and breathe: they are beautiful. (NOS, 133)

This was a perceptive homage. However, Faulkner's first novel, finished only a month later, did not reveal many of the qualities that he praised in Anderson. As we have seen in comparing his poetry and his critical prose, this apparent contradiction was less paradoxical than typical.

Soldiers' Pay—or *Mayday,* as the novel was named before the publisher changed the title (FAB, 397)—brought no deep and enduring solution to Faulkner's problems. Like *The Marble Faun,* however, the work played the role of a double catalyst. If the apparent aim of the book was to dramatize the experience that had frustrated him several years earlier, Faulkner clearly is more responsive here to an immediate psychological problem, which is frustration itself. In other words, Faulkner fictionalizes an empty form. Frustration is like a container whose original contents (the war in which he had not participated) is replaced by sexual activity. The result is a bipolar novel, a fact that has irritated some critics. The part of personal projection that is inherent in any work of art is here awkwardly distributed between Donald Mahon and Januarius Jones.

Like most of Faulkner's first works (the only exception being "Nympholepsy"), *Soldiers' Pay* is rigorously symmetrical. The return of the hero in the last section of chapter 2, is reflected precisely in his death in the last section of chapter 8 (the book has nine chapters). Thus, the whole movement of the narrative results from the expectancy generated by these two events—all the more so as the reader is informed from the outset that Donald is, if not medically at least symbolically, living through a short reprieve from death when he arrives at his father's house.

Not only is *Soldiers' Pay* bipolar and symmetrical, it is built around two alternating themes, war and peace, both of which result only in disillusionment. The first chapter is entirely devoted to the return of the veterans and is probably modeled on Faulkner's own return from Canada in 1918.[5] The second, on the contrary, dwells in considerable detail on the setting (a stereotype of a Southern haven of calm and gentleness) which is "home" to the wounded hero, as it is to those who wait on him: his father, his fiancée, his lover, and a prissy, scrounging Sybarite. In the following two chapters Faulkner orchestrates with skill the tragic and futile ballet of the postwar period by using the letters of Cadet Julian Lowe as a kind of register of disillusionment. The townspeople function as a chorus, commenting on the soldier, just as young Robert Saunders is used as a witness to the prestige of the declining hero. Here Faulkner experiments with what will later be the hallmarks of his success—point of view and narrative distancing. Donald becomes blind at the end of chapter 4 and he dies at the end of chapter 8. The duration of his agony is thus spread out from the moment of his return home over seven full chapters.

Chapter 5 is the keystone of the arch and is itself composed with a scrupulous respect for bipolarity. The first three sections are concerned with stories of the war which are apparently evoked so as to cast a raw and lurid light on the soldier's current sufferings. The rest of the chapter is concerned with the ball, the civilian counterpart of the soldiers' fighting. Between the two Faulkner pertinently places mothers and crones, who continue to bestow their affections upon their dead sons as personified in their wounded neighbor, picturing to themselves military scenes so shameful that no heroism can survive them (sections 4 to 7). This central chapter, which the whole structure of the novel depends on, does not display a writer in control of the very scenes he has invented. The chapter is different from the initial scene, with its moving description of the veterans, and from the final one, a bittersweet "dying fall" perfectly in keeping with the literary ideal found by the author of "Pilgrimage" in Housman's *A Shropshire Lad*.[6] Neither the war scenes nor the ball succeeds convincingly; they are heavy, awkward, and confused. Such failures can be analyzed in several ways. One need only compare the war scenes with that in "Crevasse" in *These 13* to see that Faulkner in *Soldiers' Pay* is still cramped by what could be called the tyranny of verisimilitude: he wants to record life and he fails. In the case of the ball, on the contrary, the firsthand familiarity with postwar socials seems to take priority and somehow to stop him from transforming the event into a memorable literary scene, as in *War and Peace*. In both cases one recalls Faulkner's later remark, "The writer has three sources: one is observation; one is experience, which includes reading; the other is imagination, and the Lord only knows where that comes from."[7] The relationship between the three may well be what was still wrong, and the formally impeccable balance of the novel may still have represented a certain refusal to choose between observation, experience, and imagination.

In chapters 6 and 7 Faulkner accelerates the cadence of the futile, tragicomic ballet, particularly by increasing the pace of Julian Lowe's letters to Margaret Powers. The reader follows the shilly-shallying of Cecily, her parents' inability to agree to a common attitude toward her, and Januarius Jones's exasperated desire. Immediately after a citizens' chorus, it is announced that Donald is going to die. This announcement is followed by his melodramatic marriage to Margaret Powers, once Cecily has forfeited her opportunity to marry him and Emmy has refused the same. Margaret is a femme fatale in that she attracts "the slings and arrows of outrageous fortune" upon all those who come near to her emotionally: "Bless your heart, darling. If I married you you'd be dead in a year, Joe. All the men that marry me die, you know" (SP, 306). This marriage is an empty form. It is supposed to close the circle so as to allow Mrs. Powers to expiate her lack of sympathy to her first husband, Dick. The episode is an ironic echo of the end of chapter 3, in which Cecily promises the much awaited consummation in a note to George Farr. The rumor that this sets off—that Cecily was observed nude in the street—is also an echo of the nighttime love scene Emmy tells Margaret about. The two scenes, the nocturnal pastoral idyll and the exasperated exhibitionism in an urban landscape, both seem to owe something to *Winesburg, Ohio* (and to Joyce?) but even more to such early writings as "Adolescence" and "Moonlight."

The last two chapters are constructed in a falling curve, underscored ironically by the waxing spring and interrupted in the middle by Donald's death, which follows immediately after his recollection of his wound. Next comes the epilogue, in a minor and wistful key, which brings a new tone to the farce, just as, at the outset, a pathetic note had altered it. At the end black chants occur to provide a soft "dying fall" to this pagan novel full of religious allusions and images.[8]

Soldiers' Pay is very much a "period piece," both because of the First World War and of the postwar period. It is a novel about frustration since hope is everywhere in it deceived. In this sense the last scene (between Margaret Powers and Joe Gilligan) must be considered as a success, because it expresses perfectly the taste of bitterness that peace had for those who had known the war. But to say this is also to say that whatever sense of evil there is in the novel is very contemporary—and very superficial. This is still the *mal du siècle* or, more precisely, the sickness of the "first year of the century."[9] (The novel lasts only a few weeks during the spring after the end of the war; all the action thus occurs in April 1919.) Beyond the denunciation of the effects of the war and the terrible irony that colors the treatment of Donald Mahon and that is implicit in the grotesque ball of peace, Faulkner has no original vision to dramatize besides the first instance of a typically Faulknerian form of evil, amnesia, the absence of any relationship between the individual and his own experience because of the loss of the sense of time. This weakness in the novel can be explained by the fact that at this stage Faulkner was writing out of a persistent sense of frustration, which escapes scrutiny or analysis since it is the effect of the experience of an absence. In other words, one might say that Faulkner is more compromised by his first book than he is engaged by the subject matter. The novel's form is left, as it were, to compensate for the author's inability to deal with experience. The writing most often lacks a feeling of volume and substance. However, one must add that, exactly as with *The Marble Faun*, the goal— to express the experience of an absence—was hardly attainable, especially for such a young writer.

The symmetry of the novel thus reveals a mind that is still preoccupied by the aesthetics of novelistic form, as set against experience (even if it is the experience of the absence of experience). As Michael Millgate points out, form takes the lion's share of Faulkner's attention in *Soldiers' Pay*: "The whole book, indeed, affects us in formal, almost balletic, terms, rather than as a direct presentation of human experience" (*Achievement*, 66). In the same way, one of the early critics wrote of it rather aptly as "a farandole of desire and repulsion."[10] Indeed, *Soldiers' Pay* is a farandole or a ballet: nothing more, at bottom, than the animation of *The Marble Faun*. And, if one looks closely enough, it is not just Donald (who is so shocked as to appear to be little else than a medical case), but all the characters who represent more or less extreme cases, because they too are subject to the involuntary tyranny of a creative mind that is itself tyrannized by incompleteness and frustration.

One should first note that the creative consciousness is represented here by a trinity of projections: Julian Lowe, the historical "yardstick" of the novel, must somehow be considered along with Donald Mahon, who, probably against Faulkner's will, must share the protagonist's part with Januarius Jones. All three are frustrated: the first—who recalls Cadet Thompson, the protagonist of "Landing in Luck," Faulkner's first published fiction—because he is deprived of heroic action; the second, because memory and therefore consciousness elude him, whereas he should have gleaned the rewards of his heroism, specifically in successful love; and the third, because he is angry by his inability to transform desire into sexual possession. Even the Rector, who is a widower, is frustrated by his son, even at the moment of meeting him again. Emily is frustrated by her shopgirl hero. Margaret is frustrated twice by a husband. Gilligan is frustrated by Margaret. Even George Farr is frustrated in his desire for Cecily, and Robert Saunders is frustrated by his schoolboy image of the hero.

However, among all those thwarted by love, surely Januarius Jones is the most prominent. A wasp on the forbidden peach, he is a man of perpetual desires who comes from nowhere, is apparently going nowhere, and has to prove himself by besieging women or, failing that, by covering up for his failures by a rhetoric which is sometimes convincing but which serves above all to disguise his retreats. His sexual gratification in extremis is ludicrous, especially as it was to be expected after Cecily's blunder. Jones's case is poles apart from what Faulkner praised, even while he was writing the novel, in Sherwood Anderson's *Poor White* and from what he went on to explore himself in "The Hill" and "Nympholepsy": "Here again is the old refulgent earth and people who answer the compulsions of labor and food and sleep, *whose passions are uncerebral*" (NOS, 134–35; my emphasis). Jones is quite the opposite: he is the caricature of the eternal student, flitting about like a housefly, philosophizing like a pedant without experience, and chasing after women while talking ceaselessly. He is a real case, one might say, of regression (or flight) into words. However, with his "yellow" eyes (noted seven times) he is on five occasions compared to a goat. He represents a mixture of eroticism and verbalism which must have been hateful—as well as familiar?—to Faulkner himself.

In front of him, at once immobile and vainly active, is the faun, Donald Mahon. His sexual past is as sound, lusty, and innocent as Jones's is perverse and even depraved. Yet both are, as Olga Vickery says of the faun and the satyr, "followers of the great god Pan who flouted tradition and social respectability."[11] Everything takes place as if Januarius Jones were the puny master of the ballet being danced by the characters around Donald. This is exactly how *The Marble Faun* is constructed, though now, in the novel, the dance is animated by overabundant but purposeless movement. The chassé-croisés, the escapes and pursuits, the scenic games, the confusions and the quid pro quos, the rejections, the romantic maid devoted to the memory of the local Adonis, the tolerant father, a Latin scholar, sceptic and cleric, the exciting little ninny, the messages, the nocturnal meetings, the parodies of dueling—all this calls to mind a drawing-room comedy in the finest tradition.[12]

This is not exactly what, in retrospect, one might have expected in Faulkner's first novel. Yet the world *Soldiers' Pay* shows us is a world of cathexis in which the author has, not without irony, placed his fauns and satyrs. The irony does not save the book from the adolescent's obsessive fears and exasperated desires. The comedy is not intentionally satirical: Faulkner was not Aldous Huxley (whom he may have been trying to emulate),[13] nor was he Proust, of course. Yet this half of *Soldiers' Pay* seems not so much a satire on the *comédie sociale* as a comedy, enacted for the author's sake, through which he attempts to set free, if not resolve, powerful tensions in his own life—much in the same way as Joyce, according to John Cowper Powys, did in *Ulysses: "Ulysses* rippled and simmered and gurgled and heaved and hissed with a thousand ill-suppressed personal grudges, vicious self-pity and vindictive aesthetic vendettas."[14]

The fact that this personal aspect of *Soldiers' Pay* is exteriorized in juxtapositions rather than in syntheses, especially in the theme of the mutilated and absent hero, should not be surprising. The faun at the center is still made of marble. Idealizing himself according to his heroic dream, Faulkner freezes yet again. He equivocates once more, as in *The Marble Faun*. This equivocation is just what Olga Vickery appreciated, without trying to go beyond the contradiction: "his passionate engagement is continually at odds with his ironic detachment . . . his preoccupations become gigantic irrelevancies disturbing the tone and texture which he was ostensibly imitating" (*Novels,* 1–2). For her, Faulkner was imitating Huxley and Eliot in everything that concerns Januarius Jones. Only in the character of Donald Mahon, she thought, was Faulkner himself in everything that concerns "time and the individual consciousness." Her schematic division minimizes the importance of Jones, who serves an almost therapeutic function. Jones marks another stage along the road of the development of "the subject."

In regard to sexuality Jones and Mahon form a neat pair of opposites. The opposition is between sound and virile sexuality (inevitably blended with nostalgia, as shown in Donald's copy of *A Shropshire Lad* in the few things left by his son) and the exacerbated eroticism of Jones, who is described as a "sybarite," living only for pleasure, in the present moment. In other words, everything takes place as though the present could not possibly contain love or as though true love had been destroyed, along with other values, in the postwar period.[15] The opposition is so clear that, if one admits that Donald embodies goodness in sexual matters, it follows that Jones is the villain, being both bestial (the goat) and cerebral. He is the one whose obsessive desire gets "completely out of the realm of sex into that of mathematics, like a paranoia" (SP, 283).

The character of Mahon can be explained as a portrait of the "other self" of his author, that is, both ideal and (melo)dramatized. Wounded to death, he nonetheless comes back home in order to live the rest of his life and die. In a sense he is doomed both by the unsustainable glamour of the veteran and by a love which he can no longer enjoy. Such is the impasse with which the author's persona is confronted. Once more, the "figure" is one of immobility. In *Soldiers' Pay* the hero takes part in the action (the ball) as little as the marble faun did in nature's "antics." Moreover, as in Swinburne's *Atalanta in Calydon,* the movement occurs all in one place; in fact, the novel is static.

Emmy, Donald's only true partner, also plays her part in the orchestration of personal themes. She too is profoundly asocial (for instance in her confession to Margaret Powers in chapter 3, section 8). She runs up violently against her father's will. Hers is the passionate approach to life: immediate and total and, in one word, romantic. It is interesting to note that the little section devoted to her in chapter 4 (section 4), a single page in which Faulkner borrows from the themes of Anderson and from the style of the Symbolists, repeats nearly word for word the end of "Adolescence."[16]

With *Soldiers' Pay* death, time, and love become Faulkner's principal favorite considerations. It is not surprising to find that the introduction of the last chapter was much amplified in the typescript. The words italicized here were added in the margin: "Sex and death; *the front door and the back door of the world.* How indissolubly are they associated in us! *The youth they lift us out of the flesh, in old age they reduce us again to the flesh; one to fatten us, the other to flay us, for the worm.* When are sexual compulsions more readily answered than in war or famine or flood or fire?" (SP, 295).[17] Between the two (rather clumsy) initial metaphors, there seems little place left for social dynamism, for the influence of mature individuals upon the society which they make up or, more generally, for any sort of action. This is why the society described in *Soldiers' Pay*, just like that later described in *Mosquitoes,* is perfectly otiose. These first novels seem to reflect the young writer's total absence of social perspective.

Soldiers' Pay also embodies the duality of sexual responses that seem to have been William Faulkner's own. These are most frequently represented, of course, by the faun and the satyr. The conflict between the two in the novel becomes an outright battle between Januarius Jones, who "fought like a woman" (SP, 314), and Gilligan, who takes up the torch of virility from Donald's hand. Gilligan is a more important character than most commentators have recognized. His role grows proportionately as that of Julian Lowe's decreases. He also is trying to discover his path; apart from Donald, he is the only male who experiences an authentic and mature feeling of love toward a woman in a book where all is semblance and dissembling. Gilligan's pain is, moreover, ironic, since he wants to take Donald's place and conquer Margaret Powers. Clearly, he belongs to the fauns. Indeed, as far as characters between 20 and 40 are concerned, the novel hardly establishes any criteria for distinguishing between the good and the bad. We have to rely on the way Faulkner appropriates for himself "values" like colors, for example: the color yellow, which is consistently associated with Jones, always has rather derogatory or at least negative connotations in Faulkner's fiction.[18] In later novels the reader's judgment is influenced by numerous commentaries made by the characters about each other. But this is not the case as yet. For the characters who are neither young nor elderly (as Donald's father is) the relationship with sexuality seems to be the only measure of their worth. Even for the early Faulkner sexual behavior is identical with moral conduct.

One is struck in *Soldiers' Pay* by the recurrence of two words which later play a considerable role in the history of Faulkner's imagery and thought (one and the same thing for a "poetic" novelist). These are "compulsion" and "epicene." "Compulsion" had already appeared in 1922 in "The Hill," concerning the trees and "the quiet resistless compulsion of April in their branches" (EP&P, 91). In *Soldiers' Pay,* one finds it used a dozen times in a sense almost synonymous with contingency; anything that may thwart or frustrate ideal liberty, such as clothing, shelter, food, sex, time, space, etc., is a "compulsion," whether it comes from the inside, that is, from the subject himself, or from the outside. Thus, the U.S. mail service itself is called "one of the most enduring compulsions of the American nation" (SP, 111). Most often, though, physical needs such as shelter are at issue. Sex also figures prominently here and takes on the characteristics of an intolerable attachment, almost an enslavement.

It is in this sense, it seems to me, that one must interpret the story and the meaning of the buzzard in the novelist's imagery and thought. Faulkner made the animal famous by telling Jean Stein during the *Paris Review* interview in 1956: "you know that if I were reincarnated, I'd want to come back a buzzard. Nothing hates him or envies him or wants him or needs him. He is never bothered or in danger, and he can eat anything" (LITG, 243). Clearly, the bird of prey here is defined by an absence of ties. It is "tieless," as the casual laborer in "The Hill" is said to be; it is free—even, apparently, of its own "compulsion."

Soldiers' Pay is the first text in which the buzzard makes an appearance, although indirectly, in discourse. In the mouth of Januarius Jones the image of the bird obviously conveys antithetical associations. Gilligan develops the image further: "Regard the buzzard . . . supported by air alone: what dignity, what singleness of purpose!" (SP, 63). " 'I always thought I'd like to be a buzzard,' he remarked, 'but now I think I'd like to be a woman' " (SP, 304). Jones adds a further thought in this frequently quoted passage:

He told her. " 'For a moment, an aeon, I pause plunging above the narrow precipice of thy breast' and on and on and on. Do you know how falcons make love? They embrace at an enormous height and fall locked, beak to beak, plunging: an unbearable ecstasy. While we have got to assume all sorts of ludicrous postures, knowing our own sweat. The falcon breaks his clasp and swoops away swift and proud and lonely, while a man must rise and take his hat and walk out." (SP, 227)

This comparison is taken word for word from poem XVII of *A Green Bough*, which is a dream of sexual sublimation. This dream originates well beyond the novelistic context, as for Faulkner, in the words I have used elsewhere,

> the flesh and its afflictions are bound up with the earth, which is essentially the place of greenness, of peeping and creeping, of stertorous breathing and reptilian desires. The blue of the sky, on the other hand, is where desire is free from the 'compulsions' which keep us rooted in the earth and embedded in time. It is not the place of non-desire (but perhaps the non-place or *utopia* of desire); it is the *locus* of ideal desire, whose satisfaction is pure, direct, not oblique.[19]

This is the ideal, the azure where all impurity is eliminated. Soon, the reader finds himself in the midst of Baudelairean glances, but first there is the Mallarméan gaze. What is important is the indebtedness of Faulkner's first novels to his poetry. In both the poems and the early novels, to quote from "Le Regard et le désir" again, "the sky and its bestiary are to the dream of the absolute and of the self emptied of its desires, what the earth and night are to the dreamings of the earthbound desires, the bucolic and sylvan bestiary, the 'leafed and hidden' [AGB, XLI, 64] world of the satyr and the wild flight of the faun: subjective correlatives" (41).

The use of the adjective "epicene," beginning with *Soldiers' Pay,* is no less personal and revealing. Both in his fiction and in his correspondence Faulkner showed a pronounced attraction for the physical quality and age of people "of indeterminate sex." As F. G. Riedel notes at the end of a study of the recurrence of the word, "according to Faulkner, *epicene* may mean anything from bisexual to sexless."[20] Cleanth Brooks writes of Laverne in

Pylon that "she is 'epicene' also in Faulkner's special meaning of 'unattainable.' "[21] In *Soldiers' Pay,* as distinct from *Mosquitoes,* the first meaning dominates. Thus, Faulkner writes: "This was the day of the Boy, male and female" (SP, 196); "This, the spring of 1919, was the day of the Boy, of him who had been too young for soldiering" (SP, 188); "Boys of both sexes swayed arm in arm" (SP, 190). Still referring to the ball, he also writes: "Dancing with the more skilled [girls] was too much like dancing with agile boys" (SP, 202).

But in this respect the most interesting passage is the paragraph that follows a dialogue between Jones and Cecily. Like the very first story Faulkner wrote, "Moonlight," the passage deals with the imminent sexual union between the young satyr and the "flapper." The theme of epicenism is developed through the analogy with the poplar:

> She shrugged delicately, nervously, and her lax hand between them grew again like a flower: it was as if her whole body became her hand. The symbol of a delicate, bodyless lust. Her hand seemed to melt into his yet remain without volition, her hand unawakened in his and her body also yet sleeping, crushed softly about with her fragile clothing. Her long legs, not for locomotion, but for the studied completion of a rhythm carried to its *nth:* compulsion of progress, movement; her body created for all men to dream after. A poplar, vain and pliant, trying attitude after attitude, gesture after gesture—"a girl trying gown after gown, perplexed but in pleasure." Her unseen face nimbused with light and her body, which was no body, crumpling a dress that had been dreamed. Not for maternity, not even for love: a thing for the eye and the mind. Epicene, he thought, feeling her slim bones, the bitter nervousness latent in her flesh. (SP, 224)

"A thing for the eye and mind": the appeal of epicenism is part of the mechanism of fascination. Could the source of Faulkner's interest be the seventh stanza of "Mr. Eliot's Sunday Morning Service"?

> Along the garden-wall the bees
> With hairy bellies pass between
> The staminate and the pistillate
> Blest office of the epicene.[22]

And yet epicenism can in no way be limited to such a literary borrowing, however likely it may be. At bottom the word conveys the essence of this ambiguous postwar period in which Faulkner, after Eliot and at about the same time as F. Scott Fitzgerald, diagnosed the erosion of traditional values, one of which was for him, as we know, the sane and sound polarity between the sexes. This itself stands as a guarantee of an ethical order in Faulkner's work. There is always a problem when the poles are indistinct or the border between the two blurred, as is the case of the many feminine men and masculine women in his novels: Charles Bon and Henry Sutpen in *Absalom, Absalom!* and Charlotte Rittenmeyer in *The Wild Palms,* for example.

The ballet or rather the farandole ("La Ronde")[23] of *Soldiers' Pay* ends with disorder. Only the Rector in his biblical peace (which in fact is quite pagan, being a stoicism colored with epicureanism), Emmy, who remains faithful to the memory of her pure and wild love, and the Negroes (who are hardly more than stereotypes) emerge from the general confusion. At different levels they all embody the values that are implicit in the word "home." The latter is spoken gravely by the dying man ("I've got to go home, Joe" [SP, 172]), and it can already be seen to serve to distinguish between characters. For example, Joe is typically a *homeless* person. Gilligan is *rootless.* This is just a hint of what later becomes a major feature in Faulkner's fiction, where strangers or "intruders" abound. The worst plight is reserved for characters who, like Bayard Sartoris, feel like strangers at home; indeed, much like Faulkner's own, his return home signifies nothing but a choice of interior exile. His case is clearly one of existential separation.

Gradually the whole set of well-known values comes into being. Understanding the evolution of these values is a key to the writing as a whole. As V. S. Pritchett wrote in a review of the British reprint of *Soldiers' Pay* in 1951, "he has shown here the power to grow out of the bitterness and cynicism and bragging sentimentalities which Hemingway never advanced from."[24]

If Faulkner attempted to organize a masquerade of sentimental and sexual attitudes in *Soldiers' Pay,* the mask he gave himself in the unfinished novel *Elmer* is quite transparent. Faulkner brought *Elmer* back from Paris at Christmas 1925. Even more than *Soldiers' Pay, Elmer* is focused on the

postwar period and its ruling feelings of ambivalence, attraction, and refusal. Faulkner was attracted both sexually and aesthetically to what he felt
to be this period's epicene quality; at the same time he was repelled by its
ethical ambiguity and futility. It soon became apparent to him that he
needed to distance himself from his fictional subjects and the immediate
contingencies that affected them in order to probe human conflict more
deeply. According to his friend, the painter William Spratling, in Europe
Faulkner "would be discoursing to the effect that for him there were 'only
two basic compulsions on earth; i.e., love and death'."[25] This is just what he
added in the margin of the typescript of *Soldiers' Pay*. Everything depends of
course on the way these compulsions are perceived. In all events Faulkner
was not long in realizing that the postwar scene offered only one perspective. He realized the insincerity of being carried away by a cultural tide in
which one could only be passively involved. Authentic and original writing
depended on a return to oneself. This is precisely what Faulkner tried to do,
albeit superficially, in *Elmer*.

After New York and New Orleans Europe was for Faulkner the last
attempt at escape, and there can be no doubt, from reading Spratling's
account of his misadventure in Genoa, that *Elmer* has a strong autobiographical dimension, at least insofar as the present of the narrative is
contemporary with the time when Faulkner began the novel: 1925. The
same is true of the various other versions or fragments of versions of the
story which have survived, such as "Elmer and Myrtle" and "Growing
Pains."[26] Both begin chronologically with an evocation of the protagonist
in his childhood, respectively in "Johnson City, Tennessee" and in "Jefferson, Mississippi." But the longer versions, the unfinished novel *Elmer,* and
the completed short story "A Portrait of Elmer" are set, both in manuscript
and typescript versions, in Montparnasse. Outside a café on the boulevard
Elmer is sitting with Angelo, an Italian who has got him out of jail after the
same misadventure that Spratling refers to (and which, according to him,
Faulkner would have liked to claim as his own). To express his gratitude
Elmer has been supporting Angelo in Paris. They look at girls passing by,
while Angelo's voice sounds "as if he were making love to [him]" or as if his
words possessed "an aesthetic significance" (*Elmer*, 90).

By contrast, two single manuscript pages entitled "Elmer" (located in
Paris) as well as the single manuscript page called "Elmer and Myrtle"
(located in Johnson City, Tennessee) contain an immediate reference to the

protagonist's brothers and sister, as if Faulkner had been tempted by beginning his story with a description of the family. Although there are long sections involving the family, they are treated as flashbacks in *Elmer,* the 136-typescript-page unfinished novel published not long ago by James B. Meriwether. The eponymous title can hardly fail to recall Sherwood Anderson, one of whose characters in *Winesburg, Ohio* was named Elmer Cowley. The subject is also Andersonian: it concerns a painter's childhood (one even thinks of Enoch Robinson). Faulkner writes about Elmer's family—an epicene sister and two brothers who have left home—and the death of the mother while the protagonist is away at war in Europe. Then he deals with sexual and professional experiences. If one overlooks the last section and its highly improbable turn (the action is moved to England, a country Faulkner explores poorly, and thus achieves a somewhat contrived irony in the Jamesian evocation of British aristocracy), the framework of the narrative is that of a bildungsroman.

Like the *West Ivis* in Genoa (FAB, 446), the ship on which Elmer is seen at the beginning of the novel drops anchor in Italy in August. Elmer reminisces about his childhood and his recent past on the bridge during the crossing. Once ashore, he is taken to a nightclub where, drunk and surrounded by an easy woman and the ship's second officer, he has a dream made of fantasies which Faulkner used again, almost verbatim, at the end of *Mosquitoes.* Next, following an incident that he can hardly remember but which recalls the one told by Spratling in his autobiography, Elmer finds himself in jail. Angelo Marina, the young Italian, helps free him from his plight. This is the same young man we find at the beginning of the other drafts sitting in Montparnasse.

Wounded accidentally during the war, Elmer has come back to Europe with the vague idea of finding Myrtle, a young woman by whom he has had a child. Myrtle left the United States in 1922 and has been in Europe for three years. Thus, the action takes place in 1925, the very year of the writing of the novel. Elmer's sexual education began much earlier, however, when, as a child, he slept next to his sister Jo-Addie. Next, his attention was transferred to a schoolboy hero, a sort of athletic and cruel Adonis:

> In the young male there still lingers a trace of the old pagan worship of the body, of beautiful physical articulation, which the Roman was later to taint with an admiration for prowess, superi-

ority. So it ran the scale in Elmer, from his young pleasure in watching his sister undress, to his blind adoration of this boy slender and beautiful as any god, and as cruel. A boy up to and through adolescence runs the whole gamut of civilization, anyway, getting in brief episodes the whole spiritual history of man. (*Elmer*, 25–26)

Shortly after, Elmer meets and has intercourse with Myrtle, whom he asks to marry but who answers, untroubled, that she is already engaged to marry another man. Elmer then leaves for war without participating in it, being wounded while handling a grenade on board the boat taking him to Europe. However, in contrast with Myrtle's "young body seemingly on the point of bursting out of its soiled expensive dress in soft rich curves," a new "image within him had become quite definitely alive; a Dianalike girl with an impregnable integrity, a slimness virginal and impervious to time or circumstance. Dark-haired and small and proud, casting him bones fiercely as though he were a dog, coppers as if he were a beggar, looking the other way" (*Elmer*, 38).

This image, which Mario Praz would have recognized, recurs four times in the text. It is clearly meant as another, ideal pole, in contrast with the figure of the women Elmer actually knows. Thus there is more than just a cultural osmosis in the recurrence of this image of woman according to the subject's inmost desire. As the goddess of hunting, she calls forth the eroticism of the Greco-Latin myth; devoted to the moon, she recalls the iconography of the Symbolists and Decadents. Moreover, she may well have had a name—probably not Estelle Oldham, but Helen Baird.

If the young, rather unheroic hero does not appear here with all the characteristics of the faun, his idea of Woman is nonetheless unequivocal. This Woman is the Diana figure who is only here at the beginning of her novelistic career. After *Soldiers' Pay* (Margaret Powers) and *Mosquitoes* (Patricia Robyn) she appears triumphant in *Sanctuary,* where, in Temple Drake's epicene figure, she carries the perversity of ambiguity to its limit. Antithetically, the recollection of the carnal unions with Myrtle-like, soft-bodied females seems to leave Elmer somewhat disillusioned: "all the intimacies could but leave them strangers despite abnegation and wanting and striving, each within the unbreakable armour of self" (*Elmer*, 104).

Faulkner only made one remark about *Elmer*, in response to a question posed by James B. Meriwether: "According to Faulkner (interview 12 March 1958), he wrote it in Paris on his trip abroad after being in New Orleans, but left it unfinished—it was 'funny, but not funny enough'" (*Career,* 81; FAB, 479). Either Faulkner did not remember his text clearly or he was hiding his true opinion beneath his flippant judgment: whatever one's personal sense of the comic may be, few readers are likely to find *Elmer* "funny" (except, perhaps, for the circumstances that lead to the protagonist's arrest in Venice). On the contrary, it may be argued that, like *Soldiers' Pay,* this is a text that simply fails to conceal the gravity of the topic in spite of its stylistic mannerisms and the disenchanted tone of its philosophical (or pseudophilosophical) reflections. Faulkner's comment might be explained both by the lapse of time and by the distance that he had managed in the meanwhile to put between himself and his fiction, especially this kind of thinly veiled bildungsroman. Perhaps the real sense of Faulkner's remark is that *Elmer should* have been funny; that is, from the point of view of the mature artist its subject should have been treated with levity rather than left as an embarrassing witness of the protagonist's "growing pains"—as the story was called at one stage (*Career,* 81).

The much shorter version entitled "Portrait of Elmer" is no doubt a later reworking of the same material, adapted for publication ten years later in 1935. Not only has the style changed (it is less precious, firmer and more economical), but the story itself is much more sober and less scattered. Moreover, several manuscript corrections not by the author's hand prove that the typescript passed through a literary agent for submission to magazines. (In fact, it was offered to Random House, who might have published it in a limited edition, had they not received it too late for Christmas 1935; in the meantime Faulkner had become a Random House writer with the publication of *Idyll in the Desert* in 1931.)

Faulkner's comment of 1958 concerns the short story entitled "Portrait of Elmer" more than the unfinished novel, especially as regards Elmer's *Bildung*. The ending is a good example: Elmer is seen seated next to Angelo outside a café on the Boulevard Montparnasse. Elmer still wishes to become a painter and still thinks of Myrtle. He is, however, unable to meet her in the Rue Servandoni,[27] being overtaken by an urgent need at an inopportune moment. He satisfies nature's call in a place which, lacking certain basic commodities, forces him to use his first canvas, which he has been working on laboriously during the preceding week in Meudon.

Generally, however, this portrait of the young man as an artist is still centered on sexual initiation and, perhaps even more so than in the unfinished novel, on puberty. At stake here are his "apprenticeship to manhood" (us, 626) and on several occasions *"fame. And then Myrtle"* (us, 635, 638). As in *Elmer,* the taste of the protagonist for painting has such a sensual character that the word hermaphroditism is used.[28] Certain details in *Elmer* have disappeared in "Portrait of Elmer," such as the hero's taste for the shape of cigars; others have been amplified, such as the invitation from the schoolmistress. The latter forces Elmer to flee her house, since his passion for her is "fine"—apparently because it is "sexless" (us, 616). As with so many other of Faulkner's characters, this confrontation with the reality of sex leaves Elmer nauseated. New episodes in Elmer's education have appeared: for instance, his initiation with young Velma, whom he chases into a barn loft. Faulkner had also added a Hemingway-like sojourn in a lumberjack camp in Michigan.

Elmer's family situation is not changed, however: both brothers have left, the father is sedentary and ineffectual, and the mother, "that passionate indomitable woman" (us, 621), dies before Elmer's return from war. His sister has not changed at all from *Elmer;* she is still "fiercely erect," standing "starkly poised as a young thin ugly tree" (us, 615). Her image coincides with the ideal feminine image which is formulated in the text, in much the same terms as in *Elmer,* though without the allusion to Diana: "Later still, the shape in his mind became unvague concrete and alive: a girl with impregnable virginity to time or circumstance; darkhaired small and proud, casting him bones fiercely as though he were a dog, coppers as though he were a beggar leprous beside a dusty gate" (us, 620). "Portrait of Elmer" also contains a very interesting new passage about a "vision" of the hero's deceased mother in Paris. Elmer must change his hotel; he arrives in Rue Servandoni, where he sees a little hotel:

> *It's just another hotel. The only difference will be that living here will be a little more tediously exigent and pettily annoying.* But again it was too late; already he had seen her. She stood, hands on hips in a clean harsh dress, scolding at an obese man engaged statically with a mop—a thin woman of forty or better, wiry, with a harried indefatigable face; for an instant he was his own father eight ⋅housand miles away in Texas, not even knowing that he was

thinking *I might have known she would not stay dead* not even
thinking with omniscient perspicuity *I wont even need the book*
(US, 637)

This apparition of the deceased mother, to a young man who thinks of
himself as his own father, suggests perhaps the origins of the family tensions
that are focused later on in Quentin Compson and in Addie Bundren.
Following this apparition, Elmer moves straight into the little hotel with
Angelo, where Myrtle is waiting for him. Such a play of superimposed
identities might make one believe that Faulkner had just been reading
Freud.[29] Whatever the truth may be, Thomas McHaney's final comment on
Elmer may be said to apply much better to the "Portrait": it is "a comic
gloss on Elmer's sexual coming of age" (*Miscellany*, 42).

Reading the "Elmer" material, one is above all struck by the impression
of a kind of literary exercise in self-appraisal. If this exercise is overly ironic,
as in the "Portrait," the central problem posed is no less than that of Bildung
or of ontological development. How does one *become* an artist? Does this
somehow imply ceasing to be biologically the young man that one is? This is
the question the story asks. In *Elmer* it is true that the hero's growth during
his *Wanderjahr* is more important than the development of the artist. Yet
even here there are many elements that later recur in other portraits of the
young man—particularly in that of Joe Christmas. Nothing is more serious
than a self-examination, and irony is, after all, only a way of ducking the
even more serious question asked by the protagonist, which is the question
asked of Stein at the very center of Joseph Conrad's *Lord Jim:* "How to
be?"[30]

No doubt *Elmer* played a functional role for Faulkner. The many abor-
tive attempts to start the story suggest as much. Making Elmer a would-be
painter is the thin disguise that Faulkner needed to put himself on stage as
an unheroic hero (which in itself was a far cry from the heroic histrionics he
had just been playing both in life and in his early fiction). Elmer is, therefore, Faulkner in Paris, although both the actor and the stage are doubled:
the actor fleshes out both an intention and the (ironic) sublimation of the
intention; the stage is both Elmer's Paris and, behind it, though faintly
drawn, the artist's "Carcassonne." At this point writing was still "fun"
(LITG, 255). Faulkner was still astonished at what he was becoming: after
Elmer the painter there was to be Gordon the sculptor and, even later,

Charlotte Rittenmeyer and her "collection of little figures," "the effigies elegant, bizarre, fantastic and perverse" (TWP, 87, 89). Beginning with *Flags in the Dust,* art stopped being the topic and became the substance of the discourse.

The few but crucial years between Faulkner's return from Europe and his emergence as a major writer witnessed the gradual transformation of a mere (though doubtless passionate) ego into a real, substantial narrative consciousness (*sujet de l'écriture*). Instead of the static self of narcissism, there emerges a more malleable or bending self, formed through the act of writing and through nothing else. One could speak in fact of an inflection of the self through the grammar of writing. Like all great writers, Faulkner had a strong sense of the moral and personal economy which is implicit in the act of writing. And for him, who would dedicate the rest of his life to this single, endlessly repeated act, there was no perspective left but to make it an everyday activity. Let us remember Phil Stone's only comment on the years now in front of us: "He was writing all the time."

chapter four

Perversion

Mosquitoes, "Afternoon of a Cow," *The Hamlet*

> . . . if this be humor, then I have lost my sense of it;
>
> unless humor is, like evil, in the eye of the beholder.
>
> —*"The Ivory Tower"*

There exists a photograph of the young Faulkner seated alone on a bench at the foot of a gigantic tree. He is writing *Mosquitoes.* Far off, one sees a jetty running out into the ocean. This is Pascagoula, Mississippi, in the summer of 1926. On page 464 of the typescript of the novel one reads "Pascagoula, Miss./1 Sept. 1926," and one of the cover pages carries the dedication, "To Helen, beautiful and wise." Helen is Helen Baird, with whom Faulkner tried to console himself for having lost Estelle Oldham. In fact, there is no doubt now that he actually wished to marry her.[1] Her physical importance for Faulkner is beyond doubt, since the reverse side of page 269 of the same typescript is a draft of a very personal letter in which her name and that of the novel recur like leitmotivs: "Your book is pretty near done. Just a few more things. They are nice people[:] Jenny as ineffable as an ice cream soda, and Pete with his queer golden eyes, and Mrs Talliaferro" (SL, 33).

Like *Soldiers' Pay, Mosquitoes* is a novel constructed with an extreme care that borders on cleverness and discloses the lingering influence of late French symbolism or aestheticism. But where the first novel is symmetrical, the second is concentric. Much like the *Nausikaa,* in front of whose stem "a small bow wave spread its sedate fading fan" (MOS, 58), the novel is organized around a central (though perfectly futile) event, the midnight swim, which is followed by a flight to the swamps. The episodes reflect one another on either side of the main action, which is virtually the only action in the novel: two men overboard—Ayers ("The First Day," Four O'Clock) and Talliaferro ("The Fourth Day," Two O'Clock); the breakdown ("The Second Day," Morning); and the tugging of the yacht off the sand ("The Third Day," Three O'Clock). In addition to this the longest conversations are spread equally over the four days of the cruise and between the episodes: the breakdown and the swim during the second day, the flight and the tugging during the third, the disappearance of Gordon and his return during the fourth.

Thus, one is encouraged to set the characters who act and speak little against those who speak a lot and act little (or, at any rate, who act too late, at the very moment when the tug is at last in sight). Among the first are Pete, the steward, whose theft of a steel rod in the machine room causes the breakdown; Patricia and David, who swim at midnight and escape into the swamp, and Gordon, who disappears. This opposition in the plot of the novel reflects faithfully the central thematic opposition between the mature characters (all over thirty) and the young (all under twenty): on the one hand, there are Mrs. Maurier, Talliaferro, Fairchild, the Semite, Ayers, Mrs. Wiseman, and Miss Jameson; on the other, Patricia Robyn and her twin brother Theodore, Pete Ginotta and Genevieve Steinbauer and David West. Mark Frost is more difficult to place; he is the poet who, though spending most of his time with the older people, peppering their endless chatter with biting witticisms, does not share their verbosity and seems younger than they are (perhaps only because he is less verbose). Gordon is thirty-six years old, but he is the only person capable of communicating with the two groups, even if he can do so only through the spanking he gives to the hostess's niece. Gordon is the new avatar of the Faulknerian faun: "In the yet level rays of the moon the man's face was spare and cavernous, haughty and inhuman almost. He doesn't get enough to eat, she [Patricia] knew suddenly and infallibly. It's like a silver faun's face, she thought" (MOS, 152).

Indeed, the images that recur throughout the novel are signs of a singularly persistent (even quite static) vision of the characters. Thus Gordon, a sculptor from New Orleans, who has carved "the virginal breastless torso of a girl, headless, armless, legless, in marble temporarily caught and hushed yet passionate still for escape" (MOS, 11), is compared throughout the novel to a hawk (in addition to being closely associated with the faun): "Gordon's hawk face brooded above them, remote and insufferable with arrogance" (27), "Gordon looked down at the shorter man with his lean bearded face, his lonely hawk's face arrogant with shyness and pride" (267), and ". . . brooding his hawk's face above them against the sky" (337). Moreover, he is always pictured as being alone, haughty, even arrogant: "Gordon loomed above the two shorter men, staring down at them, remote and arrogant" (49), "Gordon stood against the wall, aloof, not listening to them hardly, watching within the bitter and arrogant loneliness of his heart a shape strange and new as fire swirling, headless, armless, legless" (72), and "He released her as abruptly and stood over her, gaunt and ill nourished and arrogant in the moonlight" (154).

This hauteur is the deeply romantic arrogance of geniuses "all over the world," as Melville might have said. It is part of "the shock of *un*recognition." Gordon is no doubt meant to be an authentic artist who suffers because he stands out so much from the crass and superficial world around him. He belongs to the same species of bird with which Faulkner identified. The motif that haunts him ("your name is like a little golden bell hung in my heart"—MOS, 267–68, 274) is associated with Patricia, the irritating girl to whom he administers the spanking. Patricia's name is not quoted in the draft letter to Helen Baird mentioned above, but the same motif which haunts Gordon in the novel occurs there twice. This recurrence is enough of a coincidence, surely, to let us conjecture that Patricia is modeled on Helen Baird and that Gordon (who is taller than most every other character) is himself an idealized projection of the author.

This assumption has already been made by several critics. For instance, Raymond Queneau makes it implicitly in suggesting that Gordon is the least grotesque of all the characters: "in *Mosquitoes,* grotesqueness grows by degrees, as follows: the sculptor, the novelist, the critic, the poet, the non-artist, the patron."[2] For Joseph Blotner, however, Gordon is modeled on William Spratling (FAB, 515). Michael Millgate sees some of Faulkner's traits—beginning with his taciturnity—in Mark Frost (*Achievement,* 74). But these identifications are not incompatible with an interpretation of Gordon as the novelist's ideal self. Conrad Aiken has also noted the potential preeminence of the character: "One gets the impression . . . that when he began the book, he intended to make his sculptor, Gordon, the chief character, or, at any rate, *one* of the chief characters."[3] As we have seen, the same hesitation can be observed in *Soldiers' Pay.*

The critics who have taken an interest in *Mosquitoes* have in general been struck by the importance of both language and sexuality. Yet, curiously, they have not attempted to establish a link between these two elements. For example, Olga Vickery's remarkable study, the best on the opposition of word and action in *Mosquitoes,* strangely overlooks the sexual theme. As for the others, three of them compare *Mosquitoes* with *The Reivers* as being Faulkner's only two comic novels. A grosser error is hard to imagine. Not only do these critics overlook the masterful comedy of *The Hamlet,* but they also fail to distinguish between the comic modes of the two novels they compare, which are poles apart. It is not even certain whether the satire in *Mosquitoes* is more comic than grave. In fact the same might be said of *Mosquitoes* as Faulkner said of *Elmer:* It is "funny, but not funny enough" to be called a "comic" novel. Moreover, as is true of certain sections of *Soldiers' Pay, Mosquitoes* is a book in which the sophisticated tone and the verbal veneer conceal poorly what one senses to be the author's personal involvement in his subject. This involvement is felt to such a degree (in this novel and in most of the early writings, in fact) that the real problem of the book concerns more its prenovelistic and private quality (as Raymond Queneau shrewdly noted in his preface) than the orchestration of themes and the ways in which they are treated.

The opposition between the two age groups is crystallized in the avuncular relationship between their two spokesmen, Mrs. Maurier and her niece Patricia, whose relationship is limited to a caricature of communication: ineffectual complaints in place of authority on the one hand, insolence instead of respect on the other. This hiatus recalls the relationship between Mrs. Saunders and her daughter Cecily in *Soldiers' Pay,* as well as the total absence of communication between Mrs. Compson and her daughter Caddy in *The Sound and the Fury.* The age gap may remind us of what Faulkner said in 1955: "People between 20 and 40 are not sympathetic. The child has the capacity to do but it can't know. It only knows when it is no longer able to do—after 40. Between 20 and 40 the will of the child to do gets stronger, more dangerous, but it has not begun to learn to know yet. Since his capacity to do is forced into channels of evil through environment and pressures, man is strong before he is moral. The world's anguish is caused by people between 20 and 40" (LITG, 254). This statement is interesting because it shows how, for Faulkner, who was certainly not a philosopher in the sense that he did not deal primarily in concepts, everything had a body before having a consciousness. Even if, when almost sixty years old himself, the author imputed the reason for the individual's being "forced into the channels of evil" to the deterministic concept of "environment and pressures," it is nonetheless remarkable that he should say what, thirty years earlier, he might not have been willing to say: "Man is strong before being moral." It is not of course a question of *Macht geht bevor Recht;* if there is a rationalization, it concerns only the individual—and even, more precisely, the latter's *development.* In other terms, for Faulkner before being a form of conduct, that is, before having moral implications, every act is a form of behavior, which the body inscribes in what is always in the process of becoming the individual's history, or History in general. This is what is usually implied by such a phrase as "a historical gesture." To decipher this history through the palimpsest is one task of the symbolist writer, for whom everything is a sign to be interpreted, beginning with mere physical presence—or absence. Indeed, it is a remarkable fact that until 1927–28 Faulkner told stories of frustration and absence: only in *The Sound and the Fury* did he aim straight at the lack (*le manque*), which he explains in his own terms: "Previous to it I had written three novels, with progressively decreasing ease and pleasure, and reward or emolument . . . because one day it suddenly seemed as if a door had clapped silently and forever to between me and all publishers' addresses and booklists and I said to myself, Now I can write. *Now I can just write.* Whereupon I, who had three brothers and no sisters and was destined to lose my first daughter in infancy, began to write about a little girl" (*Miscellany,* 158–59; my emphasis).

Thus, in *Mosquitoes,* instead of allowing his characters to live in his own moment (he was just turning thirty in 1927), he cast them either in an earlier period, for which he already nurtured a poignant nostalgia, or in a later period, which he imagined in a satirical light, with a mixture of irony (Mark Frost) and confidence (Gordon). The only moment when his inveterate talkers grow serious in silence (or silent in seriousness) is when they brood about their lost youth:

> Mark Frost snored. The moon, the pallid belly of the moon, inundating the world with a tarnished magic not of living things, laying her silver fleshless hand on the water that whispered and lapped against the hull of the yacht. The Semitic man clutched his dead cigar and he and Fairchild sat in the implacable laxing of muscles and softening tissue of their forty odd years, seeing two wide curious eyes into which an inverted surprise came clear as

water, and long golden curls swinging downward above the or-
dure; and they sat in silence, remembering youth and love, and
time and death. (MOS, 234)

What is the origin of this strange epiphany? Closing the third day of the
voyage of the *Nausikaa* with a lull, it brings to a conclusion Fairchild's
anamnesis, a childhood recollection in which the whole novel is embedded.
The passage must be quoted almost in its entirety:

> "I was spending the summer with my grandfather, in Indiana.
> In the country. I was a boy then, and it was a kind of family
> reunion, with aunts and cousins that hadn't seen each other in
> years. Children, too, all sizes.
>
> "There was a girl that I remember, about my age, I reckon. She
> had blue eyes and a lot of long, prim, golden curls. This girl, Jenny,
> must have looked like her, when she was about twelve. I didn't
> know the other children very well, and besides I was used to
> furnishing my own diversion anyway; so I just kind of hung
> around and watched them doing the things children do. I didn't
> know how to go about getting acquainted with them. I'd seen how
> the other newcomers would do it, and I'd kind of plan to myself
> how I'd go about it: what I'd say when I went up to them. . . ." He
> ceased and mused for a time in a kind of hushed surprise. "Just
> like Talliaferro," he said at last, quietly. "I hadn't thought of that
> before." He mused for a time. Then he spoke again.
>
> · · · ·
>
> "This was before the day of water works and sewage systems in
> country homes, and this one had the usual outhouse. It was down
> a path from the house. In the late summer there were tall burdocks
> on either side of the path, taller than a twelve-year-old boy by late
> August. The outhouse was a small square frame box kind of thing,
> with a partition separating the men from the women inside.
>
> "It was a hot day, in the middle of the afternoon. The others
> were down in the orchard, under the trees. From where I had
> been, from a big tree in the yard, I could see them, and the girls'
> colored dresses in the shade; and when I climbed down from the
> tree and went across the back yard and through the gate and along
> the path toward the privy I could still see them occasionally

through gaps in the burdocks. They were sitting around in the shade, playing some game, or maybe just talking.

"I went on down the path and went inside, and when I turned to shut the door to the men's side, I looked back. And I saw her blue dress kind of shining, coming along the path between the tall weeds. I couldn't tell if she had seen me or not, but I knew that if I went back I'd have to pass her, and I was ashamed to do this.

. . . .

"So I shut the door quick and stood right quiet, and soon I heard her enter the other side. I didn't know yet if she'd seen me, but I was going to stay quiet as I could until she went away. I just had to do that, it seemed to me.

. . . .

"So I tiptoed across to the seat. It was hot in there, with the sun beating down on it: I could smell hot resin, even above the smell of the place itself. In a corner of the ceiling there was a dirt dobber's nest—a hard lump of clay with holes in it, stuck to the ceiling, and big green flies made a steady droning sound. I remember how hot it was in there, and that feeling places like that gave you—a kind of letting down of the bars of pretense, you know; a kind of submerging of civilized strictures before the grand implacability of nature and the physical body. And I stood there, feeling this feeling and the heat, and hearing the drone of those big flies, holding my breath and listening for a sound from beyond the partition. But there wasn't any sound beyond it, so I put my head down through the seat. (MOS, 231–34)

Note the functional precision and the obsessive character of the description—or rather of the staging, the mise-en-scène: the childhood world is blond, blue, and fresh, and clashes with the voyeur's internalization of greenery and heat. Next, one is struck by the description of the outhouse, pungent and overheated, droning with insect life. The precision extends into Fairchild's evocation of the scene—in the subtle correspondence between the girl's "blue dress" and Jenny, as well as between the narrator's reflection of himself as a child and Talliaferro. Fairchild's special use of language causes the anecdote to produce a similar effect on those who listen (one of whom is asleep). The same effect had been produced on the narrator when he was a child. Thus everyone's scopophilia is being appealed to.

This is neither the first nor the last time that Faulkner puts a voyeur on stage (see chapter 7), nor is it the first or the last time that he associates sexuality and defecation. Faulkner makes the same association in a more comic vein at the end of "Portrait of Elmer," when Elmer's surging desire to meet Myrtle in his own room in Paris is checked by his need to defecate. Yet another similar scene is the romantic tryst between Ike Snopes and the cow in *The Hamlet*, which is itself foreshadowed in "Afternoon of a Cow." There are, of course, ready-made psychoanalytical explanations for the association.

For Millgate Faulkner uses dramatic situations in *Mosquitoes* to explore "a wide variety of sexual relationships." According to him, the author brings "into constantly shifting juxtaposition his group of men and women of different ages and from widely divergent backgrounds. Thus we see Jenny and Pete together, Jenny and the young nephew, Jenny and Mr. Talliaferro, Pete and Miss Jameson, Miss Jameson and Mark Frost, Miss Jameson and Gordon, Gordon and Patricia, Patricia and David, and so on" (*Achievement*, 70). The trouble is not only that these "shifting" relationships are established on very different levels, but also that, if they have something in common, it is the fact that they are not sexual. As in *Soldiers' Pay*, the sexual act in *Mosquitoes* is a fire around which all the characters dance, without burning themselves. There is no doubt that the motivations for their ballet have a sexual origin, but in the space that separates the desire and the act, all the characters soon come to a stop, as if frozen mentally: the Word by which they live catches them in its snare, and the whole show leaves the impression that they are afraid of sexuality. In other words they do act, but they do not act out all that is in a human being. They even refrain from doing so.

As in *Soldiers' Pay*, the characters in *Mosquitoes* only experience sex as a form of frustration. Mrs. Maurier and Mr. Talliaferro are both widowed. Mrs. Wiseman has left her husband, and Miss Jameson has remained a virgin, even though she had a lover in Greenwich Village (MOS, 102. Could she be a distant cousin of Linda Snopes in *The Mansion?* This would not be the only relationship between the first and the last among Faulkner's works). Julius Kaufman and Major Ayers are single and happy to be so—at least this is what they say. The young generation has achieved little more than their elders in matters sexual. Patricia and Robyn's escape into the swamps is sexually "pure"—or noneventful. It is clear that the mosquitoes that bite them are the natural and ironic counterparts of the perennial chatterboxes on board the *Nausikaa*. Theodore, though a bit feminine, always has in his hand a phallic object, the steel rod, the pipe, or the knife. He reminds one of the child Elmer, with his taste for the shape of cigars and tubes of paint. Though no more successfully, Pete, laconic and brutal, at least has the merit of attempting to have a sexual affair with Jenny. Indeed, it is Pete and Jenny whom Faulkner cites in the draft of his letter to Helen.

However, just as *Soldiers' Pay* is a novel of misunderstanding and absence, *Mosquitoes* is one of failure and lack (*le manque*). Its language abounds with adjectives and adverbs with negative prefixes—unchaste, unmuscled, untarnished, undimensional, unemphatic, unsophisticated, untrammeled, unclean, unbearable, unreluctant, impersonal, insufferable, inscrutable, impossible, implacable, ineffable (seven occurrences), etc.— whose pervasiveness puts one in mind of Melville and Conrad and their vision of a world where a nostalgia filled with idealistic yearning is felt in the very moment when the consciousness must be reconciled with the existence of the principle of reality. All express refusal of the world as it is. The Word is obstinately opposed to experience, the Logos to practice. "Ineffable," for instance, is a word always associated with Jenny, the pole around which the male characters dance their sexual and epistemological *ronde*. But Jenny is not fascinating—no more than reality is in general. She envelops and ensnares her victims. The one who is fascinating is the tomboy, the nonwoman, Patricia the epicene.

The irony—and of course the ultimate perversion—is that between these two a serious, truly sexual relationship is established. Here, Faulkner boldly achieves a depth more compelling than the more superficial, mostly psychological and social study of the relationship between the three young women in *Soldiers' Pay*.

He went even further in the extant typescript. In a passage not to be found in the published version, Faulkner described Patricia kissing Jenny (whom she calls "woman" several times), searching for her lips and getting up abruptly so as to spit. Then, "her moving hand ceased in the valley beneath the swell of Jenny's thigh and she was quite motionless a moment." Millgate calls this scene "a notable extension of the sexual theme" (*Achieve-*

ment, 71), but it is both more and less than a deliberate extension. It takes place just before the swim ("The Second Day," Eleven O'Clock), at the end of the long dialogue between Jenny and Patricia. Indeed this scene, when set within the main action of the novel (the escape into the swamps during the third day), constitutes the exact symmetrical counterpart of the conversation on poetry that ends with the reading of a poem entitled "Hermaphroditus" by Fairchild ("The Fourth Day," Eleven O'Clock). Directly after this, Gordon appears again. A long conversation serves as an introduction to imminent action (though, in typical Faulkner fashion, not to the act itself).

Faulkner's interest in epicenism, already noted, is part of a wider interest in the trespassing of barriers between innocence and experience, between the sexes, etc. One remembers the scene in which the young Elmer is described in bed with his "elfish" sister Jo-Addie or indeed the character of Juliet in "Adolescence." Elsewhere in *Mosquitoes*, Patricia attempts to protect her twin brother Theodore from the irresistible charm of Jenny, under the pretext that he is only a child. Here one can see the first demonstration of "the law of twinship" which, as Michel Mohrt has shown, constitutes one of the mechanisms of literary creation in Faulkner's work.[4] "Twinship is a kinship," as Raymond Queneau also aptly noted in his preface to *Mosquitoes*. And for novelist Michel Tournier, author of a novel devoted to it, twinship is "the most complete literary theme"[5]—as Shakespeare knew better than anybody else.

Even if it were Faulkner and not his Boni and Liveright editor who censored the brief appearance of feminine homosexuality, he nonetheless wrote his novel under the sign of epicenism. A score of phrases refer to it, most frequently in relation to Patricia, whose knees are "bare and sexless," whose "fresh young smell" recalls "that of a young tree," and whose almost flat chest resembles that which Gordon sculpts in marble and which he studies with an artist's detachment: "Gordon examined with growing interest her flat breast and belly, her boy's body which the poise of it and the thinness of her arms belied. Sexless, yet somehow vaguely troubling. Perhaps just young, like a calf or a colt" (MOS, 24). The writer's nostalgia seems to be polarized by an almost presexual demonstration of erotic behavior. Can one speak in this context of innocence?

Yet the sexless Patricia attracts Gordon (the faun) no less than the oversexed Jenny intoxicates Talliaferro, who is clearly the satyr, a new avatar of Januarius Jones. They were born in the same anonymity, and both are symbols of absolute contingency and caricatures of destiny (they may therefore be said to be the slaves of their "compulsions"): "Jones, Januarius Jones, born of whom he knew and cared not, becoming Jones alphabetically, January through a conjunction of calendar and biology, Januarius through the perverse conjunction of his own star and the compulsion of food and clothing" (SP, 56). "He [Mr. Talliaferro] had been the final result of some rather casual biological research conducted by two people who, like the great majority, had no business producing children at all" (MOS, 31–32). Jones is a Latin teacher and Talliaferro a wholesale purchaser of women's clothing, like the protagonist of "Don Giovanni" (US, 480). They both have a spurious relationship with culture: they have a verbal appetite for it that turns them into satellites rotating around real problems, just as they rotate around women. Once more, the image of the tantalized hornet is suggested here.

Gordon, on the contrary, like Donald earlier, goes straight to the fact of Patricia's ambiguous attitude toward sexuality and her refusal (or at least her denial) of womanhood. The spanking he gives her purges him of the frustrated desire that he has long felt for her, yet he cannot find satisfaction with a being as sexless as she is. He spanks her so as to convey his "masculine," "sound" authority (to use Faulkner's own terms). The spanking is the only real contact between the two age groups. Moreover, the idea of a spanking crops up ironically on the very last page of the book, when an anonymous feminine voice that Talliaferro hears on the phone utters: "You tell 'em, big boy; treat 'em rough." For Queneau "the novel itself is built about the theme that 'one is always too good with women'," and it is not surprising that in the epilogue Gordon goes off to satisfy his exasperated desire in a whorehouse: "(A door opened in the wall. Gordon entered and before the door closed again they saw him in a narrow passageway lift a woman from the shadow and raise her against the mad stars, smothering her squeal against his tall kiss)" (338–39). In satisfying this urge he becomes the only adult to progress from Word to Act. There follows a passage which Olga Vickery was right in comparing with the "Walpurgisnacht section" of Joyce's *Ulysses*.

Meanwhile Fairchild continues to talk. He is as drunk as his nighttime walking companion, but what he says has a powerful impact, especially as it comes after their shared voyeuristic experience. Fairchild's running commentary on the "earth to ashes" theme contains an observation about

genius that Faulkner was to adopt as his own and that serves as an ex-
ordium to *A Fable:*

> It is that Passion Week of the heart, that instant of timeless beati-
> tude which some never know, which some, I suppose, gain at will,
> which others gain through an outside agency like alcohol, like to-
> night—that passive state of the heart with which the mind, the
> brain, has nothing to do at all, in which the hackneyed accidents
> which make up this world—love and life and death and sex and
> sorrow—brought together by chance in perfect proportions, take
> on a kind of splendid and timeless beauty. (339)

It would be wrong not to pay careful attention to this profession of faith by
Fairchild, alias Sherwood Anderson. Perhaps more related to the neo-
romanticism of a Conrad (or indeed of Keats himself) than to that of
Faulkner's contemporaries (except for Sherwood Anderson), the profession
affirms an allegiance to what might be called universal, almost anthropological conditions of existence. But the end of the quotation underscores, in
quasi-Joycean terms, how much the aesthetic requirement remains important. Above all, with the support of the Passion as metaphorical vehicle (to
be used again in *The Sound and the Fury* and in *A Fable*), the heart is pro-
moted here for the first time to the forefront of the hierarchy of Faulknerian
values. The gist of the speech delivered in Stockholm on 10 December 1950
thus has roots in the ending of Faulkner's second published novel, dated
1927. As we know, this ending paraphrases a passage in the unfinished
Elmer.[6]

However, if the brain is denied, the body is never absent. Even while
Fairchild expresses the universal echo that vibrates in all human experience,
even the most idiosyncratic, the Semitic man needs only to quote to him the
sentence with which the very first of the *New Orleans Sketches* began: "I
love three things: gold, marble, purple; splendor, solidity, color" (NOS, 3),[7]
to make him vomit. Many subsequent Faulknerian characters will react as
he does when faced with a revelation, generally of a sexual nature, that is
too strong to be assimilated without an evil reaction (see chapter 12 of this
book).

It may be argued that in relation to the other characters, Fairchild plays
the very role that Faulkner plays vis-à-vis his own persona: He verbalizes
situations. This is all the more true since he speaks immediately after the

return of the young couple from their escape and after Gordon's simultaneous disappearance:

> The way she went off with Da——the steward. It was kind of nice, wasn't it? And came back. No excuses, no explanations—'think no evil' you know. That's what these postwar young folks have taught us. Only old folks like Julius and me ever see evil in what people, young people, do. But then, I guess folks growing up into the manner of *looking at life* that we inherited, would find evil in anything where inclination wasn't subservient to duty. We were taught to believe that duty is infallible, or it wouldn't be duty, and if it were just unpleasant enough, you got a mark in heaven, sure. . . . But maybe it ain't so different, taken one generation by another. *Most of our sins are vicarious, anyhow.* I guess when you are young you have too much fun just being, to sin very much. But it's kind of nice, being young in this generation. (228–29; my emphasis)

This apparently harmless reflection takes us nearer the "heart" of the problem than ever before. The notion of substitution or *vicariousness* constitutes the very axis of a typically Faulknerian problem that continues, particularly in the recurrence of peeping Toms, up to the last novel, *The Reivers*.

The sexual attitudes displayed in *Mosquitoes* are a case in point. Evil, for Faulkner, first of all signals a *perverted* relation between two beings (or, worse, between an individual and his own consciousness). But at this early stage the existence of separate age groups serves both to simplify and to complicate the problem. Youth's saving grace is its ignorance. Faulkner's analysis evolved quite a bit from this perspective, particularly in *Sanctuary*. In *Mosquitoes* Patricia and Jenny avoid being branded with perversion only because of their youth. Talliaferro, by contrast, fails. He is a mediocre, would-be voyeur. Leaning over Jenny asleep, "all the time it was as though *he stood nearby yet aloof, watching his own antics*" (128; my emphasis). Later on, Fairchild shocks Mrs. Maurier with this remark: "There'd be sure a decline in population *if a man were twins* and had to stand around and *watch himself making love*" (185; my emphases).

Indeed, what is Talliaferro for Faulkner, as he writes in Pascagoula, if not the double from whom he knows he must be freed—the clown anticking in front of the mirror of the critical self? This is exactly what Fairchild denounces. On two occasions, like a deux ex machina, he mocks Talliaferro with the supremely ironic name of "the Great Illusion, par excellence" (130, 313). In the context of this novel the illusion clearly concerns sexuality. It consists in believing that one can seduce woman, when in fact the woman selects the man, and that one can indeed seduce with words. However, let us keep in mind the problem of Faulkner's relation with his own early work; if we consider that Woman becomes an emblem of the real and that words are the writer's only way of approaching it, calling Talliaferro the Great Illusion may also appear to be a way of putting one's earlier understanding of art in a critical perspective. It then becomes clear that the various artists pictured in *Mosquitoes* are so many figures representing the writer confronted with the problem of literature.

Stated another way, the young artist has accepted his aesthetic error and is living through its consequences or finding ways of drawing benefits from it. Faulkner's creation of Talliaferro, as of Januarius Jones before him, demonstrates a need to display and get rid of a spurious relationship with literature. The creation of Fairchild expresses the will to put on the same stage as Talliaferro someone who can see through this relationship. The creation of Gordon transcends that of the latter two and is meant to embody the true, active relationship implicit in the "Keatsian" relationship to art. Thus the trinity is complete, and Faulkner, or rather the *writing subject*, although fragmented, is totally involved in it. He is in the center of this group which contains both his past and his future as a writer.

The whole dialectic of *Mosquitoes* is contained in a sentence spoken by Mrs. Wiseman, which sums up (wrongly and ironically) the problem posed in the novel: "the Thing is merely the symbol for the Word" (130). The philosophy of symbolism (as expressed by any of its main theoreticians, Kant, Schlegel, Coleridge, Carlyle, or Emerson) is here perversely stood upon its head. In this phrase we detect Faulkner's shift from narcissistic aestheticism to anthropological symbolism. The lesson is given not by Fairchild, but by Julius Kaufman, who has just analyzed Fairchild's problem thus: "Life is everywhere the same, you know. Manners of living it may be different—are they not different between adjoining villages? family names, profits on a single field or orchard, work influences—*but man's compulsions, duty and inclinations: the axis and the circumference of his squirrel cage, they do not change*" (243; my emphasis).

The model in art is not Anderson-Fairchild, who is too innocent, too inhibited and too garrulous—a prophet, not a poet. The model is a powerful writer whose vision had "splendor, solidity, color," whom "even translation cannot injure," and who never fell into the trap of aestheticism—the model is Balzac (243). This demiurge of the novel had a relationship with his material, with life, as direct as appetite. Consequently, his art was "masculine" and "sound." One wonders if Faulkner-Elmer-Gordon's real reason for visiting Paris was not to pay homage to Rodin's famous statue.[8]

In September 1926, when he had finished writing *Mosquitoes,* Faulkner set to work on two different projects that were to be equally important for the future course of his career: the Sartoris material led to *Flags in the Dust,* the original version of his third published novel, and he was already at work on a novel about the Snopes family. Phil Stone wrote briefly of both in the *Oxford Eagle:*

> Since his return from Europe Faulkner has been here at home playing golf and writing two new novels which are already under contract. Both are Southern in setting. One is something of a saga of an extensive family connection of typical "poor white trash" and is said by those who have seen that part of the manuscript completed to be the funniest book anybody ever wrote. The other is a tale of the aristocratic, chivalrous and ill-fated Sartoris family, one of whom was even too reckless for the daring Confederate cavalry leader, Jeb Stuart. Both are laid in Mississippi.[9]

Faulkner himself confirmed that the idea for both the Snopes and the Sartoris families came at about the same time when, in 1959, he prefaced *The Mansion* with a note beginning: "This book is the final chapter, and the summation of, a work conceived and begun in 1925."

The first panel of the Snopes triptych is *The Hamlet* (1940). The writing and the structuring of the novel extended over a period of fifteen years; thus, its inception preceded *Mosquitoes.*

The Hamlet is a pastoral work transposed into a contemporary setting. According to Olga Vickery, Faulkner's "choice of the love story and the tale of barter as frames for the actions of his characters is directed by the fact that sex and economics involve the two primary modes of human survival, the one natural and the other social" (*Novels,* 167). These modes are oriented principally by greed and are opposed in the same way as sexuality and experience are opposed in *Soldiers' Pay* or as sexuality and language in *Mosquitoes*. In *The Hamlet*, however, Faulkner had become a master in the art of making his structures convey a meaning—as distinct from the mechanical or aesthetic approach to form and structure of earlier works. In this novel as in many others of the mature period, irony is the key to the structure.

Two of Faulkner's last faunlike characters (who are at least nominally identified as such) appear in a setting in which simple and somewhat sentimental pastoralism is combined with piercing irony. Both appear in scenes that were not present in any of the short stories, published separately beginning in 1931, that Faulkner used in making *The Hamlet*. Both scenes were written expressly for the demands of the novel, and they are portentously placed at opposite positions on either side of the keystone of the novel's thematic vault, that is, Flem Snopes's vision in Hell, beating the devil at his own game.

The hero of the first scene, in Book 2, chapter 1, is Labove. For Millgate this section is "somewhat tenuously connected with the other events and characters"—though he admits in the next sentence that "All the episodes including Labove's are related in a multiplicity of ways to the major themes of the novel and to each other" (*Achievement*, 188). Labove seems to emerge straight from the various studies Faulkner had made in his first two novels, but he is unique in his genre since he is not to be found again in any other novel or short story. (It is not impossible that Phil Stone was his model. Like him, Labove reads Latin authors, notably Horace; like him, also, he ends up earning two degrees, one in law, the other in literature.) With a willpower strengthened by social deprivation he wants to become a lawyer, and his future at the bar seems assured. But in order to be able to pay for his studies he agrees to work for a time as a schoolteacher at Frenchman's Bend, where he undergoes the supreme challenge, in the person of the queen bee, Eula Varner. It surely cannot be a coincidence that Faulkner used Labove to deliver lyrical and even mythical compliments to this young girl. His literary role consists in universalizing the character of Eula—in drawing her out of her "hill-cradled and remote" hamlet and in becoming "the crippled Vulcan to that Venus" (119).

When he is introduced to Will Varner, the Homeric master of Frenchman's Bend, Labove is twenty-one years old. He is a man who was not thin so much as actually gaunt, with straight black hair coarse as a horse's tail and high Indian cheekbones and quiet pale eyes and the long nose of thought but with the slight curved nostrils of pride and the thin lips of secret and ruthless ambition. It was a forensic face, the face of invincible conviction in the power of words as a principle worth dying for if necessary. A thousand years ago it would have been a monk's, a militant fanatic who would have turned his uncompromising back upon the world with actual joy and gone to a desert and passed the rest of his days and nights calmly and without an instant self-doubt battling, not to save humanity about which he would have cared nothing, for whose suffering he would have had nothing but contempt, but with his own fierce and unappeasable natural appetites. (119)

Olga Vickery writes pertinently that *The Hamlet* is "a study in metamorphoses" (*Novels,* 167).[10] Indeed, this ascetic character is bound to undergo an ordeal of transformation for which he is less prepared than anyone: "Then one morning he turned from the crude blackboard and saw a face eight years old and a body of fourteen with the female shape of twenty, which on the instant of crossing the threshold brought into the bleak, ill-lighted, poorly-heated room dedicated to the harsh functioning of Protestant primary education a moist blast of spring's liquorish corruption, a pagan triumphal prostration before the supreme primal uterus" (129).

For two years after this moment his class (and his life) would have "but one point, like a swarm of bees, and she would be that point, that center, swarmed over and importuned yet serene and intact and apparently even oblivious, tranquilly abrogating the whole sum of human thinking and suffering which is called knowledge, education, wisdom, at once supremely unchaste and inviolable: the queen, the matrix" (131). "Poor Labove"[11] becomes the stage of the ancient battle between knowledge and the flesh, a battle of irreconcilable appetites in which Faulkner, having lost his dream of an epicene Narcissus, relives the stupefied discovery of the supreme feminine serenity (serenity being the key quality of a character like Narcissa in *Sanctuary*). Eula is Jenny raised to the nth power.

Three years pass and Labove grows into "the virile anchorite of old times": "he would lie prone and sweating in the iron winter nights, naked, rigid, his teeth clenched in his scholar's face and his legs haired-over like those of a faun" (124). Yet he only has the legs of a faun: he is neither Donald nor Gordon. Irony separates this new avatar of the faun from myth. He would rather be part of a monastic order. He thinks for a while that he might marry Eula, but then he renounces the idea as being absurd. Having no satyr qualities either, he reiterates pathetically Talliaferro's gesture. At the end of his lessons he walks "with his calm damned face to the bench and lay[s] his hand on the wooden plank still warm from the impact of her sitting or even kneel[s] and lay[s] his face to the plank, wallowing his face against it. . . . There would be times when he did not even want to make love to her but wanted to hurt her, see blood spring and run" (135). This wild eroticism is no more natural to him than is the magic thought to which he next resorts in his imagination:

> It would now be himself importunate and prostrate before that face which, even though but fourteen years old, postulated a weary knowledge which he would never attain, a surfeit, a glut of all perverse experience. He would be as a child before that knowledge. He would be like a young girl, a maiden, wild distracted and amazed, trapped not by the seducer's maturity and experience but by blind and ruthless forces inside herself which she now realised she had lived with for years without even knowing they were there. He would grovel in the dust before it, panting: "Show me what to do. Tell me. I will do anything you tell me, anything, to learn and know what you know." He was mad. (135–36)

Thus Labove, in the course of an evolution so rapid as to be a caricature of the history of man, undergoes all the torments associated, since the Bible, with the knowledge of Woman. His adventure describes a complete circle. After the near bestial attack he launches against Eula, she, contrary to his expectation, does not even denounce him to her brother Jody: "She never told him at all. She didn't even forget to. She doesn't even know anything happened that was worth mentioning" (143–44). The orgy of experience that the tortured adolescent's imagination associates with Woman leads only to a monstrous innocence, and Labove's melodramatic adventure leads only to farce. His crucifixion is followed by neither death nor resurrection. Symbolically, all he can do is drive a nail in his door in order to hang up the key to the school. Then he disappears from the novel and from

Faulkner's fiction altogether (unless one considers that he is reborn under the name of Gavin Stevens).

At the end of this Dionysiac hand-to-hand combat that both unites and irremediably opposes Labove and Eula, the latter demands with irony: "Stop pawing me . . . You old headless horseman Ichabod Crane" (138). This is the only allusion Faulkner ever made to Washington Irving, whose well-known "The Legend of Sleepy Hollow" suggests many points in common with this episode in *The Hamlet*. In both works the schoolteacher with a grotesque body (which is said to be reminiscent of Don Quixote's in Irving's tale) is a stranger to the scene. He falls under the spell of a being "that causes more perplexity to mortal man than ghosts, goblins, and the whole race of witches put together, and that was—woman."[12] His desire for her is expressed by Irving in the repeated metaphor of appetite, which is echoed ironically in Faulkner by the sense of satiety and even nausea which Eula transmits to Labove. However, because he is biologically inferior to the local Don Juan (Brom Van Blunt, Hoake McCarron), the knight errant of idealism (Ichabod Crane, Labove) must leave. He is driven out, according to Cecil Eby, by the rural community.[13] The similarity of detail goes as far as the pumpkin that crashes on Ichabod on the bridge of sexuality and which is depicted as the head of the legendary horseman. The potato that Eula brings every day to school plays the same role in Faulkner's work. Both the tuber and the fruit convey the quiddity of sexuality (and of experience in general), which cause the two heroes to fall. In both stories, however, once the circle is closed, gravity turns into levity. The adolescent drama modulates into a fable with a moral.

In the Panic pastoral of *The Hamlet* there is another episode with a faun that functions both formally and symbolically as a pendant to the Labove episode. The love story between the idiot Isaac Snopes and the cow stolen from Jack Houston is told in various tempi: it begins with an andante movement and passes to an unbridled allegro that relates Ike Snopes's rescue of the cow from a prairie fire. Faulkner had already treated this topic as a farce in "Afternoon of a Cow."[14] In this sketch the comic element stems from several sources.[15] The first source is the distance the author manages to maintain in placing himself on stage and in handing the storytelling over to his secretary, Ernest V. Trueblood, alias Ernest B. Toogood. A second comic source is the attribution of the feminine sense of prudery to the cow: "she knew by woman's sacred instinct that the future held for her that which is to a female far worse than any fear of bodily injury or suffering: one of those invasions of female privacy where, helpless victim of her own physical body, she seems to see herself as object of some malignant power or irony and outrage" (US, 430). Lastly, there is slapstick farce reminiscent of the scatological ending of "A Portrait of Elmer": "In a word, Mr. Faulkner underneath received the full discharge of the poor creature's afternoon of anguish and despair" (US, 430).

"The role played by William Faulkner in 'Afternoon of a Cow'," writes Maurice Edgar Coindreau with reference to *The Hamlet,* "is supported here by an idiot, Isaac, whose attachment to his cow shows all the signs of love."[16] Ike's vision of the cow, which belongs to Houston, a widower who also owns a highly virile horse, is described in such natural and feminine terms in Ike's vision of it that in the novel the cow becomes the thematic counterpart of Eula in the Labove episode: she is "the flowing immemorial female" (HAM, 189), like Eula, the "integer of spring's concentrated climax" (192). The climax of the episode is the same as in "Afternoon of a Cow": "he, lying beneath the struggling and bellowing cow, received the violent relaxing of her fear-constricted bowels" (198). The irony is that, immediately after the "violent relaxing," the late Lucy Pate's inconsolable husband tells the cow: "Git on home, you damn whore!" (200).

Faulkner's orchestration of this perverse parody of a pastoral idyll is subtle, especially in the way it ends with an extraordinary lyrical adagio showing Ike, previously described as a "hulking shape . . . with its hanging mouth and its pointed faun's ears" (99), now in love with his cow:

> Blond too in that gathering last of light, she owns no dimension against the lambent and undimensional grass. But she is there, solid amid the abstract earth. He walks lightly upon it, returning, treading lightly that frail inextricable canopy of the subterrene slumber—Helen and the bishops, the kings and the graceless seraphim. When he reaches her, she has already begun to lie down—first the forequarters, then the hinder ones, lowering herself in two distinct stages into the spent ebb of evening, nestling back into the nest-form of sleep, the mammalian attar. They lie down together. (213)

This is a far cry from the pale and derivative eroticism of "L'Apres-Midi d'un Faune" and from the impotence that so afflicted the marble faun. Yet, this about-face is precisely what is interesting: Faulkner is using irony for a personal end as much as for a thematic one. He is settling some old scores with himself and ridding himself of a few youthful errors. The very title, in English this time, "Afternoon of a Cow," recalls the parody which had appeared almost twenty years earlier, under the title "Une Ballade d'une Vache Perdue" (EP&P, 16), in *The Mississippian*—following the publication in the same magazine of his own (poor) poem inspired by Villon and entitled, in French, "Une Ballade des Femmes Perdues" (EP&P, 54). A joke like this at the expense of such a self-conscious young writer as Faulkner (anyone who reads his poetry can hardly fail to agree on this point) must have come as a sharp shock. That it was so is clearly shown by the letter, at once acid and self-critical, entitled "The Ivory Tower" (EP&P, 9) which he had published two months earlier in answer to one of his detractors (probably the author of this sarcastic "Ballad").

For anyone interested in the genesis and process of literary creation, as well as in the author's own thoughts about these, this letter is a document of considerable interest. After quoting Ben Jonson, Faulkner acknowledges that "mirth requires two things: humor and a sense of humor. I flatter myself that I possess the latter." More important is the curious aside with which the letter ends. It conveys several points relevant to our own dual focus, on the writer and on the work: "if this be humor, then I have lost my sense of it; unless humor is, like evil, in the eye of the beholder" (EP&P, 9). Is this not exactly how section 2 of the first chapter of Book 3 of *The Hamlet* functions? One needs only to compare the reactions of Ratliff and Lump Snopes when confronted with the amorous affair between the idiot and the cow: in short, their reactions bring to mind the old injunction "Honi soit qui mal y pense." Carvel Collins is right to say that in "Afternoon of a Cow" Faulkner has used this "motif" (the subject of "Une Ballade d'une Vache Perdue") "for thematic point, parody, pathos as well as humor" (EP&P, 16).

In *The Hamlet* Faulkner drew a lesson from the bitter experience of the years 1919–24. By combining lyricism and irony, and by using the pastoral as a means of conveying his critique of mercantilism, he revealed to what extent his writing continued to exploit what had come before it, including the writer's own temptations and perverse tendencies. This suggests how much our reading of Faulkner's works profits from understanding his development as a writer. However, the fact remains that lyricism was checked by irony, as late as in *The Hamlet*, and this suggests that Faulkner had not yet accepted his "biological inheritance" (HAM, 199). Death, time, and flesh would long remain open wounds in Faulkner's consciousness. One might even say that Faulkner spent his lifetime obsessively writing *against* these realities. For him writing never lost its function as a conjuring and exorcising activity, whether one thinks of this function as a magical one or, in the light of psychoanalysis, as a form of literary anthropology.

PART THREE

The Field of Vision

chapter five

Focusing

Flags in the Dust/Sartoris

> Old Bayard's headstone was simple too, having been born, as he
> had, too late for one war and too soon for the next one, and she
> thought what a joke They had played on him: denying him
> opportunities for swashbuckling and then denying him the
> privilege of being buried by men who would have invented
> vainglory for him.—*Flags in the Dust*

The writing of *Flags in the Dust* marked a sudden and sharp increase in
creativity that began in early 1927. However, it is not so much the acceleration of Faulkner's production that concerns us in this chapter, as it is the
marked change in his style and in his attitude to writing. Indeed, one can
easily draw a dividing line between the first two novels and the third, and
the way the writer himself accounted for it almost thirty years later, in
1955, is remembered as one of his best-known comments on his own work:

> Question: What happened to you between *Soldiers' Pay* and
> *Sartoris*—that is what caused you to begin the Yoknapatawpha
> saga?
> Faulkner: With *Soldiers' Pay* I found out writing was fun. But I
> found out after that not only each book had to have a design but
> the whole output or sum of an artist's work had to have a design.
> With *Soldiers' Pay* and *Mosquitoes* I wrote for the sake of writing
> because it was fun. (LITG, 255)

The insistence on "fun" is significant. Only with the next novel did things
become more than a game, involving the man's whole background and even
his life: "Beginning with *Sartoris* I discovered that my own little postage

stamp of native soil was worth writing about and that I would never live long enough to exhaust it" (LITG, 255).

Although this statement was not the origin of the theory that there had always been a "saga," or even several sagas, present in Faulkner's mind, it may well be appropriate to deal briefly now with the school of thought that sees Faulkner's enterprise as a kind of *comédie humaine,* usually with an appropriate reference to Balzac.

This view of Faulkner's work was encouraged, if not even initiated, by Malcolm Cowley in his introduction to the *Portable Faulkner:*

> Slowly the brooding thoughts arranged themselves into the whole interconnected pattern that would form the substance of his novels.
>
> The pattern was based on what he saw in Oxford or remembered from his childhood. . . . There in Oxford, Faulkner performed a labor of imagination that has not been equaled in our time, and a double labor: first, to invent a Mississippi county that was like a mythical kingdom, but was complete and living in all its details; second, to make his story of Yoknapatawpha County stand as a parable or legend of all the Deep South.[1]

Forty years after it was published, this conception of Faulkner's work is still active and influential among many of Faulkner's casual readers.

Much closer to the truth—in spite of the same exaggerated importance attributed to Faulkner's overall "design"—was Maurice Edgar Coindreau's careful distinction between Faulkner and Balzac. First published in French the same year as Malcolm Cowley's epoch-making anthology, the text reads: "The map to be found at the end of *Absalom, Absalom!* (1936) shows well enough that the author thinks of his books not as separate and independent works but as a sort of *comédie humaine* whose puppets are hopelessly manipulated by an implacable fatalism. Yet, unlike Balzac's work, which develops horizontally, the work of Faulkner develops vertically, in a downward direction."[2] Not only do the notions of horizontality and verticality somehow account for the predominance of space over time in Balzac—whereas it is hinted that the opposite is true in Faulkner—they also refer to the writers' goals: Balzac's ambition was clearly to cover all aspects of contemporary France; Faulkner never showed himself to be so systematic or demiurgic. Coindreau admits that Faulkner's design was not to encompass "the deep South," as Cowley asserts, but rather to probe more and more deeply into the few stories he had to tell. In this sense Faulkner's recurring characters are as different from Balzac's as are his repeated "scenes."[3] In figurative terms one could say that Balzac worked like a pioneer, reclaiming more and more land for his own, amazingly sweeping, work as a chronicler of the nineteenth century, whereas Faulkner functioned more like a driller, boring deeper and deeper into his "own little postage stamp of native soil." This is just the dimension that one must take into account so as to understand how the major works finally emerge as they do—from a long suppressed or harnessed imagination.

Flags in the Dust, completed on 29 September 1927 (according to the typescript), illustrates these preliminary remarks in an exemplary way. Certainly, in the quantitative sense, it is a panoramic work, a work that a reader might begin with—as Faulkner said of *Sartoris* in his last class at the University of Virginia—because it had "the germ of my apocrypha in it. A lot of characters are postulated in that book" (FITU, 285). But this is even more true of the original, uncut version.

This is also a work which is bound closely to the formative period that includes "The Hill" and "Nympholepsy" and *Soldiers' Pay* (rather than *Mosquitoes*).[4] Yet, the book is of interest above all because the staging of the "inner drama" begins here—and it begins with "focusing."

Michael Millgate was probably right to suggest that the major line of development runs directly from *Soldiers' Pay* to *Sartoris*—thus bypassing *Mosquitoes*, as it were. The latter novel takes us back in time to the period at which the former ends. The subject matter (the return from World War I and its aftermath), the date of the action (1919), and even the choice of the protagonist all remind one how persistent the wounded veteran motif was in Faulkner's early fiction.

The young novelist begins by looking critically at the persona of the writer. This return to a much earlier theme is remarkable since it gives credence to the image, suggested by Coindreau, of writing as a downward probing, a vertical movement which advances while turning back on itself like a spiral.

In contrast to this apparently regressive step, Faulkner was also building bridges for the future. *Flags in the Dust* prepares the way both for *The Sound and the Fury* and for *Sanctuary*. Bayard Sartoris, like Donald Mahon before him, points in the direction of Quentin Compson (all three being "sick"[5] heroes). But the Benbow material clearly unites the novel with *Sanctuary*—even more so in the original version. One may indeed say that *Sanctuary* reveals for us the hidden side of *Flags in the Dust*. Since *Flags* is a richer work than *Sartoris*, the version published in 1929, and since it has not really been studied in detail except in Millgate's chapter and in the (quite inadequate) introduction to the 1973 edition, *Flags in the Dust* is worth detailed scrutiny.

The structure of the book is essentially that of a five-act tragedy. There is, in other words, a rather formal feel like that of the two earlier novels. Each of the acts contains a key event in the story of Bayard III, the protagonist. He is introduced in a melodramatic way at the end of act 1, after a suspenseful and carefully orchestrated prelude. In act 2 he falls from his horse. In act 3 he has a first automobile accident. In act 4 he has a second one which kills his grandfather. And in the middle of act 5 he meets his own death in an airplane. This leaves space only for an epilogue whose function is to lend a temporal perspective to a brief career.

Furthermore, these successive episodes, between Bayard's first appearance (*Flags*, 38; SAR, 43) and his death (which, although it takes place off the stage, is no less theatrical than his nocturnal entrance upon the stage), are deliberately placed closer to the beginning of each act. Bayard's first appearance takes place in the sixth and last chapter of Part 1; his fall from the horse occurs in the fifth part of Part 2; his first automobile accident is placed in the fourth section of Part 3, and his second accident, in the third section of Part 4. His death occurs in section two of Part 5. In this way Faulkner manages to create the impression of an acceleration in time which is a way of making fate loom nearer and make its reality more material. Bayard's life after his return from war is objectively a "death drag."[6]

The overall structure of the work reveals another important development in the use of time. The cyclical return of the seasons is gradually decelerated. This has the effect of extending each of the acts. Thus act 1, in which we are waiting for Bayard's return, lasts only one day at the beginning of spring. Act 2, like the whole of *Soldiers' Pay*, runs parallel to the burgeoning of spring. It begins with an intimate scene (in the same pastoral setting of the first novel) and ends, as in act 1, with a night scene (here prolonged and agitated). The act (as long as the second act of *Sartoris*, but the longest act in *Flags in the Dust*) takes place at the beginning of summer: in section six, during his visit to Memphis, Old Bayard asks the date—it is July 9. Thus there is a slowing down in the flow of time by comparison to the previous act. Act 4 begins in October and ends at Christmas. It is of the same objective duration (one season) as its opposite, act 2. The final act takes us into a new year. The wandering of Bayard begins in January in Tampico and ends in mid-June in Chicago (the American version of Babylon, as in *The Wild Palms*). Like act 1, the epilogue covers one day only, beginning with the baptism of Benbow Sartoris and ending with Miss Jenny's visit to the cemetery.

The fact that Bayard arrives at the very beginning of spring and dies a year later, at the end of spring in June, is in itself significant. *Flags/Sartoris* does not last four, but five seasons. From a symbolic point of view, the difference is obvious. This is an ironic commentary on the hiatus between the natural promises of the earth (the cycle of death and regeneration) and the fate of man.

This typically Faulknerian word, "hiatus," is indeed used for the second time in the published oeuvre at the beginning of section 4 of act 3: "For a time the earth held him in a smoldering hiatus that might have been called contentment" (*Flags*, 194; SAR, 203, without "smoldering"). This is in the summer and Bayard is busy working the soil. The rather abstract notion of hiatus (from *hiare,* to gape) is paradoxically associated here with an opposite motion, contentment, and is justified by the fact that this natural activity, at one with "the sober rhythms of the earth" (*Flags,* 195; SAR, 203), runs against what Bayard believes to be his own destiny. Bayard's destiny is to be perpetually separated from reality, from time, and from himself by an abyss originating in a trauma and compounded by his fascination with the name Sartoris.[7]

The macroscopic study of the novel reveals other significant characteristics. Each part or act ends with a night scene.[8] Yet these, which make *Flags/Sartoris* one of Faulkner's darkest novels, are not identical in terms of content. The first scene concerns old Bayard and is nostalgic and meditative (or "brooding," to use Faulkner's own word). The second is exactly the opposite—noisy, agitated, almost clownish except for the "still scene."[9] The third is rather sordid, since it is devoted to the details of Byron Snopes's burglary. The fourth, the Christmas night of the poor blacks in the hills, is quiet and serene. The last twilight is filled with the loneliness and sadness felt by Aunt Jenny and Narcissa after young Bayard's death.

Faulkner places the "black scenes" judiciously at regular intervals. There is one in the middle of the first act (1, 4), another at the end of the second (2, 6), and two other similar scenes at the beginning and at the end of the fourth (4, 1 and 5). Thus, two of the four black scenes coincide with the two night scenes which are thematically opposite (the mad night of act 2 and the holy night of act 4), as if to suggest that merriness and meditation, two facets of the same authenticity, were qualities which now belong only to Negroes. In both cases Bayard is present in the scene only as an intruder, though his violent action soon makes him master of the two situations.

Act 4 is extremely rich in revelations of all kinds. It is justly celebrated for the magnificent ascension of young Bayard to the mountain dwelling of the MacCallums. The section devoted to the black Christmas is, as well, a humble but unmistakable prefiguration of the great Easter scene in *The Sound and the Fury.* The style, as if purified by the climate, transmits emotions directly. In this sense it even foreshadows certain passages of *Go Down, Moses.* Critics have failed, however, to notice that this part begins and ends with a "black" scene. The first one is comic, the second grave and religious. Moreover, the Negroes' frugal Christmas meal is the counterpart of the lavish lunch that the Sartorises and their friends have for Thanksgiving. Most astonishing perhaps is the fact that few if any critics have explored the very stark symbolic opposition between the plain and the mountain. The role played by the rain as a leitmotiv in Hemingway's novel *A Farewell to Arms,* also published in 1929, is well known.[10] Compare the beginning of a section at the end of 4, 4: "All that day it rained, and the following day and the one after that" (*Flags,* 321; SAR, 329). One might think that this was the beginning of a chapter from *A Farewell to Arms.* Moreover, the description and the examination of the puppies play a strangely similar (though not identical) thematic role to that of the ants on the burning log in *A Farewell to Arms.* Without proving or even strongly suggesting a debt owed by Hemingway to Faulkner,[11] the similarity reflects, at the very least, a common aesthetic preoccupation, particularly in the use of objective correlatives. For both writers the plain is associated with impurity, softness, and compromise. The plain is also a synecdoche for the city as well as a metaphor for temptations and traps. Moreover, women live in the plain. Except for Mandy, the cook of the MacCallums, women are not present in the hills where Bayard identifies the qualities of altitude and cold air with purity, with clear and lucid vision, and with a robust, sound life. The hunting scenes echo one another, as do the mealtime scenes. It is in the hills that Bayard becomes simultaneously aware of his responsibility and of his cowardice.

Lastly, the structure of *Flags in the Dust/Sartoris* reveals an interesting series of thematic parallels, contrasts, and oppositions. First, the characters, more than in any other novel, obey the law of twinship already alluded to.[12] There are blood twins: John and Bayard, Stuart and Rafe McCallum, and even the two mules, Roosevelt and Taft. But there are also twins by affinity: in the older generation old Bayard and Simon Strother as well as Aunt Sally and Miss Jenny are complementary pairs from the past; in the younger generation Bayard is coupled with Horace on the one hand and with Caspey on the other: all three have recently returned from the war. Finally, there is the close kinship between Bayard and Narcissa. This constant repetition of twins tends to prove that, at this stage, Faulkner's literary creation includes doubling and duplication. This is true of groups as well as of individuals: in *Flags in the Dust* as in *Mosquitoes,* there are duplications of the old (Bayard, Falls, Simon, McCallum, Peabody, Jenny, and Sally) and of the young (Bayard, Horace, Caspey, Harry, Belle, and Narcissa). In *Flags in the Dust* as in *Soldiers' Pay* and *Mosquitoes,* there are active people (the Sartoris clan) and verbal people (the social group to which the Benbows belong).

The main contrast is between Bayard and Horace. The latter returns from the war at the beginning of Part 3 and marries at the end of the novel. Thus, if Bayard's journey toward death is compared to a fatal spiral gradually engulfing the character, Horace's path, by contrast, cuts across it like a straight line. This is a pattern that recurs throughout the oeuvre, for example in *Light in August* where Lena Grove's "line" cuts across Joe Christmas's "spiraling" journey toward death. The pattern helps us understand how in Faulkner's fiction time can acquire the spatial qualities reserved for fate in classic tragedy.

In *Flags/Sartoris* neither Bayard nor Horace can be said to develop or evolve. They go through the novel like statues moved about in a play. According to Sartre, in the first of his two well-known studies on Faulkner's works, they possess a certain amount of mental "data" that, however, does not constitute a real psychology—as the word might be understood by European novelists. These data make up the characters' "nature," says Sartre, who is struck by the "psychic" existence and by the fact that they do not change.[13] Their set nature is what pushes the characters to their destiny.

Every time we see the characters, they are described in nearly the same way. They appear to be frozen in the attitude in which they have been suddenly surprised:

> [Old Bayard] watched a tall shape emerge from the lilac bushes along the garden fence and across the patchy moonlight toward the veranda where he sat. His grandson wore no hat and he came on and mounted the steps and stood with the moonlight bringing the hawklike planes of his face into high relief. (*Flags,* 38; slightly different version in SAR, 43)
>
> Horace Benbow in his clean, wretchedly-fitting khaki which but served to accentuate his air of fine and delicate futility. . . . (*Flags,* 170; SAR, 161)

Both have returned from the war. How they behave can be interpreted as Faulkner's comment on the generation of 1919 or, as Olga Vickery put it, on "post-war disillusionment, *Weltzschmerz,* and the death-wish" (*Novels,* 16). Indeed, when one examines the simple chronology of their destiny, it is clear that each is drawn irresistibly toward a different but parallel conclusion. Horace falls into the trap of marriage that, he thinks, will alleviate the insoluble problem of his incestuous penchant for his sister, while Bayard plunges violently toward his death, which at last puts an end to his "curse": the guilt springing from the constant conjunction (at least in his mind) of a glamorous but remote past (his ancestor) and the present deprived of his "heroic" twin brother. Death and marriage serve as the meeting points for a combination of movements: a linear movement of simple temporality and the spiral of fatality.

Bayard's and Horace's careers illustrate the main dimensions of Faulkner's perception of evil: "time and flesh" (SAR, 1; only "time" in *Flags,* 5). Both characters can be thought of as beings who have been alienated from an ideal liberty. The novel gives an example of this in the world of the MacCallums. Their universe appears to have been miraculously saved both from the degradation implicit in sexuality[14] and from the onslaughts of time. One feels that Faulkner has at last found an adequate structure. However, it is only a pattern, and a somewhat schematic one at that. In *Flags/Sartoris,* as opposed to *The Sound and the Fury,* the hand of the self-conscious stage manager can still be seen, whereas the later novel is a complete act of self-dramatization.

A study of time in *Flags/Sartoris* would show how the novel constitutes an advance on preceding works and points to future ones. *Soldiers' Pay* takes place in an atmosphere of sentimental compliance (though it is situated in the present). *Mosquitoes* is also situated in the present, but it avoids this plight through a double escape into exoticism and into flippant verbal pyrotechnics. With *Flags/Sartoris* Faulkner reaches a point of no return. His quest for a fictional locale—one might even say a fictional "home"[15]— was not a search for lost time, as with Proust, but rather a recuperation of a historical background capable of furnishing what was lacking in the first two novels, namely a *perspective*.[16]

As opposed to Dos Passos and Hemingway, who sought to understand the contemporary scene through their own experience of war and of its bitter aftermath, Faulkner, who did not have this key experience, sought to recreate the past not for its own sake, but to use it as a permanent backdrop against which to measure the present scene. This theatre or setting provided the focal point which he did not have before. (Faulkner's own life makes clear that he was himself, for a while, the wanderer whom Bayard becomes in the last chapter.) As suggested by the repetition of the words borrowed from Théophile Gautier, Faulkner had been looking for "form, solidity, color." In fact he was searching for a perspective with which to structure his future work, a touchstone as much for organization as for value.

In the latter part of the well-known statement that I have already quoted, Faulkner wrote that: "by sublimating the actual into apocryphal I would have complete liberty to use whatever talent I might have to its absolute top. It opened up a gold mine of other peoples, so I created a cosmos of my own" (LITG, 255). He had heeded the "lesson" of Sherwood Anderson, to whom he dedicated the book. Of course, the language of this statement about the origin of Yoknapatawpha has the feel of 1956, that of a writer who had become a tried hand at the novel. Yet it is important to underscore the relationship Faulkner establishes between what he calls sublimation and liberty. There is hardly any doubt that he recalled the writing of *Flags/ Sartoris* as a kind of liberation into fiction. The novel paid off the writer's debts. Faulkner did not need to—nor did he—dedicate the next novel to anyone.

Written at a time when Faulkner had made two constrasting and yet complementary decisions—to become an exile in his own country and to pursue a literary career—*Flags in the Dust* was the first of many attempts to solve his main problem: how could writing help him cope both with his principal source of frustration, the present, and with his principle source of fascination, the past? Nearly everything one knows about Faulkner's childhood, his education, and his life lead to the image of a man placed under the sign of this polarity and of this ambivalence. His novel develops under this sign as well. It expresses the difficult and even heartrending coexistence of contradictory feelings: a guilty life and an attraction to death, on the one hand; the ordering of the past and the affirmation of the will to survive and to leave a mark, on the other.

Faulkner begins with a significant gesture: he simply denies being trapped in the present so as to grasp the essence of the past that he then exploits as a guide to the present. This is the beginning of a crucial process which is like focusing on one's own tragic past:

> As usual, old man Falls had brought John Sartoris into the room with him, had walked the three miles in from the county Poor Farm, fetching, like an odor, like the clean dusty smell of his faded overalls, the spirit of the dead man into that room where the dead man's son sat and where the two of them, pauper and banker, would sit for half an hour in the company of him who had passed beyond death and then returned.
>
> Freed as he was of time and flesh, he was a far more palpable presence than either of the two old men. (SAR, 1; a much briefer version in *Flags*, 5)

This evocation of the late John Sartoris by his humble double is a remarkable way of starting a novel. The passage contains in miniature both the temporal structure of the novel and its moral structure, divided here into the separate treatment of time (Bayard) and flesh (Horace), the double evil from which the ghost is now freed.

After using a bipolar structure in *Soldiers' Pay,* where the wounded war hero was only the antithetical aspect of a group of civilians, and a concentric structure in *Mosquitoes,* Faulkner next went to work with a structure that best served his interest. The structure is still bipolar, but this time the past is not used just in opposition to the present, as in the earlier works. Apart from several flashbacks, which are certainly important from the thematic point of view, both *Soldiers' Pay* and *Mosquitoes* are ordered—even overordered—chronologically. In the new novel, on the contrary,

Faulkner makes it clear that the chronology of the living is not the only time scale that matters in the book. With the motif of the return of the dead he introduces a bipolar theme and a structure developed in a series of echoes. This structure is based on correspondences that the living establish with the past.[17] These correspondences are simple in *Flags/Sartoris*. But if one thinks of *The Sound and the Fury* and, above all, of *Absalom, Absalom!* and *Go Down, Moses,* it is clear that the reason for the simplicity is Faulkner's relatively unsophisticated technique—rather than the absence of the theme itself.

After an introduction dedicated entirely to the ghost, one has no other yardstick for measuring the great-grandson, Bayard III, than his prestigious ancestor, John Sartoris. Faulkner's well-known penchant for patronyms/homonyms is here given a literal explanation. His heroes are born as doubles of the same prototype. This law is not metaphorical. It is expressed in physical terms on the first page and is accompanied by the assumption that the past is superior to the present in terms of the (paradoxical) immediacy of the former. This theme recurs repeatedly throughout the narrative: "Freed as he was of time and flesh, he was a far more palpable presence than either of the two old men who sat shouting periodically into one another's deafness. . . . He was far more palpable than the two old men cemented by a common deafness to a dead period. . . . John Sartoris seemed to loom still in the room, above and about his son, with his bearded, hawklike face" (SAR, 1; also briefer in *Flags,* 5—in which, however, the text has the words "and the bold glamor of his dream"). It is through the very same image of the hawk or falcon face (which is also used for Gordon in *Mosquitoes*) that old Bayard soon feels the presence of his grandson, some forty pages and approximately twelve hours later. What is this image of themselves which the Sartorises are vowed to perpetuate? What urge does young Bayard seek to answer from the moment of his return?

In this encounter with the dead as a much more "real" presence than the living, one finds an avatar of the first stage of Faulkner's development as a writer: the stasis, the paralyzing effect of fascination, the "still scene" reminiscent of the aesthetic temptation in the earlier works. Note how the double archetype, the ancestor and the model whose death must be imitated, is described: he is petrified, of course, as he has become a "pompous effigy" (SAR, 119) with a "florid stone gesture" (304), "his carven eyes gazing out across the valley where his railroad ran, and the blue changeless hills beyond, and beyond that, the ramparts of infinity itself" (375). Just as the prestigious paternal figure of Robert E. Lee has remained on center stage in the mind of the South, as John Corrington has observed, so the ancestor stands at the center of the stage of Faulkner's fiction.[18] Yet there is more to the matter than just this. The ancestor also loomed like a giant, dark sun—long extinguished, but still active—in the writer's imagination: only he could transform the landscape of the real into the space of an inner drama, that of Faulkner's fiction.

chapter six

Glamour

Flags in the Dust/Sartoris

> For there is death in the sound of it, and a glamorous fatality,
> like silver pennons downrushing at sunset, or a dying fall of
> horns along the road to Roncevaux.—(*Flags in the
> Dust/Sartoris*)

What is glamour? Originally, the word meant "a magic spell," "an enchantment," or "the supposed influence of a charm on the eyes, making them see things as fairer than they are."[1] Faulkner uses the word in its adjectival form quite often, particularly right at the end of *Flags in the Dust/Sartoris:*

> The music went on in the dusk softly; the dusk was peopled
> with ghosts of *glamorous* and old disastrous things. And if they
> were just *glamorous* enough, there was sure to be a Sartoris in
> them, and then they were sure to be disastrous. Pawns. But the
> Player, and the game He plays . . . He must have a name for His
> pawns, though. But perhaps Sartoris is the game itself—a game
> outmoded and played with pawns shaped too late and to an old
> dead pattern, and of which the Player Himself is a little wearied.
> For there is death in the sound of it, and a *glamorous* fatality, like
> silver pennons downrushing at sunset, or a dying fall of horns
> along the road to Roncevaux. (*Flags,* 369–70; SAR, 380; emphases mine)

Glamour is an "attractiveness that stirs the imagination," "a strangely alluring atmosphere of romantic enchantment," or "a bewitching intangible irresistibly magnetic charm" (Webster). One can associate the word with André Malraux's analysis of another word in the lesser-known but more interesting part of his preface to *Sanctuary:* "Fascination is a psychological state on which almost all tragic art depends and which has never been studied because aesthetics do not reveal it."

Like fascination, glamour isolates, immobilizes, tends to paralyze. In attracting the subject away from oneself, it prevents that person from moving, both physically and mentally, in any direction other than toward an identification with the object. This is precisely the uncanny force of glamour: like fascination, it reverses the relationship between subject and object.[2] The contemplator embellishes the object contemplated; by doing this, he defines himself as experiencing some shortcoming, and the relationship with the object becomes, from his point of view, a pouring out or emptying of the self as the seat of emotions and free will.

Glamour functions like a vampire. By emptying the subject of its substance, it creates a disembodied being, robbed or dispossessed of its status as subject by the glamorous object, which establishes itself as the subject through a process that is literally *sub-versive*.

Since there is surely no natural glamour, the power of glamour seems to derive from the fact that glamour can appear to be natural. Here, one has to raise the problem of genetics and structure. Genetically, glamour is a psychic phenomenon; structurally, it is a social one because it cannot be analyzed without being considered as a relationship. A flag, for example, cannot be glamorous without some social consensus (structure), itself probably explicable in historical terms (genesis). Faulkner's "silver pennons downrushing at sunset" refer the reader to a legend, that of Roland's death at Roncevaux.

> The legend of the French epic hero Roland (transferred to Italian romance as Orlando) is based on authentic history. Charlemagne invaded Spain in 778, and had captured Pamplona, but failed before Saragossa, when the news of a Saxon revolt recalled him to the banks of the Rhine. On his retreat to France through the defiles of the Pyrenees, part of his army was cut off from the main body by the Basques and entirely destroyed. . . . These incidents no doubt served to strengthen the tradition of the disaster of Charlemagne's rearguard in 778, the importance of which was certainly magnified in popular history.[3]

It is hardly necessary here to stress the crucial part played by the word magnified. Without this magnification Faulkner would probably not have used a reference to one among thousands of minor military incidents in European history to end his first ambitious novel.

In the same way Edgar Morin has distinguished between Sarah Bernhardt, the actress, and Marlene Dietrich, "a myth like Phryne," the Greek courtesan: "the dialectic of the actor and the role," he writes, "cannot account for the star unless the notion of myth intervenes."[4] Roland Barthes has also written that "myth is always a theft of language," "a language that will not die," and that "nothing can be sheltered from myth" because myth is a "metalanguage," or "a second language, in which one speaks about the first"; thus it is not difficult to agree with his conclusion that "myth can be rooted in any meaning."[5]

What is glamorous for Faulkner the writer? *Mosquitoes* tells us nothing about this, no more than do the early stories. In the poems one only finds the obverse of glamour, or glamour "hollowed out," so to speak. In *A Green Bough,* for example, the sequence of poems referred to in chapter 2 of this book as the postwar poems, tells of the poet's frustration on returning from a war in which he did not fight, the shame he feels about this, and the aimlessness of his life after his return. As we have also seen, the first, "Prufrockian," poem of this sequence is built on the same theme as *Soldiers' Pay.* Is there any sign of the phenomenon of glamour in this first novel? The answer is strangely inconclusive. There is no glamour in the novel because, somewhat paradoxically, the brilliant object of attention leads the reader's gaze only to an absence: Donald Mahon is, as the expression goes, only a shadow of himself, the opposite of a living myth. A tragic dignity is for certain bestowed upon him in extremis, so that he does not die like a run-over dog, without being conscious of "imminent nothingness." The advent of dignity takes place in the scene in which Donald recalls the air battle which results in his being wounded beyond repair. The scene ends with these words: "He knew sight again and an imminent nothingness more profound than any yet, while evening, like a ship with twilight-colored sails, drew down the world, putting calmly out to an immeasurable sea. 'That's how it happened,' he said, staring at him" (SP, 294). Faulkner, however, did not develop or magnify the dramatic potential of the traumatic scene. It would have been too late, in fact, since this recognition is relegated to the end of the novel. Instead, at the beginning of the same section (8) of chapter 8 he wrote the following: "And suddenly he found that he was passing from the dark world in which he had lived for a time he could not remember, again into a day that had long passed, that had already been spent by those who lived and wept and died, and so remembering it, this day was his alone: the one trophy he had reft from Time and Space. *Per ardua ad astra*" (SP, 292–93).

The notion of glamour is touched upon in *Soldiers' Pay*, but obliquely, as nearly a caricature—not only through the naive admiration young Robert Saunders feels for all aviators, but also in the unabashed curiosity of children for the horribly maimed veteran. This caricatural aspect is demonstrated in the comic scene showing Robert Saunders climbing a fence and, to his immense disappointment, falling down on Joe Gilligan and not on Donald Mahon (Part 3, ch. 2, 100–103).

Thus one has to wait for *Flags in the Dust* (as suggested by the title itself) to see glamour become not only material for fiction, but the working principle of a particular novel.

Miss Jenny had two brothers, John and Bayard Sartoris (1823–76 and 1838–62). With "his bearded, hawklike face" and "a far more palpable" presence than either of the two old men who celebrate his cult from the very first page of the novel, the former serves to direct the fiction toward the past; but it is the latter Sartoris (perhaps because of his death during the Civil War) who fixes the focus of the legend:

> She [Miss Jenny] has told the story many times since (at eighty she still told it, on occasions usually inopportune) and as she grew older the tale itself grew richer and richer, taking on a mellow splendor like wine; until what had been a hair-brained [*sic*] prank of two heedless and reckless boys wild with their own youth, was become a gallant and finely tragical focal-point to which the history of the race had been raised from out the old miasmic swamps of spiritual sloth by two angels valiantly and glamorously fallen and strayed, altering the course of human events and purging the souls of men. (*Flags,* 12; slightly different in SAR, 9)

In making Miss Jenny responsible for the perpetuation of the myth—in her capacity as narrator—Faulkner distances himself from it. In this way fiction differs distinctly from history (at least from history as fact) from the very beginning. The discreteness of fiction is the real theme of this "first" novel.

One critic, writing about the narrative of Bayard's death, which takes place a few pages after this introduction (*Flags,* 14–20; SAR, 9–19), says, apparently without irony, that in Miss Jenny's mouth the event becomes "worthy of Homeric poetry."[6] It does indeed play the role of a primitive epic to which all later versions refer. One should, however, remember that the pretext for the glamorous feat concerns anchovies: irony interferes at the very birth of the myth. There is even a second degree of fictional discreteness, or isolation, by which one can measure the myth, the gap between Bayard's glamorous gesture and its utterly futile purpose. It is the same gap as that which separates rhetoric and truth, or theatre and life. The narrative ends with the wise judgment of General "Jeb" Stuart: "He said he was a good officer and a fine cavalryman, but that he was too reckless." Those who listen are nonetheless enthralled: "They sat quietly for a time, in the firelight. The flames leaped and popped on the hearth and sparks soared in wild swirling plumes up the chimney, and Bayard Sartoris' brief career swept like a shooting star across the dark plain of their mutual remembering and suffering, lighting it with a transient glare like a soundless thunderclap, leaving a sort of radiance when it died" (*Flags,* 19; SAR, 18). The description of the effect of "Bayard Sartoris' brief career" upon his younger sister is as good an analysis of glamour as can be found in literature.

If the part played by Bayard I in history is, to say the least, ambiguous, there is no doubt that he actively plays the part allotted to him in the novel. This part is that of the mythmaker. During the years after his death his brother John takes up the role in terms of drama by being the author of a series of beaux gestes, the last of which are placed *before* the narrative of his brother's death in the original version of the novel: "It showed on his brow, the dark shadow of fatality and doom, that night when he sat beneath the candles in his dining room and turned a wine glass in his fingers while he talked to his son. . . . 'And so,' he said, 'Redlaw'll kill me tomorrow, for I shall be unarmed. I'm tired of killing men. . . . Pass the wine, Bayard'" (*Flags,* 6; SAR, 23). It should be noted that John Sartoris's last utterance concerns (a) an object almost as futile as his younger brother's anchovies and (b) the very object with which the tale of the latter's death is compared in the same chapter: "as she grew older the tale itself grew richer and richer, taking on a mellow splendor like wine." Aesthetically, John's last utterance is therefore quite comparable to Bayard's: " 'Anchovies?' repeated Bayard Sartoris who galloped nearby, and he whirled his horse" (*Flags,* 18; SAR, 16).

In terms of the formal structure of the myth the two brothers have behaved similarly. But as far as the meaning of the myth is concerned, John's gesture is as pregnant as Bayard's is sterile. Faulkner returns to this at length in *The Unvanquished*, particularly in "An Odor of Verbena," in which John Sartoris's son, the aging Bayard we see in *Sartoris*, breaks the absurd chain of violence by repeating his father's gesture: he refuses to kill his father's killer. In this way he extricates himself from the myth at last.[7]

Such a positive gesture is quite foreign to the spirit of *Sartoris*—and even to the name: "For there is death in the sound of it." In *Sartoris* one is present at both the inception and the apotheosis of the myth. As can be inferred from the first quotation of this chapter, the final commentary leaves no doubt as to the "outmoded" character of "the game."

Fallax Fatum: even while he builds a prodigious verbal destiny upon the mere name "Sartoris," Faulkner makes it clear (to himself, to begin with) that even if man deludes himself with words, the tribute he must pay to glamour is often his life. In Jenny's narrative Faulkner's renowned rhetoric emerges. It is already clear to what extent his work tends towards dramatic expression. For example, in the passage where old Bayard is seen climbing up into the loft, opening the trunk of souvenirs, and taking out of it the family Bible so as to inscribe in it the date of the death of his grandson John III (5 July 1918), the location is described as carefully and lovingly as a stage setting: "The room was cluttered with indiscriminate furniture— chairs and sofas like patient ghosts holding lightly in dry and rigid embrace yet other ghosts—a fitting place for dead Sartorises to gather and speak among themselves of glamorous and old disastrous days. The unshaded light swung on a single cord from the center of the ceiling. He unknotted it and drew it across to a nail in the wall above a cedar chest. He fastened it here, and drew a chair to the chest and sat down" (*Flags*, 79; slightly different in SAR, 89–90). Next follows a passage which remained un-published until the appearance of *Flags in the Dust* in 1973:

> Thus each opening was in a way ceremonial, commemorating the violent finis to some phase of his family's history, and while he struggled with the stiff lock it seemed to him that a legion of ghosts breathed quietly at his shoulder, and he pictured a double line of them with their arrogant identical faces waiting just beyond a por-tal and stretching away toward the invisible dais where Something

sat waiting the latest arrival among them; thought of them chafing a little and a little bewildered, thought and desire being denied them, in a place where, immortal, there were no opportunities for vainglorious swashbuckling. Denied that Sartoris heaven in which they could spend eternity dying deaths of needless and magnificent violence while spectators doomed to immortality looked eternally on. (*Flags*, 80)

The ancestral epic, even though more and more isolated from its historical context, is from now on something hallowed, as every evocation of the family history henceforth will remind us. Indeed, each new death in the family is a pretext for a similar elegaic recollection. In other words the mediation of the word confers a posteriori an aesthetic gloss on the new death.

What is the meaning of all this? Behind the mask of old Bayard's grumbling observance of the family tradition, is not Faulkner trying "to kill two birds with one stone," that is, to lend his voice to the rite of evocation and at the same time find out what is wrong in the Sartoris tradition? In front of the Bible, whose once immaculate last page is now inscribed with the names of all his ancestors, "Old Bayard sat for a long time, regarding the stark apotheosis of his name. Sartorises had derided Time, but Time was not vindictive, being longer than Sartorises. And probably unaware of them. But it was a good gesture, anyway" (*Flags*, 82; SAR, 92).

At this point, however, the Ancestor himself draws old Bayard away from the growing fascination: "And he recalled his father's words. 'In the nineteenth century,' John Sartoris had said, 'chortling over genealogy anywhere is poppycock. But particularly so in America. . . . Yet the man who professes to care nothing about his forbears is only a little less vain than he who bases all his actions on blood precedent. And a Sartoris is entitled to a little vanity and poppycock, if he wants it' " (*Flags*, 82; slightly different version in SAR, 92). Old Bayard can now repeat his last sentence. No longer fascinated, he "muse[s] quietly" on Time in a reflection on the past tense:

Yes, it was a good gesture, and Bayard sat and mused quietly on the tense he had unwittingly used. Was. Fatality again: *the augury of a man's destiny peeping out at him from the roadside hedge, if he but recognise it;* and as he sat and gazed with blind eyes at the page, Time rolled back again and again he ran panting through undergrowth while a Yankee cavalry patrol crashed behind him, crashed fainter and fainter until he crouched with spent, laboring lungs in a bramble thicket and heard their fading thunder along a dim wagon road. Then he crawled forth again and went to a spring he knew that flowed from the roots of a beech tree; and as he leaned his mouth to it the final light of day was reflected onto his face, bringing into sharp relief, forehead and nose above the cavernous sockets of his eyes and the panting animal snarl of his teeth, *and from the still water there stared back at him for a sudden moment, a skull.*

The unturned corners of man's destiny. (My emphases: *Flags,* 82; slightly different version, SAR, 92–93)

The real topic in this page is history itself and its teaching. By concentrating on a scene (even if it is truly tragic) the passage seems to say that one runs the risk of reducing history to a "gesture," and that this gesture, being the seed of myth, attracts narrators like a decoy. This is truer for Miss Jenny than for old Bayard because, though she treats history sarcastically, she nonetheless cultivates it by telling it again and again as a story; it is also true of old man Falls (the narrator of the scene of John Sartoris's escape from the Yankees), who overwhelms history with his trusting tenderness and of old Bayard, who lets himself be taken despite his grouchiness. The problem with the Sartorises is that, from generation to generation, they reduce history to a series of gestures—or to a gallery of characters arrested, like statues, in their last movement. In the place of history they substitute a chronicle of heroic and vain deeds the value of which is derived only from the oral tradition that keeps them alive. To Faulkner, however, this was the essence of literature. In *Sartoris* he was already speaking of the equivocal power of all narrations. He was not narrating about himself, but rather about himself narrating.

For the Sartorises the present (the time during which the narration is being uttered, as opposed to the past time that is evoked by the narrative) is clearly devoted to discourse. This has already been shown in the jabbering characters of *Mosquitoes* as well as in Januarius Jones's countless aphorisms in *Soldiers' Pay.* Yet, an entirely new kind of discourse can be seen to begin with the character of Horace Benbow in both *Sartoris* and *Sanctuary* and to culminate in Quentin Compson's monologue in *The Sound and the*

Fury. Quentin's mind is filled with his father's empty, perverted rhetoric. In Faulkner's world rhetoric is often the prerogative of men, and more particularly of fathers, who use it to rationalize the experience (most often of failure) for which they are incapable of preparing their sons. Thus Mr. Compson's reported speech at the end of the first paragraph of Quentin's section of the novel: "Because no battle is ever won he said. They are not even fought. The field only reveals to man his own folly and despair, and victory is an illusion of philosophers and fools" (TSATF, 93; CT, 86).[8]

This is substantially the same reflection as that which old Bayard voices by the trunk. The pretext for it, the watch given to Quentin by his father as "the mausoleum of all hope and desire," plays the same part in *The Sound and the Fury* as the page of the Bible inscribed with family names in *Flags in the Dust/Sartoris*. It is the symbol of the vanity of battles that men wage against their common enemy, time. Against time there can only be illusory or false victories. This is why the long vertical list of yellowed names is found by Bayard to be the perfect antidote against the grandiloquence of the gestures perpetuated in marble statues. Indeed, Faulkner's oeuvre is punctuated by scenes in which writing is made to appear as something dead and inert—as dead as the dead mechanisms which are also to be found here and there in his fiction.

The following passage from *Sartoris,* although in a sense a description superfluous to the narrative in which it occurs, is revealing if only because it adumbrates the broken down, ghostly world of the Old Frenchman place:

> Beyond the bordering weeds a fence straggled in limp dilapidation, and from the weeds beside it the handles of a plow stood at a gaunt angle while its share rusted peacefully in the undergrowth, and other implements rusted half concealed there—skeletons of labor healed over by the earth they were to have violated, kinder than they. The fence turned at an angle and Suratt stopped the car and the youth stepped down and opened the warped wooden gate and Suratt drove on into the barnyard where stood a wagon with drunken wheels and a home-made bed, and the rusting skeleton of a Ford car. Low down upon its domed and bald radiator the two lamps gave it an expression of beetling and patient astonishment, and a lean cow ruminated and watched them with moody eyes.
> (SAR, 137)

This is what one reads in *Sartoris;* but the same passage in *Flags in the Dust* contains three significant words that were deleted from *Sartoris:* "the two lamps gave it an expression of beetling and patient astonishment, *like a skull*" (emphasis mine; *Flags,* 123). Here again is the object whose sudden apparition earlier interrupted old Bayard's meditation over the trunk. Faulkner's fiction returns to such evidence of human impotence (*memento mori, vanitas vanitatum*) as to an unvarying truth such as that expressed in the third chapter of Ecclesiastes.

In vain have the Sartorises tried to turn glamour into a value, but they, like everybody else, have gone only as far as the cemetery. This is where the chronicle of their "heroic" deeds ends—though not without a final flourish, a "gesture of haughty arrogance which repeated itself from generation to generation with a fateful fidelity" (*Flags,* 365; SAR, 375). Indeed, they are so perfectly faithful to their tradition that Miss Jenny is the only one to perceive the irony of the repeated vanity. Thanks to her and to her wise mediation between the Sartorises and the reader, Faulkner ends his novel as he began it, by dramatizing glamour and debunking it at the same time: "He stood on a stone pedestal, in his frock coat and bareheaded, one leg slightly advanced and one hand resting lightly on the stone pylon beside him. His head was lifted a little in that gesture of haughty arrogance which repeated itself generation after generation with a fateful fidelity, his back to the world and his carven eyes gazing out across the valley where his railroad ran and beyond it to the blue changeless hills, and beyond that," (*Flags,* 365; different version in SAR, 375).

Miss Jenny's undeniable superiority over all these men who, even beyond death, remain vain despots with pompous genealogies, comes from her ability to see clearly into and even through their grand chronicle—and to put this vision into words. Faulkner could hardly have found himself a better model, either for narrating or for evaluating.[9]

Bayard Sartoris had a twin brother, John Sartoris III. By the end of the novel both are dead. But something has changed since the generation of their forefathers. World War I—during which the latter was killed and the former wishes he had been killed—was, unlike the Civil War, hardly an occasion for acts of heroism. The best proof lies in the brothers' burial site: John's life is recorded by an inscription in the cemetery, but his body is not in the grave; Bayard's body lies in its grave, but there is no inscription on it, for the good reason that no one is left to write one for him—no male Sartoris, that is. Once more, Miss Jenny sets the matter into perspective:

> Bayard's grave too was a shapeless mass of withered flowers, and Miss Jenny had Isom clear them off and carry them away. The masons were just beginning to lay the curbing around it, and the headstone itself sat nearby beneath a canvas cover. She lifted the cover and read the clean, new lettering: Bayard Sartoris. March 16, 1893—June 5, 1920. That was better. Simple: no Sartoris man to invent bombast to put on it. Cant lie dead in the ground without strutting and swaggering. Beside the grave was a second headstone; like the other save for the inscription. But the Sartoris touch was there, despite the fact that there was no grave to accompany it, and the whole thing was like a boastful voice in an empty church. Yet withal there was something else, as though the merry wild spirit of him who had laughed away so much of his heritage of humorless and fustian vainglory, managed somehow even yet to soften the arrogant gesture with which they had said farewell:
>
>
>
> LIEUT. JOHN SARTORIS, R.A.F.
> Killed in action, July 19, 1918.
>
> *'I bare him on eagles' wings and brought him unto Me.'*[10]
> (*Flags*, 364; different version in SAR, 373–74)
>
>

Unlike their ancestors, neither twin ends up petrified in a baroque statue.[11] This is not, however, because of any lack of effort to emulate tradition. John died like a Sartoris in a gesture of supremely elegant defiance. The efficacy of his gesture is nonetheless contested by his brother. It is true that Bayard, crushed by the guilt he feels in surviving his brother after being the powerless witness of his death, is moved to criticize his action through the enraged, furious tone he uses to tell the story to his grandfather, old Bayard:

> "Tell us about Johnny."
> "He was drunk," young Bayard answered harshly. "Or a fool. I tried to keep him from going up there, on that damn Camel. You couldn't see your hand, that morning. Air all full of hunks of

cloud and any fool could a known that on their side it'd be full of Fokkers that could reach twenty-five thousand, and him on a damn Camel. But he was hell-bent on going up there, damn near to Lille. I couldn't keep him from it. He shot at me," young Bayard said. "I tried to drive him back, but he gave me a burst. He was already high as he could get, but they must have been five thousand feet above us when they spotted us. They flew all over him. Hemmed him up like a damn calf in a pen while one of them sat right on his tail until he took fire and jumped. Then they streaked for home." (*Flags*, 39–40; slightly different version in SAR, 45)

Was this jump, following an act more foolhardy than courageous (note the ambiguity: "He was drunk . . . or a fool"), the modern equivalent of John Sartoris's self-decreed death or of Bayard's futile death by pursuing anchovies? Whatever the truth may be, on his return from World War I Bayard III finds himself confronted with a triple inheritance, which an intolerable state of indebtedness makes all the more ironic. Insofar as his life seems to be devoted to finding a tragic focus, everything outside of this is bound to be a form of alienation. Such is the figure he cuts throughout the novel after emerging from the lilac bushes at the end of Part 1. Like that of his great-grandfather Bayard, his career could be described as a "colorful, if not always untarnished, pageant" (*Flags*, 50; SAR, 59). The description of his destruction-bent behavior contains features that will later be found in such characters as Thomas Sutpen. Here, for example, is Bayard as seen by Narcissa after his fall from a horse. The passage was deleted during the rewriting of the novel: "All of Narcissa's instincts had been antipathetic to him; his idea was a threat and his presence a violation of the very depths of her nature: in the headlong violence of him" (*Flags*, 368). Later, after his first automobile accident, she looks once again at his face: "It was again like a bronze mask, purged by illness of the heat of its violence, yet with the violence still slumbering there and only refined a little" (*Flags*, 232; SAR, 244–45). Of course, Narcissa's view of Bayard is a privileged one, just as Miss Jenny's view of his great-grandfather continues to be, and as Miss Rosa's view of Sutpen will be. The manner in which the women see their "heroes" is an important index to Faulkner's experiments in the technique of point of view (the passage emphasized below, for example, was deleted in *Sartoris*): "The long shape of him lay stiffly in its cast beneath the sheet, and she examined his bold immobile face *with a little shrinking and yet with fascination,* and her own patient and hopeless sorrow overflowed . . ." (*Flags,* 237; a different version in SAR, 250; my emphasis). The myth is essentially virile (the typical objects that embody it are weapons, horses, automobiles, airplanes). By having a woman contemplate the object, Faulkner found a perfect way of dramatizing the effect of fascination.

This effect is just what is confirmed in the second account given by Bayard, this time for Narcissa, of the death of his brother. Here one finds a significant detail that was not to be found in the first account. It is the fact that John "thumbed his nose" at Bayard before jumping from his Camel— without a parachute:

> It was a brutal tale, without beginning, and crassly and uselessly violent and at times profane and gross, though its very wildness robbed it of offensiveness just as its grossness kept it from obscenity. And beneath it all, the bitter struggling of his stubborn heart; and she sitting with her arm taut in his grasp and her other hand pressed against her mouth, watching him with terrified fascination.
>
> "He was zig-zagging: that was the reason I couldn't get on the Hun. Every time I got my sights on him, John'd barge in the way again. Then he quit zig-zagging. Soon as I saw him side-slip I knew it was all over. Then I saw the flame streaming out along his wing, and he was looking back at me. The Hun stopped shooting then, and all of us just lay there for a while. I couldn't tell what John was up to until I saw him swing his legs outside. Then he thumbed his nose at me like he always was doing and flipped his hand at the Hun and kicked his machine out of the way and jumped. (*Flags,* 238–39; slightly different version in SAR, 252)

One must note that, as written here, the narrative is not at all "profane and gross," as the preamble describes it. Again, what we hear is influenced by Narcissa's high-strung nerves. And it is only after Narcissa intervenes that the image of the lofty peak first appears, to be associated with Bayard (and contrasted with the valley) throughout the rest of the novel. The sexual symbolism of this polarity finds ample confirmation here: "Far above him now the peak among the black and savage stars, and about him the valleys of tranquillity and of peace" (*Flags,* 240; SAR, 254).

Young Bayard is bound to drift with no pleasure at all from one absurd gesture to the next, from one *acte manqué*, an automobile accident, to another, in order to compensate for the chronicle of heroic deeds he has been unable to inscribe upon the wall of oblivion. He does not even have the help (or the excuse) of war as his ancestor and namesake did. Like his great-grandfather who was "tired of killing," he is doomed to repeat military gestures in a civilian setting. His sickness is a kind of terminal fascination with glamour.

The arrival of the shabby though tragic stunt-aviators fascinates the community in the same way in "Death-Drag" (*Doctor Martino*) because the experience of the flyers is fundamentally alien to that of the ground crew. So it takes a connoisseur, the former airman Warren, to see through the incomprehensible prestige of the flying trio, to turn them back into something human and even try to save the nervous wreck that one of them has become. Glamour is exclusive; it robs people of their liberty; it freezes life, which is movement.

Yet "the aim of every artist is to arrest motion, which is life, by artificial means and hold it fixed so that, 100 years later when a stranger looks at it, it moves again since it is life" (LITG, 253). Such was the (Keatsian) "paradox" of art according to Faulkner. Although admittedly a later, and even an a posteriori formulation of his poetics, the quotation expresses unambiguously the importance of the act of looking in Faulkner's work.

chapter seven

Shame

Flags in the Dust/Sartoris

Pure shame is not the feeling of being this or that, a
reprehensible object, but, in general, of being *an* object, that is,
of recognising myself in this degraded, dependent and fixed
being that I am for others.—Jean-Paul Sartre, *Being and
Nothingness*

At the same time he dramatized what I have called the aesthetic temptation,
Faulkner set out to explore the ground from which his "flowers of evil"
would blossom, that fertile area of the unconscious, at the opposite pole
from glamour, which is reflected in glances filled with *shame*.

In *Soldiers' Pay*, as we have seen, the full effects of glamour are not
developed. Faulkner's first voyeur, little Robert Saunders, is hardly more
than a sketch. He does climb the fence by night in order to look at his
mutilated idol (3, 2), and his idée fixe certainly does have a morbid quality:
"I just want to see his scar" (SP, 152). Yet if he technically turns himself into
a voyeur, he does so only to seek revenge for having been surprised by
Margaret Powers and Joe Gilligan as he swam naked behind the undergrowth (4, 5). Nevertheless, Robert Saunders is the first in a series of young
voyeurs who, though "innocent," are extremely disturbing, especially in
this case as he is associated with the villain George Farr. This evil character
would be destined for the same voyeur's hell that is dramatized by Byron
Snopes if it were not for his amorous relation with Robert Saunders's sister,
Cecily. In *Soldiers' Pay* the frustration of desire is represented in a somewhat
contrived and abstract manner, perhaps because the motifs which dominate
Faulkner's early poetry also dominate here:

> He drank fiercely, feeling the fire in his throat become an inner grateful fire, pleasuring in it like a passionate muscular ecstasy. (Her body prone and naked as a narrow pool, flowing away like two silver streams from a single source.) Dr. Gary would dance with her, would put his arm around her, anyone could touch her. (Except you: she doesn't even speak to you who have seen her prone and silver . . . moonlight on her like sweetly dividing water, marbled and slender and unblemished by any shadow, the sweet passion of her constricting arms that constricting hid her body beyond the obscuring prehensileness of her mouth—) Oh God, oh God! (SP, 212)

There is more to this than an adolescent's prurience. The "analysis" is followed by a section in chapter 6 where the voyeur's night is cut up into one-hour, then half-hour, segments that are meant to echo George Farr's ordeal of desire. Moreover, the whole section is orchestrated against the backdrop of a crowd of people flooding out of a moviehouse. Soon, only "tiny red eyes [passing] along at mouth-height" punctuate the night's darkness. Farr, however, notices that "fireflies have not yet come."

The ordeal begins at ten-thirty and culminates at eleven o'clock. It is the first full-length version of the voyeur's passion that we know in Faulkner's work (excepting the draft of it to be found as early as 1919 in "Landing in Luck"), the ordeal of suffering that precedes a final (and ironic) disembodiment:

> . . . Eleven-thirty.
>
> He had lost his body. He could not feel it at all. It was as though vision were a bodiless Eye suspended in dark-blue space, an Eye without Thought, regarding without surprise an antic world where wanton stars galloped neighing like unicorns in blue meadows. . . . After a while, the Eye, having nothing in or by which to close itself, ceased to see, and he waked, thinking that he was being tortured, that his arms were being crushed and wrung from his body. (SP, 236)

Torture results from a glance that, overwhelmed by desire, falters or dissolves. Like a weapon turned back against the one who wields it, the glance exposes the eye ("the organ") to pure and defenseless nakedness, leaving it atrociously vulnerable, cut off from the body to which it belongs. The physical organ is abandoned to the very forces it has called forth—the empire of pure or disembodied vision. And even though such vision may begin with pleasant images ("like unicorns in blue meadows"), it ends in the emptiness created by the failure to embody the desire of the Other, to possess the Other—the emptiness of impotence.

The scene has the feel of a first attempt; it is still shaky, a bit abstract and hesitant, like a draft or a preliminary drawing. And yet it foreshadows the real thing in *Flags/Sartoris*. The scene points towards the ultimate development of this theme in *Pylon*.[1] Indeed it may also be related to a dominant concern in American literature, as Robert C. Davis has argued in an article about the "Ocularity of American Fiction."[2]

Byron Snopes is a remarkably unremarkable character. His authorship of the anonymous letters he sends to Narcissa Benbow is his only noteworthy act. Faulkner gives him a minimum number of sociological and psychological identifying features: "The book-keeper was a hillman of indeterminate age, a silent man who performed his duties with tedious slow care and who watched Bayard constantly and covertly all the while he was in view" (*Flags*, 7). Later in the novel three scenes that lead to a crescendo recount the career of old Bayard Sartoris's meticulous bank accountant. In the first he dictates to Virgil Beard (they are both named after poets!) one of the letters that poisons the life of Narcissa. She, however, does not react in the blunt, straight-forward manner Miss Jenny counsels. Here is Byron's letter, quoted verbatim:

> "I thought once I would try to forget you. But I cannot forget you because you cannot forget me. I saw my letter in your hand satchel today. Everyday I can put my hand out and touch you you do not know it. Just to see you walk down the street To know what I know what you know. Some day we will both know to gether when you got use to it. You kept my letter but you do not anser. That is a good sign you do. . . ."
> "—not forget me you would not keep it. I think of you at night the way you walk down the street like I was dirt. I can tell you something you will be surprised I know more than watch you walk down the street with cloths. I will some day you will not be surprised then. You pass me you do not know it I know it. You will know it some day. Be cause I will tell you." (*Flags*, 99–100)

This is a remarkable analysis of the way voyeurism naturally leads to blackmail and, eventually, to even more serious offenses. The two poles of Byron Snopes's mental universe are the glamorous object of desire and himself as a shameful subject; his only feeling is a penchant for rape, and blackmail is his only way of establishing a communication. Through him and in a few lines, Faulkner gives the reader the whole psychology of a voyeur.

The second scene in the crescendo takes the dramatic progression one step further. It is the last section of Part 2 and it tells of the nighttime serenade by Bayard and his friends at Narcissa's window. Thus, after Dr. Alford's first visit, Narcissa is visited a third time. The contrast between these three approaches to Narcissa is summarized thus:

> She had received three callers that night. One came formally and with intent; the second came informally and without any particular effort to remain anonymous or otherwise; the third came anonymously and with calculated intent.
>
> . . . .
>
> When they [Bayard and his friends] had gone she came to the window and parted the curtains and stood for a while in the dark fallen wings of her hair, looking directly into his hidden eyes.
>
> Then the curtains fell again, and once more she was a shadowy movement beyond them. Then the light went off, and he lay face down on the steep pitch of the garage roof, utterly motionless for a long time, darting from beneath his hidden face covert ceaseless glances, quick and darting and all-embracing as those of an animal. (*Flags*, 139–40)

Covert is the best word for describing the motionless activity of the Faulknerian voyeur in his first appearance on the stage of fiction. It is in every way the opposite of the Sartoris style. Since the voyeur is compared with an animal, it is worth paying attention to the latter's nature, since Faulkner always attaches a symbolic value to the bestiary in his works.[3] Whatever animal the voyeur is related to, it would be opposed to the falcon or the hawk, which is the emblem of the Sartorises from father to son.

The animal evoked by the character called "the Snopes" is revealed in an extraordinary scene which almost completely disappears from the novel in its published version of 1929. The scene comes at the end of the third part of the earliest version, after Narcissa draws close to the wounded Bayard and the possibility of marriage is even evoked. The scene basically deals with the "hell," the sordid mediocrity, of a voyeur's life. The scene takes place in four movements:

(1) Byron Snopes's minute, morose preparations, including the writing of the last anonymous letter addressed to Narcissa;

(2) his breaking into Narcissa's bedroom to steal an undergarment;

(3) the burglary at the bank;

(4) the escape to Alabama, including a feeble attempt to rape his girlfriend.[4]

Of this sequence only the last part has completely disappeared from *Sartoris*. Yet it is precisely the last which is the most interesting from my point of view, since only such sexual frustration can push the Snopes's frenzied night to a logical conclusion. I am giving extracts from each of the four movements.

> [1] But the Snopes crouched over his desk after his sleepless night, with jealousy and thwarted desire and furious impotent rage in his vitals.
>
> His head felt hot and dull, and heavy . . . He had thought it dreadful when he was not certain that there was another; but now to know it, to find knowledge of it on every tongue . . . and young Sartoris, at that: a man whom he had hated instinctively with all his sense of inferiority and all the venom of his worm-like nature. Married, married. Adultery, concealed if suspected, he could have borne; but this, boldly, in the world's face, flouting him with his own impotence. . . . He dug a cheap, soiled handkerchief from his hip pocket and wiped the saliva from his jaws.
>
> . . . .
>
> It was his final letter, in which he poured out his lust and his hatred and his jealousy, and the language was the obscenity which his jealousy and desire had hoarded away in his temporarily half-crazed mind and which the past night and day had liberated.
>
> [2] He found a match in his pocket and struck it beneath the shelter of his palm, and by its light he chose one of the soft garments, discovering as the match died a packet of letters in one corner of the drawer. He recognised them at once and he threw

the dead match to the floor and removed the letter he had just written from his pocket and put it in the drawer and put the other letters in his pocket, and he stood for a time with the garment crushed against his face. . . .

[3] He entered the grilled cage. His left heel showed yet a bloody print on the floor, but no blood ran from beneath the bandage. The vault door opened soundlessly; without striking a match he found the key to the cashbox and opened it. He took only the banknotes. . . . He passed out the rear door, threw the latch so it would lock behind him. The clock on the courthouse rang midnight.

[4] She let him draw her forward and down the steps, but as they moved further and further away from the house she began to resist, with curiosity and growing alarm. "Byron," she said again and stopped. His hands were trembling upon her, moving about her body, and his voice was shaking so that she could not understand him.

"You aint got on nothing under here but your nightgown, have you?" he whispered.

"What?" He drew her a little further, but she stopped firmly and he could not move her; she was as strong as he. "You tell me what it is, now," she commanded. "You aint ready fer our marryin' yet, are you?"

But he made no answer. He was trembling more than ever, pawing at her. (*Flags,* 249–59; SAR, 264–69)[5]

Byron Snopes disappears as he first appeared, with "madness and helpless rage and thwarted desire coiling within him" (*Flags,* 260).

To add the finishing touch Faulkner flanks Byron with Virgil Beard, who writes his letters for him. The little boy completes and enriches the portrait of the voyeur in a clever, convincing way. His relationship with Byron is that of a little slave, who in turn can become a source of unbearable torture for his master: he and he alone can blackmail the blackmailer. Virgil, who is indebted to Robert Saunders, allows us to see ahead, as far as *The Reivers.* In this last novel Otis appears as the final avatar of the Faulknerian boy with innocent, "periwinkle" eyes, brought up in immorality and led astray by money. These boys end up embodying the most troubling form of evil—the evil that is inextricably bound to innocence (an association which Henry James had explored before Faulkner). Moreover, because of a feature which did not appear in *Flags in the Dust* but which figures prominently in *Sartoris*, Virgil Beard adumbrates a future character named Popeye. The last chapter of *Sanctuary*, in which Faulkner gives a naturalistic account of Popeye's childhood, contains a particularly odious detail, namely the vivisection of two "lovebirds." After copying the last anonymous letter of his master/slave Byron, Virgil kills a mockingbird with the gun Byron gives him as a reward. In *Sartoris* this is related in a brief coda, which is as factual as the account of Popeye's gesture in *Sanctuary*.[6] In *Flags* Virgil's gesture is less evil. He simply goes and buys the gun that Byron has long promised him.

There is hardly any doubt that voyeurism is one of the most disturbing aspects of Faulkner's literary creation. Voyeurs abound to such an extent that one asks whether their recurrence is not the sign of a thoroughly subjective, that is personal, "compulsion" rather than of a conscious or deliberate "objective" concern. It is, of course, doubtful if any "clinical" proof will ever be found to show that William Faulkner had a tendency to scopophilia, or to the "contrasting pair" known to psychoanalysts as voyeurism/exhibitionism. Rather than risk a highly conjectural psychobiographical explanation, I would like to introduce a more general, and, in fact, more radical hypothesis. This hypothesis is not founded on Faulkner's case alone, but on the observation that the same phenomenon can be detected in various forms in many other writers. The hypothesis assumes an analogy between the voyeur and the writer. Both have a secretive and static occupation that involves the expression of visual fantasies. By definition these fantasies cannot be actualized without changing radically, in fact without annihilating, the subject's status. As shown by the use of the pair of opposites "overt/covert," the subject is therefore in constant jeopardy as far as his/her own status is concerned—particularly as to whether his fantasies are legitimate. What is revealed here is the fundamental ambiguity involved in the act of seeing, an ambiguity that is best clarified with reference to the phenomenology of perception.

Certainly one is tempted to think, as Sartre puts it, that one cannot at once perceive and imagine. However, the singular quality of Faulkner's fiction lies precisely in the fact that the reader is presented simultaneously with the effects of perception and of imagination. The most concise example of this is to be found in Vardaman's words in *As I Lay Dying*, "My mother is a fish." In this remarkable expression of the boy's desperate state of mind the concrete and objective merge with the intensely subjective. In other words there is a concatenation or an overlapping of two undeniable realities: a dead fish lies in front of him and he has heard that his mother has just died. At this point Vardaman finds himself so unable to rationalize death that a gap opens in his reasoning—a gap into which his fantasy rushes in the form of the heavily symbolic equation, "My mother is a fish."

In the same way the opening scene of the final version of *Sanctuary*, in which a man (Horace Benbow) is perceived as being ensnared by a voyeur's covert glance, immediately introduces the reader to both a realistic setting (at the spring) and its dream (or nightmare) equivalent—which can only be part of a fantasy. Sartre's words in fact sound like an analysis of the beginning of *Sanctuary*:

> Something happens here that is analogous to what I have at-
> tempted to demonstrate with regards to the imaginary: I said that
> we cannot perceive and imagine at the same time, that it has to be
> one or the other. To perceive is to look at, and to take in a glance is
> not to apprehend a glance-as-object from the outside (unless this
> glance is not directed at us); it is to grow conscious of *being
> looked at*. The look that eyes can convey, whatever their charac-
> ter, is a pure reference to myself. What I take in immediately when
> I hear branches snap behind me, is not that there is someone, but
> that I am vulnerable, that I have a body which can be hurt, that
> this body occupies a portion of space, and that I cannot in any way
> escape from the space in which I am without defence—in short,
> that I *am seen*. (B&N, 258–59)

Thus, one could say that the reality of Faulkner's characters derives from a double presence, which is the effect of both looking and being looked at. Perhaps one should add that the reader always stumbles upon the scene like an intruder into a theatre of sudden apparitions, *"un théâtre de surgisse-ments"* to quote Sartre's phrase, or, to borrow one of Faulkner's, a theater of materializations. The well-known phenomenon called déjà vu is part and parcel of Faulkner's fiction from the start. Let us simply juxtapose three passages for demonstration's sake:

There is a spectacle to *be seen* behind the door only because I am jealous, but my jealousy is nothing if not the simple objective fact that there *is* a spectacle *to see* behind the door—this we shall call a *situation*. (B&N, 259)

He could feel that 'ere Yankee a-watchin' him, lookin' right 'twixt his shoulder blades whar the bullet would hit. Cunnel says that was the hardest thing he ever done in his life, walkin' on thar acrost that lot with his back to'w'rds that Yankee without breakin' into a run. He was aimin' to'a'rds the corner of the barn, where he could put the house between 'em, and Cunnel says hit seemed like he's been walkin' a year without gittin' no closer and not darin' to look back. (SAR, 21; slightly different version in *Flags*, 4)

In the same way, shame is only the original feeling of having my body *outside*, engaged in another being and as such without defence at all, illuminated by the absolute light that is sent out by a pure subject. It is the awareness of being irrevocably what I always was: deferred (*en sursis*), in the sense of "not yet" or "already no more." Pure shame is not the feeling of being this or that, a reprehensible object, but, in general, of being *an* object, that is, of recognising myself in this degraded, dependent and fixed being that I am for others. (B&N, 288)

Everything depends on the relationship one has with another person's gaze. *Flags in the Dust* is an excellent case in point since it dramatizes both glamour and shame and since both glamour and shame are crucial elements in the game of glances. Old Bayard is no more free of the effect of glamour than his grandson is. As "There Was A Queen" makes clear, even Narcissa is not an innocent party in Byron Snopes's shame.

The example of Bayard Sartoris is useful in carrying the analysis one step further. He is haunted by a sense of being under constant observation. What causes his death is not a persecuting sense of being peered at by both his brother John and by his ancestor? Shame is no more negotiable than glamour: as Horace puts it in *Sanctuary*, "Dammit, say what you want to, but there's corruption about even looking upon evil, even by accident; *you cannot haggle, traffic, with putrefaction*—" SAN, 152; CT, 134; my emphasis).

As an idealist Bayard strives to link the family saga with his own conception of goodness. In this he is motivated by his own failure, which he equates with evil. Thus he locks himself in an absolute contradiction, since from his point of view good and evil have the same origin: "Sartoris . . . the name of the game itself" (*Flags*, 369). The way out of this impasse should in dialectical terms be a way beyond. But Bayard is doomed as soon as he comes home, since he has seen his brother jump from his plane. He cannot escape from the guilt that surviving his twin brother makes him feel. He is doomed simply because he returns alive. In order to satisfy the tyranny of the Sartoris myth, he should have returned like his brother, as an effigy. He should have died in the skies of France, as in Faulkner's early poem:

> I hear their voices as from a great distance—Not dead
> He's not dead, poor chap; he didn't die—
> (AGB, 11).

However, the Sartoris anecdote is relatively unimportant, being only the first of a series: Bayard's fate is virtually the same as Quentin's in *The Sound and the Fury*—at least in his father's version of it at the end of the third section of the novel: "you are not thinking of finitude you are contemplating an apotheosis in which a temporary state of mind will become symmetrical above the flesh and aware both of itself and of the flesh it will not quite discard you will not even be dead" (TSATF, 220; CT, 203). Like so many other characters in Faulkner's fiction, Bayard is burdened with his own future as soon as he enters the stage in this typically theatrical way. His intolerable responsibility comes from inheriting a past that goes beyond the temporal and spatial context of the novel's setting. In a Calvinistic theological context this would be called preordained destiny; in a psychoanalytic context it is clearly a case of overdetermination.

By making Bayard a simple representative of postwar weltschmerz, many critics have failed to recognize other aspects of the character's significance. To say that he is a sick hero limits his problem to psychology. He suffers from a dual relationship with the Sartoris myth, unlike those around him, who have only a simple relationship with it. Old Falls tells tales and weaves myths innocently. Miss Jenny uses tales and myths for simple pleasure, the pleasure of telling them. Even old Bayard, who sneers at mythmaking, falls nonetheless under the spell when faced by the shimmering contents of the chest.

In his February 1938 article on "Faulkner's *Sartoris*," the very first in a long series later published under the generic title *Situations*, Sartre writes that he was struck by Bayard's "mournful arrogance." Faulkner, he says, tells us too little about his character. Sartre's all too well-known reproach of "disloyalty" therefore rests on the technicality that Faulkner leaves too much unstated and thus limits his character's behavior to gestures. This is in part true, and it is interesting to notice how often Sartre repeats the word "gesture" in the course of his article—no fewer than ten times: "One is tempted to say 'too many gestures' as one said to Mozart, 'too many notes.' Too many words, too. Faulkner's volubility, his superbly abstract style, anthropomorphic like a preacher's: these are as many *trompe l'oeil*. The style thickens the ordinary gestures." However, as Sartre must immediately admit, "this is all deliberate. It is indeed this sickening, pompous monotony, the ritual of everyday life, which Faulkner aims at. The gestures are the world of boredom. . . . Faulkner's landscapes grow as bored as his characters.[7] Here Sartre is too voluble. We find ourselves characteristically trapped by enticing but arbitrary formulas. As we read him, we cannot help but note how a penetrating reading is combined with a subtle lack of fairness, which may be due to the fact that, at the time, Sartre had already begun to let others (other novelists, that is: Mauriac, Faulkner, later Flaubert) carry the responsibility of his own future repudiation of a novelistic career. Moreover, the impression left by Sartre's first study of Faulkner is one of a mixture of rejection and fascination, into which may also have entered some jealousy, or at least some irritation. His final remark, in which he seems to wish he knew the novelist personally ("*Il faudrait le connaître*") is almost absurd, as it cannot be proof of anything but an intense personal curiosity and moreover is without theoretical justification whatsoever. Better trust D. H. Lawrence in his famous piece of advice ("Trust the work, not the artist"), or smile with William Carlos Williams when he writes, in "Portrait of a Lady":

> Agh! what
> sort of man was Fragonard?
> —as if that answered
> anything.

"The true drama," Sartre goes on, "is behind: behind the bored life, behind the gestures, behind the consciousnesses. All of a sudden, from the depths of this drama, the Act looms up, like a meteorite. An Act—at last something has happened, there is a message. But here again, Faulkner disappoints us: he seldom describes acts." "Like Sherwood Anderson," Sartre argues, "he is tale-teller, a liar. Only he dreams of a world in which stories might be believed, in which they might influence the world of men. And his novels describe the world of his dreams." One is really surprised at such naïveté: What else did Sartre expect to find in a novel but fiction? And yet, as usual, Sartre was in a sense a shrewd reader. As we have seen, it cannot be denied that Faulkner did find in storytelling a compensation for "acts" he had dreamed of but was unable to accomplish. If this is what Sartre calls a "message," then it could indeed be the message of Faulkner's early fiction.

From the point of view of someone who, like Sartre and Faulkner, is interested in the relationship between literature and action, the draft of an introduction to *Sartoris* written in 1928, after the completion of *Flags in the Dust*, is particularly revealing. Probably for the sake of Ben Wasson, who was his agent then, Faulkner argues with humor and vehemence against "trimming off" the manuscript. He invents (or remembers) a dialogue with his editor:

> I said, "A cabbage has grown, matured. You look at the cabbage; it is not symmetrical; you say, I will trim this cabbage off and make it art; I will make it resemble a peacock or a pagoda or 3 doughnuts. Very good, I say; you do that, then the cabbage will be dead."
>
> "Then we'll make some kraut out of it," he said. "The same amount of sour kraut will feed twice as many people as cabbage." A day or so later he [the editor] came to me and showed me the mss. "The trouble is," he said, "that you had about 6 books in here. You were trying to write them all at once." He showed me what he meant, what he had done, and I realized for the first time that I had done better than I knew ... *and I contemplated those shady but ingenious shapes by reason of whose labor I might reaffirm the impulses of my own ego in this actual world without stability, with a lot of humbleness, and I speculated on time and death and wondered if I had invented the world to which I should give life or it had invented me, giving me an illusion of greatness.* (My emphasis)[8]

In thus describing his first Yoknapatawpha novel, Faulkner begins by using the romantic metaphor of the plant as an image of organic development. Then, in a typically modern way, he undercuts it by making fun of it. The tone becomes that of a sardonic comment on his own writing, much like the better-known 1932 introduction to *Sanctuary*. However, one should be attentive to the reversal that occurs midway through the passage; there is pride in these words, albeit mixed with a self-confessed humbleness and a sense of wonder. The last and most important sentence can be seen as an adumbration of the now well-known description of the effect of writing *The Sound and the Fury*: "So when I finished it [*As I Lay Dying*] the cold satisfaction was there, as I had expected, but as I had also expected, *that other quality which THE SOUND AND THE FURY had given me* was absent: that emotion definite and physical and yet nebulous to describe: that ecstasy, that eager and joyous faith and anticipation of surprise which the yet unmarred sheet beneath my hand held inviolate and unfailing, waiting for release" (my emphasis).[9] What is striking in these comments is the repeated reversal of the relationship between author and work, of the classic concept of the creator giving life to his creation. Here, on the contrary, the author seems to hesitate as to whether he "invented a world . . . or if it invented him." In the case of *Flags in the Dust* the book may have given him "an illusion of greatness." In the case of *The Sound and the Fury* it may have given "that other quality" that he describes at length. Faulkner had never gone so far, nor would ever go that far again, in analyzing retrospectively the effects of writing on himself. These must have been nothing short of magic, since they made him feel "great."

Of course, this way of interpreting the relationship between literature and action was poles apart from the way Sartre would study the problem in a later, though today very much dated, contribution to a debate entitled "What Can Literature Accomplish?" ("*Que peut la littérature?*").[10] He rejected, because he thought it was merely rhetorical, the reflexive use of language, and he rejected as an "alienation" the idea that literature has its end in itself and nowhere else. These statements can hardly be reconciled with what the late Faulkner said at the end of his interview with Jean Stein: "I like to think of the world I created as being a kind of keystone in the Universe; that, as small as that keystone is, if it were ever taken away, the universe itself would collapse" (LITG, 255).

PART FOUR

The Optical Rape

chapter eight

Fascination

Flags in the Dust, Sanctuary

Thus we stood:—snake and victim: life ebbing out from me, to
her.—Herman Melville, *Mardi and a Voyage Thither*

How do you know? they said, and she said because the Snake
was there before Adam, because he was the first one thrown out
of heaven; he was there all the time.—*Sanctuary*

It is not difficult for a reader to perceive the "poetic justice" that extermi-
nates the arrogant Sartorises and makes their last descendant a Benbow as a
kind of objective judgment. The author has no need to cast a look of
condemnation on the other victim of the gaze, Byron Snopes. As chapter 7
of this book has shown, once Byron Snopes leaves the scene, it is clear that
his voyeur's inferno has been punishment enough. Henceforth, our attention is increasingly directed toward Horace Benbow, especially as he appears in both *Sartoris* and *Sanctuary*—and perhaps, with the new name of
Gavin Stevens, in a half-dozen of the novels that follow.

Here again, a passage from *Flags in the Dust* that has completely disappeared from *Sartoris* serves as a useful starting point. The passage belongs
to a dozen pages placed between chapters 2 and 3 in the fourth part of the
version published in 1929. It is Thanksgiving and the hunting season. For
the first time since her marriage to Bayard, Narcissa has come to spend a
day at her brother's house. Her continued shameful feelings of affection
toward him are suggested at the end of what is left of the scene in *Sartoris:*
"Oh! Horry, I've been a beast to you" (*Flags*, 287; SAR, 303). In the ensuing
dialogue in *Flags in the Dust* the "serene" Narcissa expresses a revulsion
from the young woman (Belle) that her brother is about to marry, and the
restless Horace thinks aloud:

"That may be the secret, after all. Not any subconscious striving after what we believed will be happiness, contentment; but a sort of gadfly urge after the petty, ignoble impulse which man has tried so vainly to conjure with words out of himself. Nature, perhaps, watching him as he tries to wean himself away from the rank and richly foul old mire that spawned him, biding her time and flouting that illusion of purifaction [*sic* in both manuscript and typescript] which he has foisted upon himself and calls his soul. But it's something there, something you—you—." (*Flags*, 288–89)

Nowhere else in Faulkner's fiction can one find—in a nutshell—such a "theory," or rather a vision, of evil. For evil, and nothing else, is the subject of this passage: what else could this "gadfly urge" be that pushes a person toward the petty and ignoble? Horace, however, is hardly in a position to "screw his courage to the sticking place." As the waning energy at the end of the quotation shows, he is only capable of *brooding* (one of Faulkner's favorite words). Horace himself confesses to Ruby Lamar at the beginning of *Sanctuary:* "You see," he said, "I lack courage: that was left out of me. The machinery is all there, but it wont run" (SAN, 18; CT, 18).

In spite, or perhaps because, of his being weak in willpower, Horace Benbow has often been properly considered as a central consciousness through which we have access to the roots of evil. Indeed, in both the second chapter of the published version of *Sanctuary* and, more confusedly, in the first six chapters of the original version, Horace explains to Ruby how, once he had decided to leave his wife, he found himself at the spring where Popeye surprised him. Ruby apparently understands nothing of what he says. She interrupts him with remarks such as "He's crazy," "The poor fool!" etc. What makes this passage particularly interesting is the fact that it is full of non sequiturs and confusion. Belle, Little Belle, the Virginia creeper, the shrimp, the Delta of the Mississippi itself, are cited by turns as reasons for his gesture (once again, Horace is capable only of making a gesture). It is this confusion that makes the passage sound like a stream-of-consciousness monologue in which the lucid voice of intelligence is upset by the most irrational components of the character's (one is tempted to say the patient's) psychic life. These components remain unordered by either experience or willpower.

The following paragraph allows a first glimpse at the related problems of Evil and Innocence as perceived by Faulkner's enfeebled idealist:

> "From my window I could see the grape arbor, and in the winter I could see the hammock too. But in the winter it was just the hammock. That's why we know nature is a she; because of that conspiracy between female flesh and female season. So each spring I could watch the reaffirmation of the old ferment hiding the hammock; the green-snared promise of unease. What blossoms grape have, this is. It's not much: a wild and waxlike bleeding less of bloom than leaf, hiding and hiding the hammock, until along in late May, in the twilight, her—Little Belle's—voice would be like the murmur of the wild grape itself." (SAN, 13–14; CT, 14)

The unstable perspective, typical of Horace's vision, results from a confused or blurred focus—or no focus at all. The association that Horace wants to establish between woman and nature (obviously an age-old motif in Christian and Western mythology)[1] is hopelessly mixed up with the connivance that he detects between woman and evil. In this sense what is usually called the "puritanism" of the Faulknerian idealist derives in fact from a syllogism—Woman is Nature; Nature includes Evil; therefore Woman is bound up with Evil—which is as absurd as it is arbitrary if considered outside the context in which it is conceived. This context is, in fact, entirely visual. It gives rise to a set of problems that can all be placed under the rubric of fascination. ". . . and then I saw her face in the mirror. There was a mirror behind her and another behind me, and she was watching herself in the one behind me, forgetting about the other one in which I could see her face, see her watching the back of my head with pure dissimulation. That's why nature is 'she' and Progress is 'he'; nature made the grape arbor, but Progress invented the mirror" (SAN, 15–16; CT, 16).

Shouldn't this latter-day Adam realize that the focus of his glance, however confused, is in the mirror and not in "the green-snared promise of unease"? The mirror ensnares the gaze, both of Little Belle, who is caught unawares, and of Horace, who not only "surprises" the insinuating gaze of his daughter-in-law at the back of his head—but who is himself surprised by the surprise. This leads him to charge her with "pure dissimulation" (in reality, only the compounded effects of the two mirrors) and to jump to the absurd conclusion just noted.

The episode that triggers off the outrage is described in the ensuing dialogue:

> "Why did you leave your wife?" she said.
>
> "Because she ate shrimp," he said. "I couldn't—You see, it was Friday, and I thought how at noon I'd go to the station and get the box of shrimp off the train and walk home with it, counting a hundred steps and changing hands with it, and it—"
>
> "Did you do that every day?" the woman said.
>
> "No. Just Friday. But I have done it for ten years, since we were married. And I still don't like to smell shrimp. But I wouldn't mind the carrying it home so much. I could stand that. It's because the package drips." (SAN, 18–19; LA, 191)

In the scene alluded to in this dialogue—a scene that Faulkner was apparently so anxious to see in print that, after it was deleted from *Flags in the Dust,* he reinserted it into the first version of *Sanctuary*—there is more than just the nausea of the repeated gesture, the loathing of being "sunk in the everydayness of [one's] own life," as Binx in Walker Percy's *Moviegoer* puts it.[2] The breeding ground of the nausea is the object itself, the shrimp, which not only ceaselessly drips and smells, but which is also pink.

A study of the role played by colors in Faulkner's fiction would be revealing. One would focus not on their symbolic meaning (as Melville did in "The Whiteness of the Whale" in *Moby-Dick*) but on their phenomenology, and their organizing function within Faulkner's literary production. Pink, for example, usually connotes an object to be found at the "dead center" of fascination. In order to illustrate this point one can hardly find a more explicit passage than the one that follows. Originally placed at the beginning of chapter 3 of the third part of *Flags in the Dust,* it tells of Horace's relationship with Belle's sister, Joan Heppleton:

> Horace had seen her on the street twice, his attention caught by the bronze splendor of her hair and by an indefinable something in her air, her carriage. It was not boldness and not arrogance exactly, but a sort of calm, lazy contemptuousness that left him seeking in his mind after an experience lost somewhere within the

veils of years that swaddled his dead childhood. . . . Then, as he lay in bed thinking of Belle and waiting for sleep, he remembered it.

He was five years old and his father had taken him to his first circus, and clinging to the man's hard, reassuring hand in a daze of blaring sounds and sharp cries and scents that tightened his small entrails with a sense of fabulous and unimaginable imminence and left him a little sick, he raised his head and found a tiger watching him with yellow and lazy contemplation; and while his whole small body was a tranced and soundless scream, the animal gaped and flicked its lips with an unbelievably pink tongue . . .

That was it, and though that youthful reaction was dulled now by years, he found himself watching her on the street somewhat as a timorous person is drawn with delicious revulsion to gaze into a window filled with knives. (*Flags,* 290–91)

Horace, then, is about to know (in the biblical sense) a "lady tiger in a tea gown" (*Flags,* 292). Compared to her, her sister Belle is but a flimsy replica. Indeed, in *Sanctuary* the only pink associated with her is a vulgar bedroom:

He walked out of the mirror and crossed the hall quietly and looked into Belle's room. It was pink, the bed piled high with pink pillows frosted with lace. On the night-table beneath a pink-shaded lamp lay a box of chocolates and a stack of gaudy magazines. The closet door was ajar, the symmetry of the dressing-table broken where she had paused again to don her hat. He went to the table and looked. In a moment he found what he knew he should: a soiled handkerchief with which she had removed surplus rouge from her mouth and stuffed between the mirror and the wall. He carried it to the closet and put it in a bag for soiled linen and closed the closet and left the room. (STOT, 18–19)

In spite of her righteousness the "serene" Narcissa is correct in asserting that Belle is "filthy" and that she "will always smell of the pantry." At the end of *Sanctuary* Belle herself seems to confirm this judgment by ordering Horace to "lock the back door." Belle's nest (one could call it a den or even a lair) is the same in *Flags* and in *Sanctuary:* "Before he reached the house, he saw the rose colored shade at his wife's window. He entered the house from the back and came to the door and looked into the room. She was reading in bed, a broad magazine with a colored back. The lamp had a rose colored shade. On the table sat an open box of chocolates" (SAN, 358; CT, 313–14). Repetition persuades the reader that this rose colored shade hides a carnivorous reality.

Miss Reba's establishment is also associated with pink in the minds of the two hairdresser apprentices: "Fonzo thought of himself surrounded by tier upon tier of drawn shades, rose-colored, beyond which, in a murmur of silk, in panting whispers, the apotheosis of his youth assumed a thousand avatars" (SAN, 233; CT, 203). Temple herself has been taken by Popeye to a pink nest/den/lair: "The whole room had an air of musty stodginess, decorum; in the wavy mirror of a cheap varnished dresser, as in a stagnant pool, there seemed to linger spent ghosts of voluptuous gestures and dead lusts. In the corner, upon a faded scarred strip of oilcloth tacked over the carpet, sat a washstand bearing a flowered bowl and pitcher and a row of towels; in the corner behind it sat a slop jar dressed also in fluted rose-colored paper" (SAN, 186; CT, 163). The temple of lust, the apotheosis of the flesh, Eros's altar, each is a name for a shabby brothel where all the spent desires of mankind, themselves but degraded specimens of moribund and "defunctive" Desire, founder like shipwrecks on a polluted beach. Were Venus to be born again, as Harry Wilbourne puts it in a later novel, she would be a shabby travesty: "if Venus returned she would be a soiled man in a subway lavatory with a palm full of French postcards" (TWP, 136). Under the "fainting surges of a final saffron-colored light" that falls on the capital city of crime, the haven of middle-class frustrations reveals itself to be as "dingy" as a rubbish dump, as "niggardly" as it is wretched (see the final scene of chapter 18). There is something abject in the kingdom of the flesh. This is made obvious by the two ridiculous Cerberuses trimmed with ribbon at the gate: "In the grimy grassplot before it two of those small, woolly, white, worm-like dogs, one with a pink, the other a blue, ribbon about its neck, moved about with an air of sluggish and obscene paradox" (SAN, 170; CT, 149). Surrounded "by a ghostly promiscuity of intimate garments, of discreet whispers of flesh oft-assailed and impregnable" (SAN, 172; CT, 151), Temple recalls an episode from her own adolescence. The reader senses another debunking of desire—this time from the point of view of Eve herself:

The worst one of all said boys thought all girls were ugly except when they were dressed. She said the Snake had been seeing Eve for several days and never noticed her until Adam made her put on a fig leaf. How do you know? they said, and she said because the Snake was there before Adam, because he was the first one to be thrown out of heaven; he was there all the time. But that wasn't what they meant and they said, How do you know, and Temple thought of her kind of backed up against the dressing table and the rest of them in a circle around her with their combed hair and their shoulders smelling of scented soap and the light powder in the air and their eyes like knives until you could almost watch her flesh where the eyes were touching it, and her eyes in her ugly face courageous and frightened and daring, and they all saying, How do you know? until she told them and held up her hand and swore she had. That was when the youngest one turned and ran out of the room. She locked herself in the bath and they could hear her being sick. (SAN, 181–82; CT, 159)

This evocation is embedded in the archetypal setting—the silky, sordid den of a brothel—the symbolism of which could not be more blatant. The setting seems to capture one's glance and hold on to it like a regressing set of mirrors. The glance that the serpent directs at Eve is evoked by the plain Jane character in the middle of the circle of staring girls. They pierce her with their inquisitiveness. But their own glances are reversed by the contemplation of the "primitive scene," which the plain Jane character is apparently proud to have witnessed. The conclusion one draws has far-reaching implications for those interested in the general laws of Faulkner's creation: (a) the fascinated person is also someone who fascinates; (b) the innocent person vomits when confronted with experience.

When Horace Benbow affirms that nature is woman and progress is man, and when he symbolizes the one by the Virginia creeper and the other by the mirror, he underscores the point that what was absent from paradise at the time of the Fall was a mirror. Had they had a mirror, Adam and Eve would have discovered that they were naked, since they would have been able to see, if not even admire, their nudity. Do we conclude that the mirror performs the same role as the serpent, perpetuating the Fall each time the eyes are enticed by their own reflection? Given the role that mirrors play in the novels of Faulkner (a role common to many other reflexive, symbolist novels),[3] such a conclusion could well be justified.

In *Sanctuary* both Horace Benbow and Temple Drake are associated with mirrors, though in quite different ways. For the former the mirror is so associated with the repetitive shock of being confronted with the phenomenon of fascination/repulsion[4] that, mutatis mutandis, the photograph of Little Belle functions in the same way (that is, as a mirror) on two occasions. For Horace, the photograph is what leads him to discover that female sexuality ensnares:

> Upon the glazed surface a highlight lay. He shifted the photograph until the face became clear. He stood before it, looking at the sweet, inscrutable face which looked in turn at something just beyond his shoulder, out of the dead cardboard. He was thinking of the grape arbor in Kinston, of summer twilight and the murmurs of voices darkening into silence as he approached. . . .
>
> He moved suddenly. As if of its own accord the photograph had shifted, slipping a little from its precarious balancing against the book. The image blurred into the highlight, like something familiar seen beneath disturbed though clear water; he looked at the familiar image with a kind of quiet horror and despair, at a face suddenly older in sin than he would ever be, a face more blurred than sweet, at eyes more secret than soft. In reaching for it, he knocked it flat; whereupon once more the face mused tenderly behind the rigid travesty of the painted mouth, contemplating something beyond his shoulder. (SAN, 199–200; CT, 174–75)

This must be one of the most unequivocal examples of fascination not only in Faulkner's fiction, but in the history of literature. Horace is literally mesmerized by his daughter-in-law's photograph. Because of the absence of a clear focus (see the repetition of the key word *blurred*), all notion of reality disappears. First, the reality of the object of contemplation, the photograph itself, fades away. This, in turn, opens the possibility of a vision that sublimates sensuous reality in the way a revelation does. The revelation, however, retains a specific visual context—the one that belongs to Horace's eye. The fully subjective nature of the revelation is amply confirmed, moreover, by a typical Faulknerian juxtaposition in the passage that immediately follows. Horace is attracted to Temple, as he is to Little Belle, but to such an extent that he confuses the former with the latter in his erotic fantasy at the end of chapter 23. In the train on the way to Oxford he sees everything with eyes still in the grip of fascination: "He changed again. The waiting crowd was composed half of young men in collegiate clothes with small cryptic badges on their shirts and vests, and two girls with painted small faces and scant bright dresses like artificial flowers surrounded by bright and restless bees" (SAN, 202; CT, 177). The association of women with flowers, with a landscape, with nature in general, is so constant in Horace's mind that, if we take him as a sesame to the novel, *Sanctuary* might well be thought of as an extended metaphor based on the diseased Garden of Eden: a blighted pastoral.

However, the second moment of fascination reveals even more clearly the power of an imaginary gaze:

> The photograph sat on the dresser. He took it up, holding it in his hands. Enclosed by the narrow imprint of the missing frame Little Belle's face dreamed with the quality of sweet chiaroscuro. Communicated to the cardboard by some quality of the light or perhaps some infinitesimal movement of his hands, his own breathing, the face appeared to breathe in his palms in a shallow bath of highlight, beneath the slow, smoke-like tongues of invisible honeysuckle. Almost palpable enough to be seen, the scent filled the room and the small face seemed to swoon in a voluptuous languor, blurring still more, fading, leaving upon his eye a soft and fading aftermath of invitation and voluptuous promise and secret affirmation like a scent itself. (SAN, 267–68; CT, 234)

The passage demonstrates better than a rational explanation could the extreme ambiguity that fascination generates. This ambiguity could be called the "mirror effect." It induces a deep and enduring doubt as to the reassuring precedence of reality over appearance—a doubt only to be accounted for by an explanation of perception as a form of seduction.[5]

Moreover, the scene conveys a strange impression of literary intertextuality. Through the use of such a magnetic word as *communicate* and through the interplay of light and shadow, the passage provokes the same feeling of uneasiness and homelessness, of alienation or estrangement of identity as that analyzed with graceful care in Hawthorne's chapter 19, entitled "The Child by the Brook Side" of *The Scarlet Letter:*

> By this time Pearl had reached the margin of the brook, and stood on the farther side, gazing silently at Hester and the clergyman, who still sat together on the mossy tree-trunk, waiting to receive her. Just where she had paused the brook chanced to form a pool, so smooth and quiet that it reflected a perfect image of her little figure, with all the brilliant picturesqueness of her beauty, in its adornment of flowers and wreathed foliage, but more refined and spiritualized than in reality. This image, so nearly identical with the living Pearl, seemed to communicate somewhat of its own shadowy and intangible quality to the child herself. It was strange, the way in which Pearl stood, looking so steadfastly at them through the dim medium of the forest-gloom; herself, meanwhile, all glorified with a ray of sunshine, that was attracted thitherward as by a certain sympathy. In the brook beneath stood another child—another and the same—with likewise its ray of golden light. Hester herself in some indistinct and tantalizing manner, estranged from Pearl; as if the child, in her lonely ramble through the forest, had strayed out of the sphere in which she and her mother dwelt together, and was now vainly seeking to return to it.

This admirable scene, at once delicate and penetrating, can be compared to more than one passage in *Sanctuary,* beginning with the first scene by the spring. I shall later return to the problem raised by the victim of these effects of fascination. Clearly, he/she is an avatar of the perennial double or doppelgänger, analyzed by such authors as Poe, Stevenson, Otto Rank, and recently Clément Rosset.[6] It should be pointed out, however, that Faulkner does not make use of the doppelgänger theme for metaphysical reasons (as is typical of German romanticism), but for reasons that are physical, like hypnotism for example. If Horace is repeatedly trapped by his own gaze, there is something physical in him that not only does not want to resist the attraction, but also secretly begs for it.

The difference between Horace and Temple lies in the fact that, for Temple, the mirror has nothing secret about it. Though admittedly thrown into a disturbing situation in the room in which she spends her first night at Miss Reba's, Temple is surely looking for more than composure when she takes out her compact and (the gesture that is repeated in the final scene of the novel) begins to tease her hair in front of the small mirror inside. There is an urge to seduce even in the dungeon of her seclusion—a fact clearly demonstrated in chapter 8 of the novel. The words used are revealing: is her hat not "rakishly" inclined? And when she lies down with "her hands crossed on her breast, her legs straight and close and decorous, like an effigy on an ancient tomb" (84, 75), is she not acting out her own death like a child, "as in a theatrical scene, where life is a disguise and death a living person"?[7] In other words, even her immobility is a show.

In Popeye's car as they drive to Memphis, she also takes out her mirror. Then again, at Miss Reba's: "It was twilight; in a dim mirror, a pellucid oblong of dusk set on end, she had a glimpse of herself like a thin ghost, a pale shadow moving in the uttermost profundity of shadow" (177, 155). She is not yet aware of what is happening to her. But then, in her room, the clock itself turns into what might be called a looking-trap:

> From beneath the shade the smoke-colored twilight emerged in slow puffs like signal smoke from a blanket, thickening in the room. The china figures which supported the clock gleamed in hushed smooth flexions: knee, elbow, flank, arm and breast in attitudes of voluptuous lassitude. The glass face, become mirror-like, appeared to hold all reluctant light, holding in its tranquil depths a quiet gesture of moribund time, one-armed like a veteran from the wars. Half past ten oclock. Temple lay in bed, looking at the clock, thinking about half-past-ten-oclock. (SAN, 179–80; CT, 157)

This is the jump in time that makes her remember how she prepared for the dance in the passage quoted above. It is important to note how the *vacant gaze* functions. This is what shifts the mind from the actual time to remembered time. The real is so unreal! The vacant gaze is entirely absorbed by what stands on the mantelpiece, the motionless eye of the clock and the four voluptuous caryatids. At this point Temple is no longer thinking. She is what her languid body is, that is, an imitation of the scene under her gaze. Both are dominated by pure expectation and obstinate refusal, by the memory of a nightmare as well as a vague, conceited, unattached availability that shocks Horace when, in chapter 23, he learns of "the night she had spent in the ruined house. . . . That was the only part of the whole experience which appeared to have left any impression on her at all: the night which she had spent in comparative inviolation" (257–58; CT, 225). This is what frequently takes the place of psychology in Faulkner's fiction: a slightly perverse juxtaposition and a cluttering of nearly traumatic scenes, the contemplation of which gradually fascinates the character and takes possession of his/her consciousness and will to act.

Temple's vision, after the description of her gaze wandering around the mantelpiece and before her recollection of preparing for the dance, pre-figures in all details the vision that Horace has after becoming fascinated for a second time: "She watched the final light condense into the clock face, and the dial change from a round orifice in the darkness to a disc suspended in nothingness, the original chaos, and change in turn to a crystal ball holding in its still and cryptic depths the ordered chaos of the intricate and shadowy world upon whose scarred flanks the old wounds whirl onward at dizzy speed into the darkness lurking with new disasters" (SAN, 180–81; CT, 158). Aesthetically, there is something baroque about the play with depths and surfaces, the dominance of the circle and even the globe image, and the abrupt equation of the world of familiar objects with the cosmos. Faulkner is, of course, also playing with psychology. The vision of the scarred flanks of Mother Earth is not new in his work; we have already seen it in "Carcassonne." But where do these wounds come from—which "whirl onward at dizzy speed"—if not from the association of Temple's own bleeding with the doctor's recent visit ("Behind the glasses his eyes looked like bicycle wheels at dizzy speed; a metallic haze" [SAN, 179; CT, 157])? Faulkner writes with a deeper though cruder logic than the omniscient positivist realists of the late nineteenth and early twentieth centuries. Jean-Jacques Mayoux pointed this out when he noted that Faulkner's writing was "expressive and even over-expressive."[8] Very often, indeed, the sheer visual intensity of his "psychological" scenes results in a surreal representation of reality, as in the passage above. Otherwise, as in the case of many descriptions of Miss Reba's house, one passes into something quite unreal, for instance: "The house was full of sounds. Indistinguishable, remote, they came in to her with a quality of awakening, resurgence, as though the house itself had been asleep, rousing itself with dark" (SAN, 186; CT, 163).

In this respect much of chapter 18 of *Sanctuary* could be compared with chapter 18 of *The House of the Seven Gables,* in which Hawthorne describes a room occupied only by a dead man, Judge Pynchon, as night gradually creeps in, "rousing itself with dark." In both cases the effect of *Unheimliche* originates in fascination.

Temple, however, never vomits. She does not vomit either at the old Frenchman's house or at Miss Reba's, at the courthouse or in the Luxembourg Gardens where, after a yawn of boredom, she opens her compact once again "upon a face in miniature, sullen and discontented and sad" (SAN, 379; CT, 333). She does not have the otherwise typically Faulknerian defense-reaction of an "innocent" organism confronted by an experience harsher than it can take. The absence of physical reaction does not mean, of course, that she does not know (like Joe Chistmas in *Light in August*) that "Something is happening to me! . . . I told you all the time!" (122, 107), but that her defensive reaction is rooted in a mixture of fascination and repulsion. Faulkner's attitude to Temple is quite reminiscent of Baudelaire's virulent invective: "What is a young girl in reality? She's a young ninny and a little bitch; she is the grandest stupidity wedded to the deepest depravity. There is, in the young girl, all the abjectness of the gutter-snipe and of the schoolboy."[9] To explain the two writers' apparently hostile attitudes toward the other sex as a kind of "puritanism" would be glib. The fact that one writer was a Catholic and the other a Protestant denies the facile association of Puritanism with Protestantism. This hostility harks back to such an age-old and well-known Judeo-Christian conception of the woman as part virgin and part whore that it seems better to refer it to the whole West's collective consciousness than as belonging to a particular individual's obsession. Nowhere else in his work, moreover, does Faulkner express such a vision of a young woman. As André Bleikasten writes about *Sanctuary:* "Whether repulsed by horror or anguish or aroused by desire, the body speaks the same language: the convulsions of terror resemble sexual spasms, and erotic scenes make one think of scenes of torture. An ambiguity carefully nurtured throughout the novel repeatedly links desire with horror and death. Ultimately, terror, nausea and sexuality are joined in the same poisonous sheaf."[10] My only objection to this analysis is that I am not sure, as Bleikasten seems to be, that this ambiguity is deliberately calculated. As he remarks in the same article, "There is in this book a concentrated harshness which is no doubt unique in Faulkner's novels. A sort of haste and brutality which leads the writer to harden his touch, to go for easy effects, and to multiply his simplifications." Indeed, "concentrated" is the word. But, as we know, this concentration is at least partly the result of the reconstruction of the first, far looser version of the novel. Even so, the first version contains all the mechanics of fascination. The only difference is the degree to which the (melo)drama and the rhetoric are emphasized in the final version. The first version of Horace's initial fascination bears witness to this change:

> The curtains billowed steadily and faintly, as though to the shrill pulsing of the cicadas, and he thought how darkness is that agent which destroys the edifice with which light shapes people to a certain predictable behavior, as though by the impact of eyes; thinking of the grape arbor, of the murmur of young voices darkening into silence, and into the pale whisper of Little Belle's small white dress, of the delicate and urgent mammalian whisper of that curious small flesh in which was vatted delicately a seething sympathy of the blossoming grape. He drew a chair to the table and moved the photograph until the face was clear of the highlight, gazing at the sweet, veiled enigma. As though there were in the events a fatality which takes its color from the minds privy to the events, he thought. As though a disaster not a part of the plan could be engendered by his lack of concern and my fundamental pessimism and her furious woman's desire for retributive justice. . . . . He rose quickly, his chair scraping on the floor. Again the face blurred into the highlight, yet the familiarity of the face's planes enabled him still to see it, as though beneath disturbed water or through steam, and he looked down at the face with a sort of still horror and despair, at a face more blurred than sweet, at eyes more secret than soft. He reached for it so quickly that he knocked it flat, whereupon once more the face mused tenderly behind the rigid travesty of the painted mouth. (STOT, 145–46)

There is really no room for doubt here: in Faulkner's work, as in myth generally, fascination is the link between the gaze and sexuality—and this is also true for many another writer. Hawthorne has already been quoted. Melville also comes to mind in this superb scene from *Mardi:*

Returned from the cave, Hautia reclined in her clematis bower, invisible hands flinging fennel around her. And nearer, and nearer, stole dulcet sounds dissolving my woes, as warm beams, snow. Strange languors made me droop; once more within my inmost vault, side by side, the Past and Yillah lay:—two bodies tranced;—while like a rounding sun, before me Hautia magnified magnificence; and through her fixed eyes, slowly drank up my soul.

Thus we stood:—snake and victim: life ebbing out from me, to her.[11]

And even Emerson, who—as so often—bravely, though reluctantly, addresses the heart of things in his *Journals:*

In a right state the love of one, which each man carried in his heart, should protect all women from his eyes as by an impenetrable veil of indifference. The love of one should make him indifferent to all others, or rather their protector or saintly friend, as if for her sake. But now there is in the eyes of all men a certain evil light, a vague desire which attaches them to the forms of many women, whilst their affections fasten on some one. Their natural eye is not fixed into coincidence with their spiritual eye.[12]

In *Being and Nothingness* Jean-Paul Sartre may well have been the first philosopher to study fascination both in terms of epistemology and in terms of what he called his phenomenological ontology. Here the gaze is related to the existence of the other. At the end of the chapter entitled "The Look" he arrives at the following conclusion: "In short, the other can exist for us in two forms: if I experience him with evidence, I fail to know him; if I know him, if I act upon him, I only reach his being-as-object and his probable existence in the midst of the world. No synthesis of these two forms is possible" (B&N, 302). And at the end of the following chapter on "The Body" one finds this well-known passage on the other-as-flesh:

What for the Other is his taste *of himself becomes* for me *the other's flesh.* The flesh is the pure contingency of presence. It is ordinarily hidden by clothes, make-up, the cut of the hair or beard, the expression, etc. But in the course of long acquaintance with a person, there always comes an instant when all these disguises are thrown off and when I find myself in *the pure contingency of his presence*. In this case I achieve in the face or in the other parts of a body the pure intuition of the flesh. This intuition is not only knowledge; it is the affective apprehension of an absolute contingency, and this apprehension is a particular type of nausea. (B&N, 343–44)

It should be noted, in passing, that earlier in the same book Sartre wrote this: "Intuition has often been defined as the immediate presence of the known to the knower, but it is seldom that anyone has reflected on the requirements of the notion of the *immediate*. Immediacy is the absence of any mediator; that is obvious, for otherwise the mediator alone would be known and not what is mediated" (B&N, 178). This helps formulate a question of immediate concern since, obviously, fascination and intuition have in common this "absence of any mediator." Is fascination therefore an intuition?

If we take *Sanctuary* as a starting point, it would seem that, ten years before Sartre, Faulkner had brought to light evidence of the nausea that emanates from the perception of the presence of the Other as "pure contingency." Of course, the difference between Sartre's conceptual analysis and Faulkner's dramatic representation lies in the fact that with the novelist fascination is acted out on the stage of his fiction so as to communicate immediately an overpowering (sometimes even a threatening, or at any rate an unpleasant) sense of some sensuous reality, for example the color pink. With the novelist the phenomenon seems to be one of the permanent data of the consciousness, the true though secret inner motivation behind so many memorable scenes. In other words it is as if these scenes arise from what in psychoanalysis is called the compulsion to repeat.

Fascination and its counterpart and extension, nausea, are indeed motifs that recur frequently in *Sanctuary*. When the process of fascination is not directly represented, as in the examples already quoted, it lies behind the relationship between the knower and the known. This is true even in the first version of the novel, which begins with the evocation of a rather striking encounter between Horace Benbow and the worst possible source of nausea ("the most horrific tale I could imagine," Faulkner wrote in his 1932 preface to the novel):

Each time he passed the jail he would look up at the barred window, usually to see a small, pale, tragic blob lying in one of the grimy interstices, or perhaps a blue wisp of tobacco smoke combing raggedly away along the spring sunshine. At first there had been a negro murderer there, who had killed his wife [; slashed her throat with a razor so that, the whole head tossing further and further backward from the bloody regurgitation of her bubbling throat, she ran out of the cabin door and for six or seven steps up the quiet moonlit lane]. He would lean in the window in the evening and sing. (STOT, 3)[13]

Although the remarkable economy of the second version of *Sanctuary*'s opening pages is lacking, this first version is neither banal nor undirected (it is in fact much more shocking than the definitive opening scene). One can hardly be unmoved by the implicit comparison of the murdered woman with a chicken. A feeling of nausea is close at hand. Indeed, this feeling grows remorselessly in the following pages, when Benbow associates "that black stuff that ran out of Bovary's mouth"[14] with, in turn, (a) Popeye, (b) Temple alias Little Belle, (c) his own mother.

Following John K. Simon,[15] Bleikasten also makes use of Sartre when writing about *Sanctuary:*

"The obscene appears when the body adopts postures which entirely strip it of its acts and reveal the inertia of the flesh" (B&N, 401). In *Sanctuary,* this obscenity can be found on most pages: it is found in the frozen, grotesque postures of fear, and in the hysterical convulsions of anguish and desire; in the ignoble abandonment of humiliated and defeated flesh as in the rigid immobility of the corpse. Nausea, in this novel, is the discovery of the body in the dull weight of its inertia and the contingency of its "being there"; it is also the horror and fascination inspired by the chaos of organic life, which, hardly conceived, already transmits death with the weight of destiny. In the final analysis, it is the revolt against this body of ours which never ceases to thwart our desire for identity and our will to master. . . . The language of the body in *Sanctuary* can ultimately be reduced to this repeated confession—the nauseous epiphany of death and sexuality which is nowhere better encapsulated than in that "black stuff."[16]

Can one really speak of an "epiphany"? Perhaps—but only in the sense that in the state of fascination one transcends the phenomena of time and space. More often than not, however, the one fascinated is in fact hopelessly trapped in these two dimensions. If fascination can lead to an escape through transcendence, the escape is always coupled with its own opposite. This is why fascination is at once precious and dangerous—one could say so deadly. Like narcissism, it harbors knowledge that contains in itself the death of all knowledge.

For example, during his fascination, Horace receives intimations of time and flesh, or of death and sex, but these can in no way be called knowledge in the biblical sense, that is, a communion with. On the contrary, Horace is never so separate or uncommunicative (in his mind) as when, through fascination (i.e., through sight), he communicates with what lies beneath his eyes, be it the woman with the slashed throat, the "black" quality in Popeye, or later the "blurred focus" of sex (Belle/Narcissa/Temple/Little Belle) reflected by the mirror and the photograph. Therefore, it is not enough to say, as Bleikasten does, that fascination "never ceases to thwart our desire for identity and our will to master": fascination is the very negation of identity and mastery.

One must give Sartre credit for having made this quite clear in the chapter on "Knowledge as a type of relation between the for-itself and the in-itself." He opposes the known, which is always there, and the elusive knower. He remarks that "this presence of the known is a presence to nothing, since the knower is the pure reflection of a non-being." After this, he concludes, and this seems essential to me, that the presence "appears then across the total translucency of the knower known—an absolute presence." Then he dedicates the following paragraph to fascination:

> A psychological and empirical exemplification of the original relation is given us in the case of *fascination*. In fascination, which represents the immediate act of *knowing,* the knower is absolutely nothing but a pure negation; he does not find or recover himself anywhere—he is *not*. The only qualification which he can support is that he is *not* precisely this particular fascinating object. In fascination, there is nothing more than a gigantic object in a deserted world. Yet the fascinated intuition is in no way a *fusion* with the object. In fact, the condition necessary for the existence

of fascination is that the object be raised in absolute relief against the background of emptiness; that is, I am precisely the immediate negation of the object and nothing but that. (Author's emphases; B&N, 177)

Returning to fascination later, Sartre defines it as a *state*, "the nonthetic consciousness of being nothing in the presence of being," and opposes it to seduction, which "aims at producing in the Other the consciousness of his state of nothingness as he confronts the seductive object" (B&N, 372). (It is worth noting here that this opposition is much the same as the one used in my chapters on "Glamour" and "Shame.")

And finally, in the same section on "Concrete Relations with the Other," one finds this observation:

> Fascination, however, even if it were to produce a state of being-fascinated in the Other, could not by itself succeed in producing love. We can be fascinated by an orator, by an actor, by a tightrope-walker, but this does not mean that we love him. To be sure, we can take our eyes off him, but he is still raised on the ground of the world, and fascination does not posit the fascinating object as the ultimate term of the transcendence. Quite the contrary: fascination *is* transcendence. (B&N, 374)

At this point we find ourselves somewhat prematurely carried forward to the argument of my chapters entitled "Dead End" and "The Metaphor of the Subject." Before proceeding, however, it may be useful to quote from another philosopher's criticism of Sartre's analysis of the gaze. Was it fair, Jean Brun asks, on the part of the philosopher thus to emphasize the aspect of conflict in his analysis? In spite of his denial,[17] has not Sartre—much like Faulkner in *Sanctuary*, in fact—endowed the gaze with a covert psychology while claiming to make an objective, phenomenological analysis?

> Sartre insisted on the threat the other's glance is supposed to insinuate in me; his glance turns me into a thing and allows him to be a Medusa, so that I have but one option left: I must answer back. The glance illustrates the topic so dear to Sartre, namely that the origins of *Mitsein* are to be found in conflict. It could be asked whether there are not some powerful biographical influences in Sartre's theory of the glance, which count as much as his

phenomenology. The reason for thinking so is the fact that Sartre has never really made clear why the other's glance should make him into a thing nor, above all, why the glance cannot have any other outcome than in conflict.[18]

Whether Jean Brun had in mind Sartre's well-known squint or something else, I do not know; nor can it ever be certain that there was "some powerful biographical influence" in Faulkner's frequent use of fascination as a mode of dramatization—indeed, as a substitute for psychology. What is clear to me, however, is that Faulkner's fiction does illustrate Sartre's point about the presence of conflict in the gaze. And yet there is no denying that Brun improves upon Sartre by returning, in his article, to Baudelaire—perhaps the greatest of all the poets of the glance. For example, Brun introduces a distinction between the sexes, which Sartre never does, a distinction that should not surprise us after our analyses of the different effects of the mirror on Temple and on Horace. Brun quotes many other fine remarks on the topic, two of which take us back to its anthropological context: "The glance that extends to the vanishing-point and beyond belongs specifically to the human realm. Two eyes open, two close: a life. Fascination, love, tears, are so many events that make up the history of the eye,"[19] and "Each pupil is the point which allows us to look at infinity *through the key-hole*."[20] I would add a statement quoted by Roland Barthes: "The eye through which I can see God is the same eye through which He sees me."[21]

Neither Brun nor Sartre resorts to psychoanalysis. Yet if there is a topic that might benefit from such an approach, it is this one. Indeed, the whole of Faulkner's work reveals "a linguistic pattern, a real circuit, which closes upon itself while including subject and object." It is the concept of the "pair of opposites," the goal of which is to "look and to show itself, and, in between, to be looked at, and, at an even earlier stage, to put into practice a kind of auto-erotic voyeurism."[22] Thanks to this notion of *Gegensatzpaar*, the problem can be situated not, as with Sartre, on the phenomenological level but on the structural level, "either on the level of psychological or psychopathological manifestations (e.g., sadomasochism, voyeurism, exhibitionism) or else on a metapsychological level (e.g., life-instinct versus death-instinct)."[23] Freud—for whom "the main instinct, along with the instinct to master, is the instinct to see"[24]—had, as early as 1910, developed "his interpretation of hysterical blindness." According to this theory, patients seized by hysteria are only blind in a conscious sense because, unconsciously, they can still see. Freud went as far as to say that an organ, the eye for instance, could assume "as a consequence of an exaggerated erogenous zone, the conduct peculiar to the genital organ."[25]

One can see easily—perhaps too easily—what interpretation can now be given to the exorbitant privilege the eye and the act of looking enjoy in Faulkner's novels and, more particularly, to impotent Popeye's "pop-eyed" exophthalmia. No doubt, such a decoding is valid. Yet all that it tells us is that perversion can be interpreted as the absence of the norm—which merely underscores and emphasizes the norm.

"We thus see," Freud writes, "that certain perverted propensities regularly appear in *contrasting pairs*."[26] He observes a psychological phenomenon which is displayed everywhere in Faulkner's fiction. Laplanche and Pontalis likewise observe that "terms paired in this way share a common factor, and cannot be reduced one to another; they cannot engender one another, but they are at the origin of every conflict and the motor of all dialectical movement."[27] If it is not "the model of all conflicts"[28] (which would only send us back to Sartre's analysis), the gaze in Faulkner's work and in psychoanalysis is nevertheless the highly privileged setting of a drama which takes place on two levels: "one where I attempt to exist outside myself" and one which leads me on "an itinerary towards hidden depths"—to cite Jean Brun's formulation.[29]

At this stage it seems inevitable that one should refer to Jacques Lacan. He has not only devoted a seminar to the subject—"Of the Gaze as *Objet Petit a*"[30]—but has also used phenomenology as the starting point of his reflections on the gaze in psychoanalysis:

> phenomenologists have succeeded in articulating with precision, and in the most disconcerting way, that it is quite clear that I see *outside,* that perception is not in me, that it is on the objects that it apprehends. And yet I apprehend the world in a perception that seems to concern the immanence of the *I see myself seeing myself.* The privilege of the subject seems to be established here from that bipolar reflexive relation by which, as soon as I perceive, my representations belong to me.
>
> That is how the world is struck with a presumption of idealiza-

tion, of the suspicion of yielding me only my representations. (Author's emphases; FFCP, 80–81)

The phenomenologist in question is not Sartre but Merleau-Ponty, whose striking image of the "turning inside-out of the finger of a glove" enables Lacan to postulate that "consciousness, in its illusion of seeing itself seeing itself, finds its basis in the inside-out structure of the gaze" (82).

The remarkable structure of fascination in Faulkner's work, which strikes one from the very early writings (for example the "inverted" grandmother who catches Juliet unawares in "Adolescence" [US, 465]) certainly stands at the opposite pole of the physiological positivism of Auguste Comte, for whom "the eye cannot see itself" (quoted in B&N, 379). "If then the gaze is the reverse of consciousness," Lacan asks, "how shall we try to imagine it?"

> The gaze, as conceived by Sartre, is the gaze by which I am surprised—surprised in so far as it changes all the perspectives, the guidelines, of my world, as it orders it, from the point of nothingness where I am, into a kind of radiating reticulation of the organism. As the locus of the relation between me, the annihilating subject, and that which surrounds me, the gaze, according to Sartre, is endowed with such a power that it obliges me, the gazing eye, to scotomize the eye of him who looks at me as at an object. In so far as I am under the gaze, Sartre writes, I no longer see the eye that looks at me, and, if I see the eye, the gaze disappears.
>
> Is this a correct phenomenological analysis? No. It is not true that, when I am being looked at, when I beg for a look, when I get it, I do not see it as a look. . . .
>
> The gaze sees itself, even the gaze of which Sartre speaks, the gaze that surprises me and reduces me to shame, since this is the feeling he regards as the most dominant. The gaze I encounter . . . is not a gaze seen, but a gaze imagined by me in the field of the Other. (FFCP, 84)

Moreover, Lacan says that he is struck (as we have seen) by the fact that, "far from speaking of the introduction of the gaze as something which concerns the organ of sight, he [Sartre] refers to the sound of rustling leaves suddenly heard while out hunting, or to a footstep heard in the corridor. When are these sounds heard, he asks? 'At the moment when he has presented himself in the action of looking through a key-hole.'" Lacan can thus conclude: "A gaze surprises him and turns him into a *voyeur*. It disturbs him, overwhelms him and reduces him to a feeling of shame. No doubt the gaze in question results from the presence of the other as some separate phenomenon." It is important to appreciate, according to Lacan, "the predominating status of the gaze in the function of desire" (84).

By moving from Sartre to Lacan, we thus seem to proceed from representation to acting-out, and indeed we find—have already found, in fact—both in Faulkner's fiction.

Replying to a question concerning his difference with Sartre, Lacan insists that "if one does not stress the dialectic of desire, one does not understand why the gaze of the other should disorganize the field of perception. And this is because the subject under consideration is *not that of reflexive consciousness, but that of desire*" (89). I have italicized what seems to me to be most relevant to the study of Faulkner's fiction; what does this express theoretically, indeed, if not the distinction I have already made between a "clear focus" and a "blurred focus," between, say, Miss Jenny (the subject as reflexive consciousness, unblurred by desire) and Horace Benbow (the subject as the origin of desire) in either *Sartoris* or *Sanctuary?*

Turning next to Descartes's *Dioptric* and to Holbein's *Ambassadors* to make his point, Lacan raises a question about the nature of desire, which is "lured and trapped in the picture" precisely because the primary function of a picture is to lure and trap the gaze. Beginning from the chiasmus "the picture is certainly in my eye. But I am in the picture," Lacan states that "what is at issue is certainly deceiving the eye [*tromper l'oeil*]. A triumph of the gaze over the eye" (103). But things are not quite so geometric in Faulkner who, in this respect, turns out to be a much subtler analyst of the gaze than either Sartre or Lacan. For in order to deceive the eye, one must seduce it, and in seducing it (i.e., in reinforcing the power of the gaze, or, to use Freud's language, in arousing the eye like the turgid organ of desire itself), one brings about a second reversal of the gaze, whereby the eye, and not the gaze, triumphs.

The last pages of Lacan's seminar on the gaze are devoted to the question "What is a Picture?" and are worth turning to briefly before concluding. Like Merleau-Ponty, Lacan asks whether, when dealing with the myriad small strokes of a painter's brush that end in the miracle of a picture, one can speak of choice. "No," he answers, one speaks of "something else. . . . Let us not forget that the painter's brushstroke is the end-line of a movement." This is what he goes on to name "the terminal moment" or "the moment of seeing." He continues:

> All action represented in a picture appears to us as a battle scene, that is to say, as something theatrical, necessarily created for the gesture.
>
> What we see here, then, is that the gaze operates in a descending curve, a descending curve of desire, no doubt. But how can we express this? The subject is not completely aware of it—he operates by remote control. Modifying the formula I have of desire as unconscious—*man's desire is the desire of the Other*—I would say that it is a question of a sort of desire *on the part of* the Other, at the end of which is the *showing* [*le donner-à-voir*]. (FFCP, 115)

Even though we may well resist Lacan's verbal legerdemain and intellectual acrobatics, we recognize nonetheless an adequate framework, if not even a theoretical model for Faulkner's fiction. This is especially true if we admit, with Lacan, that the subject of fiction is not necessarily where it is expected to be nor even where it claims to be. Real correspondences exist on both sides of the rather artificial line between the theory and practice of fiction as fantasy—just as powerful analogies abound between the way Faulkner dramatizes fascination and what ethnological research has brought to light about analogous phenomena. According to ethnologists, "fascination" defines a psychic condition of obstruction and exclusion and at the same time a feeling of domination wielded by a force as strong as it is occult, a force which limits the person's independence, his capacity to take a decision or to make a choice.

In its treatment of fascination as a psychic phenomenon, epistemology has taken us from phenomenology to depth psychology and from there on to ethnology. Yet, the phenomenon does nonetheless have an aesthetic dimension, which is hinted at in the following paragraph from Lacan. The passage can serve as a conclusion to this discussion, since there is hardly a word in it that is not relevant to Faulkner's fiction—as well as to the various "theories" of fiction he enunciated in his late years:

This terminal image of the gaze, which completes the gesture, I place strictly in relation to what I later say about the evil eye. The gaze in itself not only terminates the movement, it freezes it. . . . The evil eye is the *fascinum,* it is that which has the effect of arresting movement and, literally, of killing life. At the moment the subject stops, suspending his gesture, he is mortified. The anti-life, anti-movement function of this terminal point is the *fascinum,* and it is precisely one of the dimensions in which the power of the gaze is exercised directly. The moment of seeing can occur here only as a suture, a conjunction of the imaginary and the symbolic, and it is taken up again in a dialectic, that sort of temporal progress that is called haste, thrust, forward movement, which is concluded in the *fascinum.* (FFCP, 118)

Anyone familiar with Faulkner will recall his famous statement: "The aim of every artist is to arrest motion, which is life, by artificial means and hold it fixed so that 100 years later when a stranger looks at it, it moves again since it is life. Since man is mortal, the only immortality possible for him is to leave something behind him that is immortal since it will always move. This is the artist's way of scribbling 'Kilroy was here' on the wall of the final and irrevocable oblivion through which he must someday pass" (LITG, 253).

Symbolically, the notion of a *master* might be defined by three substitutes of the phallic organ: the hand, the voice, the eye. All three can be shown to function as substitutes in Faulkner's work. Indeed, Faulkner's work could well be represented as a triangle drawn between these three points. The extension of the concept of fascination need not be limited to the visual field: it can be audio-oral, and there can be fascinated gestures as well. Most importantly, perhaps, fascination can be considered as a "grammar of rhetoric" behind the "language" of gestures. The best example, indeed the paradigm, of this is to be found in the description of the Colonel's tombstone as Miss Jenny sees it at the end of both *Flags in the Dust* and *Sartoris:*

> But she knew where it would be, what with the *virus,* the inspiration and the example of that one which *dominated* them all, which gave to the whole place in which *weary* people were sup-

posed to rest, a hushed, orotund *solemnity* having no more to do with that of the characters, and beneath which the headstones of the wives whom they had *dragged into their arrogant orbits* were, despite their *pompous* genealogical references, modest and effacing as the song of thrushes *beneath the eyrie of an eagle.*

He stood on a stone pedestal, in his frock coat and bareheaded, one leg slightly advanced and one hand resting lightly on the stone pylon beside him. His head was lifted a little in *that gesture of haughty arrogance* which repeated itself generation after generation with a *fateful fidelity,* his back to the world and *his carven eyes gazing out* across the valley where his railroad ran and beyond it to the blue changeless hills, and beyond that. (*Flags,* 365; SAR, 375, reads: "and beyond that, the ramparts of infinity itself"; my emphases)

I have emphasized the phrases that belong to what could be called the lexis of fascination; no feat of critical imagination is required to see in this description a portrait of the artist as he would be, limned by wishful dreams, in complete control of his world of dead characters.

However, it is precisely because this page almost begs for such a reflexive reading that its intrinsic beauty cannot be dissociated from its deceptive power. In other words this description of what may well be called the original focus of Faulkner's fictional universe only sets the scene for far less serene tableaux. In the hushed pastoral of the cemetery scene, after all, the thrushes sing in spite of a curse: "beneath the eyrie of an eagle" or beneath the nest of any bird of prey—in other words, beneath Faulkner's namesake.

With Faulkner everything "human, too human" that occurs here below seems to be stolen, if not snatched, from the gaze of an ubiquitous, watchful eye: a bird's, God's, or the novelist's—they are all the same.

Now, the scene is set for the acting out of the master's most celebrated fascinations: the openings of the definitive versions of *Sanctuary* (chapter 9 of this book) and of *Light in August* (chapter 10).

chapter nine

Surprise

Soldiers' Pay, Flags in the Dust/Sartoris, Sanctuary I and II

If there is a true anthology piece in all the work of Faulkner, the
first page of *Sanctuary* surely is it.—Jean-Jacques Mayoux,
Vivants Piliers

We have already identified the group of images hill/valley/sunset as representing an important emotional structure in Faulkner's work. Indeed, each
time the combination appears, there occurs a phenomenon akin to what
psychoanalysts call "overdetermination." There are other structures of this
type in Faulkner's oeuvre. Two are particularly interesting because they can
hardly be explained except as effects of fascination. If these two structures
share a kind of predetermination with the cluster hill/valley/sunset, it is not
so much because of the recurrence as because of the principles that deter-
mine the sequence. One cannot say exactly why these scenes came into
being nor why they have such a privileged status. One can, however,
describe how they function.

As for the origin of the structures, phrases such as "matricial structures"
or "energetic compositions" can be borrowed from Jean Piaget's *Genetic
Psychology*. These are surface structures that emerge from a more or less
obscure zone of the author's experience—whether an unforgettable childhood impression, something seen in everyday life, or even something
read—who can tell? Probably not even the writer himself.

From a phenomenological point of view, what matters is the intensity of
these scenes (or tableaux, since they tend to "freeze"). This is all the more
true as every reader of Faulkner may be said to keep a few forever in his
memory. In two memorable essays Alfred Kazin and Jean-Jacques Mayoux
have drawn attention to the most celebrated and probably the most admi-

rable examples of such structures, the beginning of *Light in August* and the beginning of *Sanctuary.* These opening scenes are both kinds of conclusions since each came into being only in the final stage of Faulkner's work.

The expression "the still scene" is to be found in both *Flags in the Dust* and *Sartoris:* "Suratt's slow, plausible voice went on steadily, but without any irritant quality. It seemed to fit easily into the still scene, speaking of earthy things."[1] In the context (Suratt, young Bayard Sartoris and their friend Hub are drinking moonshine whiskey in an abandoned farm) the expression is so ambiguous as to be a possible pun on "still" (an adjective describing immobility as well as a distillery). However, the word is also a synonym of a tableau in both the first and the second definitions given by Webster: "a graphic description or visualization: image, picture," and "a striking effect or artistic grouping: arrangement, scene."

In this chapter, so as to bring into relief the organization of the first structure or type of scene (the "spring" scene at the opening of *Sanctuary* being only the best known), I have grouped together (and therefore organized) a number of recurring elements, along with quotations from the texts in which they occur; then I analyze the central meaning of the theme and its variants. In chapter 10 I have not thought it necessary to list examples of the second structure or type of scene in the same way, since they are innumerable. The scene that is analyzed, however, is the best known and most accomplished avatar of the type. It both opens and closes *Light in August.*

Whereas the first type produces surprise, the second produces astonishment.

The following tables present in a synthetic way the results of a careful reading of three occurrences of the first type, the scene at the spring: in *Soldiers' Pay* (table 1), in *Flags in the Dust/Sartoris* (tables 2 and 3), and in the original and the published versions of *Sanctuary* (tables 4 and 5).[2] This comparative reading may be called a collation in the sense of "ordered arrangement made by comparison" (Webster). It also opens up the field of internal intertextuality.[3]

If we consider the scenes from *Flags* and from *Sartoris* as variants of one scene, and the initial scene of the published version of *Sanctuary* as already present in the original version, we are confronted with three sequences (*Soldiers' Pay, Flags in the Dust/Sartoris, Sanctuary* I and II), which share the following characteristics:

(1) The site where the surprise occurs is distant from frequented roads,

Table 1 *Soldiers' Pay, 9, 6*

I. Time and Place
    A. Season: "May" (28, 286), "Summer is almost there"
       (303), "Summer hadn't quite come" (309)
    B. Moment of day: "evening" (309)
    C. Place: "into woods . . . Deep in a thicket" (309)

II. Scenery
    A. Visual elements
       1. The sun: "the cooling of sunset" (309)
       2. Water: "the small stream murmured like a faint
          incantation" (309)
       3. Reflection: "a small lake calmly repeated the calm
          sky" (309)
       4. Vegetation: "a thicket . . . willows . . . alder shoots"
          (309)
       5. Shadow: "it ran among violet shadows" (309)
    B. Sounds
       6. Water: see II, A, 2 and "a louder water" (309)
       7. Bird: "a thrush sang four liquid notes" (309)

III. Characters
     A. The surpriser: Joe Gilligan. His position: "Aimlessly he
        followed the stream" (310)
     B. The surprised: "a man" (309), a "gangling malaria-ridden
        figure" (309). His position: "squatting back on his heels"
        (310)

IV. Mode of surprise: "Parting the willows he came upon" (310)

V. Activity of the surprised: "the man's submerged arm" (310)

Table 2 *Flags in the Dust, 2, 6*

I. Time and Place
   A. Season: "the ripening spring" (102)
   B. Moment of day: "It was getting well into evening" (122)
   C. Place: "The road wound presently into the woods where the sun was intermittent, and it rose gradually toward a low crest on which trees stood like a barred grate against the western sky" (122)

II. Scenery
   A. Visual elements
      1. The sun: "The sun fell in a long slant" (123), "a leveling ray of sunlight" (124)
      2. Water: "The spring welled from the roots of the beech" (124)
      3. Reflection: "On the surface of the spring the sun lay reflected" (125)
      4. Vegetation: "a junglish growth of willow and alder" (123, 124, 125)
      5. Shadow: "the land descended into shadow" (122)
   B. Sounds
      6. Water: "the cool unceasing breathing of the spring" (125)
      7. Bird:
      8. Silence: "without wind" (122); "the limpid soundless laughing of the spring" (125)

III. Characters
   A. The surpriser: Bayard. His position: "He squatted also on his heels" (125)
   B. The surprised: Suratt (124), Hub (125). Their position: "squatting"

IV. Mode of surprise
                                    } After making Bayard drink
                                      Hub and Suratt drink too,
V. Activity of the surprised   } on either side of the spring.

Table 3 *Sartoris, 2, 6*

I. Time and Place
   A. Season: "the waxing spring" (112)
   B. Moment of day: "Evening was coming" (136)
   C. Place: "The road wound presently into the woods, where
      the sun was intermittent, and it rose to a gradual, sandy
      crest" (136)

II. Scenery
   A. Visual elements
      1. The sun: "the sun fell in a long slant" (137)
      2. Water: "the spring welled from the roots of the beech"
         (138)
      3. Reflection: "On the surface of the spring the red sky
         lay reflected" (139)
      4. Vegetation: "a junglish growth of willow and alder"
         (138, 139, 140)
      5. Shadow: "the ground descended into shadow" (138)
   B. Sounds
      6. Water: "the cool and limpid breathing of the spring"
         (139)
      7. Bird:
      8. Silence: "with no wind" (136)

III. Characters
   A. The surpriser: Bayard Sartoris. His position: "squatting"
      (139)
   B. The surprised: Suratt, Hub. Their position: "squatting"
      (138–139)

IV. Mode of surprise   ⎫ as in *Flags*. Both kinds of
                              ⎬ characters drink from the
V. Activity of the surprised ⎭ jug.

Table 4 *Sanctuary* I, 2

I. Time and Place
    A. Season: "April and May" (14)
    B. Moment of day: "It was afternoon", "the sunny afternoon" (21)
    C. Place: "in the hills at last . . . a high desolation of pines," "he left the road to seek water" (20–21)

II. Scenery
    A. Visual elements
        1. The sun: "the still sunny vistas" (21), "the sunshot jungle" (21)
        2. Water: "the spring welled up" (21)
        3. Reflection: "he knelt his face into the reflected face in the water" (21)
        4. Vegetation: "a close growth of cane and cypress and gum" (21)
        5. Shadow:
    B. Sounds
        6. Water: "the cool sound of his swallowing" (21)
        7. Bird: "a bird sang. . . . It sang again, three bars in monotonous repetition" (21)
        8. Silence: "silence suspirant with the peaceful afternoon" (21–22)

III. Characters
    A. The surpriser: "the man was standing" (21)
    B. The surprised: "Horace Benbow. His position: "kneeling" (20)

IV. Mode of surprise: "Beyond the spring" (21)

V. Activity of the surprised: "drinking" (21)

Table 5 *Sanctuary* II, 1

I. Time and Place
    A. Season: "May" (3)
    B. Moment of day: "That was about four o'clock on an afternoon in May" (3), "It was almost dark" (5)
    C. Place: "A faint path led from the road to the spring" (1)

II. Scenery
    A. Visual elements
        1. The sun: "broken sunlight" (1)
        2. Water: "the spring" (five times on p. 1)
        3. Reflection: "the broken and myriad reflection of his own drinking" (1)
        4. Vegetation: "a thick growth of cane and brier, of cypress and gum" (1)
        5. Shadow:
    B. Sounds
        6. Water:
        7. Bird: "a bird sang three notes and ceased" (1)
        8. Silence: "no sound" (1), "a suspirant and peaceful following silence" (2)

III. Characters
    A. The surpriser: Popeye, standing. His position: "then he squatted, facing the man" (3)
    B. The surprised: "the man" (1), "Horace Benbow" (4). His position: "and kneel to drink" (1)

IV. Mode of surprise: "From beyond the screen of bushes" (1)

V. Activity of the surprised: "to drink from the spring" (1) though it is accessible by a barely visible path among the thick-set trees and is sheltered from the glare of the sun (which is filtered) from both glances and noises.

(2) Each scene occurs at a specified time of day (evening) and during a specified season (spring).

(3) Details that may appear decorative are, in fact, indispensable to the structure, especially the sun, water and its reflective quality, silence, and, except in *Flags/Sartoris*, a singing bird.

(4) The characters are all men. Among them is always a stranger or at least someone new, that is, a man unused to the setting.

(5) In each scene, someone unused to the location, but who happens to be in the company of one or two others who are familiar with it, is surprised. This configuration of scenes by the spring is the exact opposite of the epiphany manqué on top of the hill. But these scenes fulfill a dramatic function, which is to bring together characters who have come to drink not necessarily water from a spring, but something (whiskey, of course) around it. Of the seven characters involved in the series, only Popeye does not drink at all, not even water. Drinking is nonetheless involved since, as Horace Benbow is quick to understand, one is in the midst of a group of moonshiners. In one way or another liquor therefore appears in the three major variations. And yet it is doubtful whether alcohol is an essential element, since thereafter, in the three minor variations that I shall study first, there is no mention of liquor at all.

I. The first variation of the spring scene occurs in *The Sound and the Fury*, during Quentin's walk along the Charles River in the company of the little Italian girl—a moment Quentin associates with the loss of his sister Caddy's virginity. As Melvin Backman has observed, the transition from one scene to the other (or from the present to the past) is brought about through the agency of three motifs: water, broken sunshine, and a bird.[4] These are precisely the motifs to be found in the three major scenes. In *The Sound and the Fury*, however, in keeping with the fragmented structure of the novel, the scene is itself scattered over a whole section. Here are just a few examples to show how easily the basic scene could be reconstructed from the elements in this part of Quentin's section:

> The road went on, still and empty, the sun slanting more and more.
>
>   .   .   .   .

There was a bird somewhere in the woods, beyond the broken and infrequent slanting of sunlight.

. . . .

The bird whistled again, invisible, a sound meaningless and profound, inflexionless, ceasing as though cut off with the blow of a knife, and again, and that sense of water swift and peaceful above the secret places, felt, not seen not heard (TSATF, 168–69; CT, 155–56).

II. In *As I Lay Dying*, in which references to the hill abound, Addie's central monologue begins with a brief but powerful evocation of the moment when school finished and she could live an intensely private experience: "In the afternoon when school was out and the last one had left with his little dirty snuffling nose, instead of going home I would go down the hill to the spring where I could be quiet and hate them. It would be quiet there then, with the water bubbling up and away and the sun slanting quiet in the trees and the quiet smelling of damp and rotting leaves and new earth; especially in the early spring, for it was worst then" (AILD, 160; CT, 155). Thus, for Addie, the spring is a place where she can "hate them." Does that mean that antithetically, the hill is the place, if not of love, at least of desire? This is just what we have seen in some of the early stories and what Horace Benbow would have us believe in *Sanctuary*. His one and only thought, during the walk that is interrupted by his stop at the spring, is of a hill.

Jewel also thinks of a hill, for him a place steeped in passion: "It would just be me and her on a high hill and me rolling the rocks down the hill at their faces, picking them up and throwing them down the hill faces and teeth and all by God until she was quiet and not that goddam adze going One lick less. One lick less and we could be quiet" (AILD, 12; CT, 14). In a general way one can say that Faulkner's landscapes, with the recurrence of hills and valleys punctuated by springs, are so idiosyncratic and insistent that a realistic reading would appear to be totally arbitrary, indeed, to fly in the face of evidence.

There are variants of the typical or Ur-landscape of the scene, of course; for instance, the bird song is absent in *Flags/Sartoris*, and in *The Hamlet* it is the "mournful measured plaint of a well-pulley" (22), which echoes "the sound meaningless and profound" of the bird in both *Sanctuary* and *The Sound and the Fury*. These variations only confirm that, with Faulkner, landscape is never there just to be seen: it has always already been seen or heard by a subject. Such variations moreover are less signs of change than of persistence in the basic structures of the author's imagination.

III. As might be expected, the third minor variation on this major rural structure is found in chapter 1 of *The Hamlet*. The very first, portentous meeting of a Varner and a Snopes occurs when Jody pays a visit to Ab in the abandoned house to which the latter has just moved with his family and to which he has brought his reputation as barn-burner:

> The path (it was neither road nor lane: just two parallel barely discernible tracks where wagon wheels had run, almost obliterated by this year's grass and weeds) went up to the sagging and stepless porch of the perfectly blank house which he now watched with wire-taut wariness, *as if he were approaching an ambush*. He was watching it with such intensity as to be oblivious to detail. He saw suddenly in one of sashless windows and without knowing when it had come there, a face beneath the gray cloth cap, the lower jaw moving steadily and rythmically with a curious sidewise thrust, which even as he shouted "Hello!" vanished again. (HAM, 22; my emphasis)

As if he were approaching an ambush: this is not only a pregnant metaphor in terms of the ensuing narrative, but it is also, in symbolic terms, a very just description of the crucial encounter between "innocent" Jody and "evil" Ab.

Let me now resume my analysis of the three major variations of the scene. As far as the words used to describe the scenery are concerned, the first (*Soldiers' Pay*) is characterized by preciosity. The date (1926) has something to do with this. The vocabulary used in the second (*Flags/Sartoris*), on the other hand, builds up a disturbing effect: two figurative uses of the word "skeleton," the comparison of the geese with "small, muddy clouds," and of a clump of saplings with "mottled ghosts," and finally the summary: "a small bowl of peacefulness remote from the world and time" (SAR, 139)— all of this casts upon the scene a kind of spell. In terms of verisimilitude this spell can of course be explained by Bayard's shock after falling from a horse. To this explanation, however, must be added the hallucination he experiences. In it is exposed the root of his feeling of guilt in relation to

Narcissa. Bayard feels this so strongly that one wonders if he does not later marry her simply in order to punish himself for having "fascinated" her: "So it [Narcissa's face] remained, aloof, not quite distinct, while the coiling shapes faded into a dull unease of physical pain from the jolting of the car, leaving about him like an echo that cool serenity and something else—a sense of shrinking, yet fascinated distaste of which he or something he had done was the object" (SAR, 136; slightly different version in *Flags*, 122).

In the third major version of the variation—the opening scene of the final version of *Sanctuary,* which is so much more effective than its first occurrence in chapter 2 of the original—the very first words throw the reader into an isolated world, at once plausible and uncanny. Here is what Jean-Jacques Mayoux has to say about it: "The primary quality of this text is the effect of immediacy; and because, as in a dream (if the sensation is strong enough), nothing can be questioned, the effect grows upon us. The feeling of immediacy is heightened by the unusual character of the scene. Accepting the unusual as something normal, we experience the uneasy feeling that in literature sometimes echoes the disturbance caused by a dream" (translation revised from *3 Decades,* 159). Indeed, this "uneasy feeling" is communicated to the reader from the outset, "as if he were approaching an ambush." The scene is set in a far-off place, as though beyond time, in a kind of natural nest or lair near a spring surrounded by trees in which one bird sings. The pastoral setting could serve for an eclogue, but appearances are misleading. The haven of peace is a den of treachery. The babbling water becomes still and unliving like the "black and lurid tarn that lay in unruffled lustre" in Poe's tale. The dialogue between the automobile and the bird is also disquieting. As it ends, day gives way to night, and, if it were not for the fact that both the time and the setting are very different, one would be reminded of the atmosphere at the very beginning of "The Fall of the House of Usher": "During the whole of a dull, dark, and soundless day in the autumn of the year. . . ."

One could cite other examples of the dramatic use of such description.[5] The outstanding quality of the present one, it seems to me, lies in the direction already signaled by Mayoux. The malaise, the almost intolerable feeling of unease that characterizes the opening of *Sanctuary,* does not really arise from the use of one particular symbol, nor from a rather heavy-handed insistence which includes the recurrent use of the adjective "weird," but from a general atmosphere, which only a closer analysis can help to elucidate.

In the first two versions of the scene, in *Soldiers' Pay* and in *Flags/Sartoris*, Faulkner wrote from the traditional, omniscient point of view; the author was responsible for the description in spite of the fact that he lent his voice to a character. This character—henceforth a type or a generic character—could be called the intruder: here, the person who intrudes on the quiet scene by the spring. One meets this anonymous character in the first version of the novel:

> Four days later he was within twelve miles of Jefferson, in the hills at last, kneeling at a spring, drinking. The night before he told her [Narcissa], "There's no hurry. You cant break into years like a footpad in an alley crashing into the fatuous moment of an oblivious pedestrian." It was afternoon. He was walking, the coat over his arm, along an empty road through a high desolation of pines in which the wind drew in long, sombre signs and where the fading crises of dogwood glinted in the still sunny vistas, while time, the sunny afternoon, brooded kindly and inscrutably about him. If he got a lift he would reach town in time to go out to the house that night, but after not having been passed by a car or passing a house himself in more than an hour, he left the road to seek water. (STOT, 20–21)

In this version the point of view clearly passes from the author to the character. In the second, much more economical—and subtle—version, everything changes: "From beyond the screen of bushes which surrounded the spring, Popeye watched the man drinking. A faint path led from the road to the spring. Popeye watched the man—a tall, thin man, hatless, in worn gray flannel trousers and carrying a tweed coat over his arm—emerge from the path and kneel to drink from the spring" (SAN, 1; CT, 3). In this new opening paragraph the point of view shifts quietly back and forth between the two characters. Moreover, the structure of the paragraph involves nearly imperceptible exchanges between the two characters and the reader. The reader sees both the man who drinks and the man who sees him drinking and then witnesses the shifting play of perspectives almost unawares. He gradually perceives that "the man" has intruded on an outpost of Popeye's hideout. For a while there is a confusion between subject and object, actor and audience. The reader perceives Popeye as he catches a glimpse of the man drinking. But this glimpse is enough to make one feel that Popeye's pop-eyed presence has always been here, in front of a stage, in front of others' actions. If in what follows the reader has difficulty in understanding what has happened, that is, that only Horace can perceive the hideout, and that Horace's point of view is thus the only "legitimate" one, as Mayoux believes, it is, nonetheless, clear that Faulkner succeeds in making him believe that Popeye has in a specific moral sense already taken charge of the perspective. Popeye has become a kind of demigod before any action occurs. In yet other words we are all semiconscious actors before a Popeyed figure.

An American critic noted this many years ago. Unfortunately, none of his successors seems to have profited from what he observed:

> The first paragraph presents a tableau. . . . But Popeye could not watch the man drinking before watching him arrive at the spring, and only the man at the spring would think of Popeye as *beyond* the screen of bushes. The point of view is actually with the man at the spring, whose name is Horace Benbow, and the first paragraph presents a situation which could not possibly occur until after the third paragraph, when Benbow first realizes that he is not alone at the spring. For the first paragraph is Benbow's reconstruction, from the vantage point of paragraph four, of what must have been the situation when he arrived at the spring moments earlier. Thus subtly is the reader introduced into a world which looks like the familiar field of everyday experience; but mechanisms of action in this world function quite unusually, and stylistic distortion of point of view, of the customary ordering of events, defines a new *locus* of significance.[6]

In his analysis of the categories of narration in the text, James Brown reaches the same conclusion as Mayoux in his "impressionistic" approach:

> Reading the passage one is aware of a completely real presence, such as one finds in first-rank novels (I think first of all of Dostoyevsky, particularly of *Crime and Punishment*); that is, the

scene does not affect us as if set in a book or through words; it is before us; rather, it surrounds us. It is around us as though we were in the process, not so much of living it as of dreaming it.

. . . .

First of all, a scene such as this at the very beginning of a work is quite rare. . . . Thus is the first quality of the "presence," this illusion which leads the reader directly into the scene instead of simply putting it on display before him.

Moreover, there is an interchange of subjective awareness among the participants that enables us to go directly to the scene and to forget the author. He has not said ten words when, in the very first sentence, the responsibility of observing is shifted to the first character. . . . In its superb economy, this passage succeeds in rendering the scene . . . by merely setting down the data enabling us to find our bearings. (3 *Decades*, 157–58)

This is why "from beyond" must be interpreted as conveying Popeye's temporal presence over everything that occurs in the ensuing narrative. Popeye occupies the reader's potential or imaginary field of vision before Benbow comes into it. This explains why a feeling of uneasiness precedes even the unappealing description, in paragraph four, of "the man of under size," with a "queer, bloodless" face, and no more depth to his body than "stamped tin." This description can only be attributed to Horace. Popeye therefore intrudes into the telling of the tale even before he materializes in the showing—to quote from Joseph Conrad's famous distinction in his preface to *The Nigger of the Narcissus*. The scene even belongs to him from the first two (not ten) words. Popeye precedes the novel as a key precedes a musical score. He exists before Horace's perception of him (which may well be unique in the history of fiction) and before the description Horace gives of him. In more abstract terms Popeye is not only "for" Horace, he is there in himself, *an sich*. But how can he precede or exist before the novel itself? Exclusively by his glance, Popeye makes his debut in the novel as a voyeur— even as the arch-voyeur. *Sanctuary* is the novel that sanctions Faulkner's obsession with the act and metaphor of vision. In it vision, and even sight, becomes a major literary theme. "The spring welled up at the root of a beech tree and flowed away upon a bottom of whorled and waved sand. It was surrounded by a thick growth of cane and brier, of cypress and gum in which broken sunlight lay sourceless. Somewhere, hidden and secret and yet nearby, a bird sang three notes and ceased." The comparison with the first version cannot leave any doubt; the strength of the scene comes from the fact that despite the lack of any explicit information until the end of the third paragraph, an exchange of glances is nonetheless implied. What Mayoux called "the interchange of subjective awareness" could, for the sake of our argument, also be called "the interplay of glances." The dominant impression of stillness, which is the main cause of our uneasiness, cannot be accounted for except in terms of an exchange of glances.

Let us look once more at the first lines of the novel. "The man," as Horace is aptly called in the revised version (he was "Horace" and Popeye was "the man" in the original version), is drinking. This sounds natural enough—except, precisely, that beneath Popeye's glance the innocence of the activity is transformed—actually perverted, or at least distorted. Totally uncovered, the man himself appears as innocent as the water he drinks. But moral values, like glances, also shift in this secluded spot. Popeye wields the weapon that later gives him his peculiar strength—the weapon of concealment and furtiveness. Popeye is only watching. But with Faulkner watching is an explosive activity. One need not return to Sartre's analysis of the glance to understand that Popeye already exerts control over the man— who is not just a "weak" man, as Mayoux writes, but is *everyman* (including the reader).

The reader identifies at once with both the character who drinks simply because he is thirsty and with the character who surprises him in this perfectly natural activity. The reader, in other words, identifies with both a natural act and a vicarious experience.

The first sentence establishes a relationship between the characters. The fact that one point of view is already given an outrageously privileged status suggests that the die is cast, that "the man" has already been transformed into Popeye's object. What one could call "fate" in the novel is in other words already prefigured in Popeye's extraordinarily privileged, semigod-like (and vicarious) vision—despite the fact that for the reader the scene is viewed most legitimately by Horace. The initial suspension of Horace's viewpoint is indeed the sign of the illegitimate character of the world into which he has fallen. What we witness is nothing short of a silent, optical rape, an abduction by the glance, a surprise in the sense of an unexpected overpowering.

To speak of "fate" in this context, moreover, is not really relevant since one encounters no psychological determinism, but a mere physical situation. Novalis's (and Thomas Hardy's) famed "Character is Fate"[7] simply does not apply here. Only Horace has a psychology—and this is why the passage is ultimately written from his point of view. Horace describes Popeye as human (even if this is by way of comparing him with objects), whereas Horace is perceived as someone neutral—"bland," as Faulkner might have written, using another of his favorite words. Horace and Popeye do not really belong in the same world.

The very first sentences are a flashback. In them the disquieting gap created by the first sentence is filled. As for the question, "How long has Popeye been there?"—the reader senses the answer at the end of the first sentence: as long as the spring.

The spring is thus repeatedly designated as the pivot of the scene because it attracts both men's glances. Besides provoking the narrative, the spring functions thematically as a reflecting surface: it mirrors Popeye and thus enables "the man" to discover him. Even though the novel has only just begun, one is tempted to comment here that, at long last, some kind of relationship or reciprocal activity has been established. Soon this is verbalized in the form of a dialogue. It is therefore not an exaggeration to say that the novel, as a development of an initial situation, grows out of the spring. The spring is the medium that brings Popeye into being for Horace. Its function is double: as a welling up, it allows Horace to refresh himself; as a reflective surface, it allows him to discover Popeye—that is, to surprise the surpriser. However, it also functions as the trap set by Popeye in order to catch Horace "in the act."

Thus Popeye is first and foremost an image: no wonder he has no depth. He is born as a disembodied figure. He is first perceived by Horace, who is hatless, as "the shattered reflection of [a] straw hat."

The spring functions as the objective correlative of the central consciousness and moral touchstone that the novel lacks. It is the only medium, in the double sense of place and means, that relates Horace and Popeye. Outside this bond, or mediation, the two characters have literally nothing in common. Their exchange of words after the initial exchange of glances demonstrates as much.

Without the spring, there would be no *Sanctuary*.

chapter ten

Astonishment

Light in August

I will rise now, and go about the city in the streets, and in the

broad ways I will seek him whom my soul loveth; I sought him,

but I found him not.

The watchmen that go about the city found me; to whom I said,

Saw ye whom my soul loveth?

. . . .

Who is this that cometh out of the wilderness like pillars of

smoke?—Song of Songs 3: 2, 3, 6

Ever since James B. Meriwether's pioneering description of Faulkner's manuscripts in 1962, it has been well known that the title planned for *Light in August* was originally *Dark House*. Faulkner's change emphasizes not only the polarized nature of his imagination, but also its spatial, and therefore visual, character; just as one title expresses closure and lack of light, the other expresses the cosmic pouring of the sun's rays at the height of its power.[1]

It has also been well known that the novel originally began with a description of Reverend Hightower at his window (now the beginning of chapter 3—not with Lena Grove on the road (chapter 1). In other words neither of the opening scenes in the two draft versions focused on Joe Christmas. And yet, no reader would deny that he is the protagonist of the book, not only because he plays the leading part in the present narration, but also because in the final version of the novel the author provides a long flashback on his childhood and youth.

Indeed, Regina K. Fadiman, in her study of the revisions of *Light in August,* contends that "Faulkner had written almost the entire version of the dramatic action of the narrative present before he added the Christmas flashback."[2] However, although the history of the novel is too complex to go into here, we must note that the manuscript pages making up what is apparently the earliest surviving draft of the novel suggest that Faulkner's original plan was to introduce the reader to Jefferson through the young clergyman Hightower and his wife; in the final version, of course, he used Lena Grove for this purpose.

According to Fadiman, the present beginning of the novel was the product of a revision Faulkner made after writing chapter 8, the chapter which narrates Joe Christmas's first affair with Bobbie Allen. After hearing from Bobbie that she is "sick," Joe rushes out into the woods by night: "In the notseeing and the hardknowing as though in a cave he seemed to see a diminishing row of suavely shaped urns in moonlight, blanched. And not one was perfect. Each one was cracked and from each crack there issued something liquid, deathcolored, and foul. He touched a tree, leaning his propped arms against it, seeing the ranked and moonlit urns. He vomited" (LIA, 177–78; CT, 208–9). Fadiman's hypothesis is intriguing in its suggestion that Faulkner may have written the famous comparison of Lena Grove's walk along the road to Jefferson with the movement of a figure around an urn immediately after this passage just quoted from chapter 8.

The story of Joe Christmas could thus have been begun after the completion of the present-tense narrative. Moreover, Fadiman writes that "diction changes from manuscript to text in the first scene between Byron and Lena suggest that this hypothetical draft of the narrative present did not include chapter 1, portraying Lena on the road to Jefferson" (p. 195). If this is true, the first chapter of the published novel is twice removed from the rest of the text, in both the spatial and the temporal senses. And yet, at the University of Virginia on 13 April 1957 Faulkner did not seem to doubt that "that story began with Lena Grove, the idea of the young girl with nothing, pregnant, determined to find her sweetheart. It was—that was out of my admiration for women, for the courage and endurance of women. As I told that story I had to get more and more into it, but that was mainly the story of Lena Grove" (FITU, 74). The question whether the story told in *Light in August* is "mainly the story" of Reverend Hightower, that of Joe Christmas, or that of Lena Grove cannot simply be dismissed as a scholastic game; Faulkner's response at Virginia hints at the possibility that there was a "structural" truth that eventually replaced the "genetic" truth in his mind. In other words he seems to have come (twenty-six years after the composition of the novel) to believe that the final state of the novel is very close to the way he had originally conceived and written it.

It is nonetheless methodologically correct to interpret the first chapter of *Light in August* as a "microstructure" or, Faulkner would have preferred to say, as a "miniature" of the whole book. Indeed, after a first paragraph written in the present tense, there begins a three-page "loop" that relates Lena Grove's earlier life. This loop is followed by a one-line "summary" of her most recent activity ("She had been [walking] now for almost four weeks"), which brings the reader to the present again: "Behind her the four weeks, the evocation of *far,* is a peaceful corridor" (LIA, 4). This backtracking structure—not unlike the way the mind itself reminisces—was one of Faulkner's favorites. He used it again and again.

In *Light in August* the snaillike progress is followed by Lena Grove. Here she is again, just before Faulkner compares her month-old movement from wagon to wagon to a figure moving across an urn. The superb passage is haunting, yet not disquieting, as though Faulkner were seeking to convey the effect of hypnosis rather than of fascination: "backrolling now behind her a long monotonous succession of peaceful and undeviating changes from day to dark and dark to day again, through which she advanced in identical and anonymous and deliberate wagons as though a succession of creakwheeled and limpeared avatars, like something moving forever and without progress across an urn" (LIA, 5; CT, 7). The Keatsian metaphor is a miniature of the whole book, just as the scene by the spring is a condensation of the whole of *Sanctuary.*

Immediately before this, as though organized by a dreamlike logic, an onlooker announces in italics the appearance of a new wagon. Lena recalls the onlooker's comment thus: "*Here's a wagon that's going a piece of the way. It will take you that far.*" No matter how far: for Lena, destiny is entirely organic. One may paraphrase her thought thus: "The child I am bearing shall find itself a father [not his father, just a father] and he shall be my man [whether a husband or a lover is of little importance to her]." And although he has a name this time (Byron Bunch), this man is but the new avatar of the aboriginal "tieless casual."

The next paragraph takes place in the past—an immediate or very recent past, this time, as Lena now sees, mounting the hill toward her, the very wagon she has just passed. Once she has reached the top of the hill, she pants a little, waiting to be fetched:

> The sharp and brittle crack and clatter of its weathered and ungreased wood and metal is slow and terrific: a series of dry sluggish reports carrying for half a mile across the hot still pine-winey silence of the August afternoon. Though the mules plod in a steady and unflagging hypnosis, the vehicle does not seem to progress. It seems to hang suspended in the middle distance for-ever and forever, so infinitesimal in its progress, like a shabby bead upon the mild red string of road. So much is this so that in the watching of it the eyes lose it as sight and sense drowsily merge and blend, like the road itself, with all the peaceful and monoto-nous changes between darkness and day, like already measured thread being rewound onto a spool. (LIA, 5–6; CT, 8)

The reader feels the different aspects of hypnosis: the lasting and yet apparently ineffectual effort (the mules plod . . . so infinitesimal in [their] progress), the abstraction (like already measured thread), and, finally, the effect of the steady gaze (the eyes lose it).

" 'That far within my hearing before my seeing,' Lena thinks." Lena's thinking is a passive projection of herself into space and time: there is no action involved. Indeed, all Lena can do is to wait: "She waits, not even watching the wagon now, while thinking goes idle and swift and smooth." What can "thinking" mean to her if not a visualization of her meeting with the "father" of her child, with the man who will no doubt "materialize," as characters do in Faulkner's fiction, before the end of the road.

Next comes a total narrative break from Lena. We have moved on a bit in space and time to two country folk who have seen Lena walk by, exchanged some thoughts and uttered a prophecy: "She'll have company, before she goes much further." After some haggling over the cultivator, Armstid takes to the road in his wagon, his path to converge with Lena's. Now the same impression of hypnosis is his: "In the instant in which he recognises the blue dress he cannot tell if she has ever seen the wagon at all. And no one could have known that he had ever looked at her either as, without any semblance of progress in either of them, they draw slowly together as the wagon crawls terrifically toward her in its slow palpable aura of somnolence and red dust in which the steady feet of the mules move dreamlike" (LIA, 8; CT, 11). In this passage is the third occurrence of the word *terrific* in the chapter. Almost always paired with *slow,* terrific describes a typically Faulknerian perception in which time is dramatized.[3] The gaze that accompanies the drama is part of someone's astonishment, in the old sense of that word— that is, a kind of paralysis, numbness, stupor, bewilderment.

Mayoux's observation about the arrested scenes in *Absalom, Absalom!* is also true of *Light in August:* "Now these scenes which, in the final analysis, depict moments when the consciousness and vital rhythms stop function- ing, are themselves curiously immobilized." In *Light in August* we feel perplexed by a number of extraordinary "thoughts" such as the one which occurs to Joe Christmas at dawn after the manhunt of chapter fourteen: " 'I have been asleep,' he thought. 'I have slept more than six hours. I must have gone to sleep running without knowing it. That is what I did' " (LIA, 315; CT, 366). The last thing Joe can remember is running, and at this point he wonders how he can have fallen asleep: *fallen* is indeed the word. What should be added to Mayoux's "psychological" explanation of that type of scene is the part played by language. Faulkner manipulates his characters so that they are made to rationalize their own experience.

Armstid, for example, lets Lena come up into his wagon. They chat. Time passes. Grammatically, all this occurs in the present tense, a present tense that Faulkner seems to enlarge into an everlasting, amorphous dreamstate. His present tenses do not describe stage directions or actions that are supposed to unroll before our eyes so much as the hypnotic effect of the actions upon our eyes. Time is therefore suspended by grammar. It is no longer a part of history, not even of fiction; it becomes the index of a state of mind characterized by astonishment—a passive, unintellectual as well as unromantic kind of wonder. The sun goes down upon them. The summer night is drawing near—is there an epiphany ahead? Not yet; Lena is simply going to spend the night at Armstid's. Enter Mrs. Armstid and with her a new point of view. She will make Lena talk. The reader is struck by the relationship between sight and voice. After Armstid has introduced Lena to his wife, "He cannot tell from her voice if she [his wife] is watching him or not." Mrs. Armstid reacts: " 'You men,' she says" (LIA, 14; CT, 18). This is much the same reaction as that of Mrs. Littlejohn in *The Hamlet.* A domes- tic comedy follows the rural comedy. The structure of chapter twenty-one is ordained.

The following morning, we are back on the road with Armstid and Lena, grammatically now in the narrative past tense. Armstid leaves her at Varner's, where she tells her story over again while looking at the road. As required by the laws of Faulkner's fiction, the road is uphill. Meanwhile, men steal glances at her. Another miniature comedy unfolds: with the pocket money given her by Mrs. Armstid, Lena can buy herself what she has long been yearning for—a can of what she calls "sour-deans." As soon as she goes out of the shop—the scene is still controlled by the dream-logic—a new wagon arrives. She climbs in: "The wagon creaks on. Fields and woods seem to hang in some inescapable middle distance, at once static and fluid, quick, like mirages" (LIA, 24–25; CT, 30). It is noon. After looking up at the sun, Lena eats:

> Then she stops, not abruptly, yet with utter completeness, her jaw stilled in midchewing, a bitten cracker in her hand and her face lowered a little and her eyes blank, as if she were listening to something very far away or so near as to be inside her. Her face has drained of color, of its full, hearty blood, and she sits quite still, hearing and feeling the implacable and immemorial earth, but without fear or alarm. "It's twins at least," she says to herself, without lip movement, without sound. Then the spasm passes. She eats again. The wagon has not stopped; time has not stopped. The wagon crests the final hill and they see smoke. (LIA, 26; CT, 31–32)

This is, outwardly at least, a repetition of the scene from "The Hill": the elements of the structure are all there: hill, valley, smoke. Only the sun is wanting. Beneath her eyes is Jefferson—and in Jefferson waits the one she has been looking for, the "father" of her child. She "knows" this, as it were, organically.

Yet what awaits Lena is not just the discovery of the place where she will give birth to her child. There are "two columns of smoke: the one the heavy density of burning coal above a tall stack, the other a tall yellow column standing apparently from among a clump of trees some distance beyond the town" (LIA, 26; CT, 32). There, as we shall only know later, are the smoke of surprise and the smoke of astonishment. " 'That's a house burning,' the driver of the wagon says. 'See?' " But Lena is not particularly interested in either smoke. She is only astonished at her own progression: "But she in turn again does not seem to be listening, to hear. 'My, my,' she says. 'here I aint been on the road but four weeks, and now I am in Jefferson already.'"

Now the novel can begin.

In his well-known essay entitled "The Stillness of *Light in August*," Alfred Kazin begins by describing the "unforgettable" opening of the novel which, he says, "ends sharply on the outskirts of Jefferson."[4] For him, "the secret of Southern writing" is to communicate "this intense sense of the earth, this superb registering of country sights and sounds as the stillness is broken by the creaking and lumbering wagon coming up the hill" (*3 Decades,* 249). But Kazin's is a simplistic, descriptive reading of Faulkner. Camus also liked the dust and the heat in books from the South, yet in concentrating on these superficial elements, both Kazin and Camus confuse William Faulkner and Erskine Caldwell. Actually, the difference between "the South"—geographical, cultural, historical region—and the first chapter of *Light in August* is the same that separates a real landscape and an inner space. Lena Grove conducts us not so much into "the South" as into Faulknerland. Kazin himself says as much, indirectly, when he remarks that at "the center" of the novel, Joe Christmas, whom he calls "the most solitary character in American fiction," is never seen "full face, but always as a silhouette" and from a distance: "And this distance is filled with the stillness of a continuous meditation. *Light in August* tells a story of violence, but the book itself is curiously soundless, for it is full of people thinking to themselves about events past" (*3 Decades,* 254).

Next Kazin quotes from Irving Howe, who compared the novel with a Renaissance painting: "in the foreground a bleeding martyr, far to the rear a scene of bucolic peacefulness, with women quietly working in the fields"; Howe's description reflects the lethargy in the novel, which takes "the form of enormous meditations by which Faulkner tries to lift his material into place" (256); Howe's phrasing here is awkward, perhaps because his thought is not clear. The difficulty with Kazin's essay is that the cognition or understanding of the whole fresco is not supported by any recognition of the motivation of the painter—a recognition of the relationship between the eye and the hand of the master. In other words, Kazin (like Mayoux) is content merely to praise the superb intuition of the nature of space under a mesmerized gaze: "Despite its violence, *Light in August* is one of the few American novels that remind one of the humanized and tranquil landscape in European novels" (256), Kazin notes, but this description goes against the "Southernness" Kazin had admired earlier in the novel. Indeed, Kazin goes on to compare Faulkner's novel with *The Mayor of Casterbridge* without a word about a crucial difference: for Hardy, fascination is purely a phenomenon of the senses, whereas with Faulkner it becomes a phenomenon of the mind.

The desire to begin his novel with a mesmerized gaze may even be the reason why Faulkner finally decided to cut out the first chapter about Hightower (a fascinated man if ever there was one—though with him, the source of fascination is not in the outside world, but in his own past) and replace it with the story of Lena Grove. As a figure drawn across an urn, she provides the best introduction possible to the tragic locus, since her part consists as it were in taking the reader by the hand in order to lead him into Jefferson.

In Faulkner's work there is a recurrent juxtaposition of horizontal and vertical space. In *Light in August,* just as Lena embodies the horizontal principle as she seems to move forever along the road, so Christmas, the tragic figure, embodies the vertical principle as a man standing up against the gods—or simply against the odds. Hightower, like Clifford Pynchon in *The House of the Seven Gables,* is the man seated at the threshold, that is, at the junction of the two spatial dimensions. One may even wonder whether there is not a relationship between the horizontal principle and the vertical principle on the one hand, and surprise and wonder on the other.[5]

Depth is the third dimension of space. In Faulkner's world it is typically the dimension which only eyes freed from fascination can see or express. Indeed, since fascination rivets together subject and object, it prevents the one from seeing the other in depth; it flattens everything out. Freed from fascination, one discovers perspective, as in a deservedly well-known passage in *The Town* where Faulkner, alias Gavin Stevens, can at last "stand suzerain and solitary above the whole sum of [his] life beneath [the] incessant ephemeral spangling" of the fireflies seen from the top of Seminary Hill (*Town,* 315).

For the early Faulkner appearances are a trap that leads to fascination. Another glance—or the glance of another—is often necessary to turn portentous appearance into something transparent and thus lift the spell of fascination. This lifting of the spell is what Miss Jenny does in both *Sartoris* and *Sanctuary.* What she brings to these novels is not so very different from what Dilsey brings to *The Sound and the Fury* by different means, or what some of Bundrens' neighbors bring to *As I Lay Dying:* a gaze or a perspective which militates against a near universal fascination with appearances.

Dealing with appearances is dealing with the subject's point of view. But what can one say about the other side of the question, about phenomena, about the real? Here, like Jean Starobinski, we might lend an ear to Montaigne: "Why did Poppaea wish to mask the beauties of her face, if not to render them even dearer to the eyes of her lovers?"[6] Can one conceive of a glance that is devoid of all desire? It is unthinkable, except for a glance cast from a considerable distance. Only in such a distant glance does the act of looking cease to be the tyrannical gathering place for all the other senses and recover its sovereignty. And since with Faulkner there is hardly ever a thought about space that does not include time, distance is irrevocably associated with the past. In fact, for Faulkner, the past is less a dimension of time than of space.

"It came to pass": the verb can be used with reference to time—and yet it is spatial. Deep in our imagination, time is always more or less spatialized (could we even conceive it otherwise?). The same is true of Faulkner, who must visualize everything, including the past, before being able to verbalize it. In order to be in the past the past must "pass," that is, it must be viewed like a spectacle set on a stage for the duration of a performance. This performance of the past is precisely what one witnesses in many of Faulkner's most memorable passages. In particular, it is what explains his penchant for apparently farfetched or recondite visual equivalences, or objective correlatives, for the notion of time passing: the movement of the wagon along the road, for instance, is likened to "already measured thread being rewound onto a spool." Beyond the physical precision of the image, there is also something metaphysical (in the sense given to the word in English literary history): who indeed can be responsible for measuring the thread, if not God Himself—or some kind of supreme "Metaphor of the Subject"? This subordination of time to space, which is inevitable if one thinks in terms of visual images, is what lies behind Faulkner's "hypnoses": "We go on, with a motion so soporific, so dreamlike as to be uninferant of progress, as though time and not space were decreasing between us and it," Darl says in *As I Lay Dying* (99; CT, 95). He is expressing what Lena Grove is only capable of wondering at, the movement of the wagon along the road.

The same subordination, however, gives rise to the cluttered and much less sunny vistas of thought opened by other passages from the present-tense monologues of the same character—"Before us the thick dark current runs. It talks up to us in a murmur become ceaseless and myriad, the yellow surface dimpled monstrously into fading swirls travelling along the surface for an instant silent, impermanent and profoundly significant, as though just beneath the surface something huge and alive waked for a moment of lazy alertness out of and into light slumber again" (AILD, 131; CT, 127)—or to the paradoxical and yet moving pathos of Darl's celebrated vision, worthy of a modern King Lear: "How do our lives ravel out into the no-wind, no-sound, the weary gestures wearily recapitulant: echoes of old compulsions with no-hands on no-strings: in sunset we fall into furious attitudes, dead gestures of dolls" (AILD, 196–97; CT, 191).

A comparison between *Light in August* and *As I Lay Dying* is instructive, all the more so because when Faulkner was writing the former (17 August 1931–19 February 1932), he named the latter as his favorite book.[7] In these novels, which may be described at least in part as stories about men and their violent conflicts *as seen by women,* the nature and function of the two young female characters, Dewey Dell and Lena (as opposed to Addie *Bundren* and Joanna *Burden*), both nubile and both pregnant, are the same: they are peaceful providers of renewal. Indeed, one may even go so far as to suggest that their pregnancy is symbolically *an effect of the male glances that are focused on them.* One may conceive of Dewey Dell's future in terms of Lena Grove's present life. Their very names are semantically close, as Joseph Blotner has noted (FAB, 703). Above all, they both have a strong relationship with the earth, and, structurally, both outlive the story: they are not "expelled" from it like Joe and Darl, either by death or madness.

In *Light in August* the narrative resumes or continues after the physical death of Joe Christmas in chapter 19 and the metaphorical death of Reverend Hightower in chapter 20. Like the road itself, the story begins again in chapter 21 with a spicy anecdote which, if it were not written in the present tense like most of chapter 1, would sound like a fairy tale: "There lives in the eastern part of the state a furniture repairer and dealer who. . . ." H. C. Nash has written an excellent little article about this coda, so that it is not necessary here to deal with its remarkably subtle mixture of humor and dramatic irony.[8] However, Nash overlooks what is, from a theoretical point of view, the main interest of the chapter, since the use of the same scene as in chapter 1—that is, Lena, now accompanied by a baby and by a man, traveling in a wagon under the eyes of the same Armstids—is a perfect example of difference in repetition.

The difference is first of all structural in nature. The point of view changes. If there are still two people watching Lena go by, this time it is a couple who are making love. This couple is also a mirror, since they are not looking at Lena alone but at Lena flanked by her knight and servant, her Sancho Panza, Byron Bunch. The difference is also one of tone. In place of the hypnotic feel of the first chapter, there is humor both in the scene itself (no less than a Holy Family passing by!) and in the spectator's imagination. The spectator, who is also the narrator and as such a precursor of Ratliff in the Snopes trilogy, seems to manipulate his topic (the story of his earlier meeting with Lena) so cleverly that he "narrates" his wife into bed.

A brief but persuasive passage will help demonstrate the importance of the act of looking in a book that was entitled *Dark House* before being renamed *Light in August*. The passage concerns the death and transfiguration of the hero. This death is also a symbolic "murder" of shadows by light (the ironic inversion of values is, of course, typical of most modern writers since T. S. Eliot). How do we perceive the murderer with a bicycle during the ritual struggle of shadows with light?[9] "He was beside the ditch now. He stopped, motionless in midstride. Above the blunt, cold rake of the automatic his face had that serene unearthly luminousness of angels in church windows. He was moving again almost before he had stopped, with that lean, swift, blind obedience to whatever the Player moved him on the Board" (LIA, 437; CT, 510). This is the supreme moment, the apogee of the bull-fight, the putting to death (and not simply the description of the death) of Joe Christmas:[10] "But the Player was not done yet. When the others reached the kitchen they *saw* the table flung aside now and Grimm stooping over the body. When they approached *to see* what he was about, they *saw* that the man was not dead yet, and when they *saw* what Grimm was doing one of the men gave a choked cry and stumbled back into the wall and began to vomit" (LIA, 439; CT, 512; my emphasis). Vomiting is also the reaction of Temple's friend in *Sanctuary* when, in the evening before the ball, among the rustles and chuckles, the ugly duckling tells the girls what the serpent had done to Eve. "Then Grimm too sprang back, flinging[11] behind him the bloody butcher knife. 'Now you'll let white women alone, even in hell,' he said." His knife notwithstanding, the converging stares of the spectators would in any event castrate Christmas—as we know from reading *Sanctuary:* "and their eyes like knives until you could almost watch the flesh where the eyes were touching it" (SAN, 182; CT, 159): "But the man on the floor had not moved. He just lay there, with his eyes open and empty of everything save consciousness, and with something, a shadow, about his mouth. For a moment he looked up at them with peaceful and unfathomable and unbearable eyes" (LIA, 439; CT, 513). This atemporal, pure gaze is the best approximation of what the gaze of God might be like. It has all the attributes of God's gaze—minus the ubiquity. But the pure gaze alone has the attributes of God's gaze; it is "on loan"; must it later be redeemed? "Then his face, body, all, seemed to collapse, to fall in upon itself, and from out the slashed garments about his hips and loins the pent black blood seemed to rush like a released breath" (LIA, 439–40; CT, 513). Christmas's blood is not black because of his race[12] nor simply because this is arterial blood. It is black symbolically, because it has finally reverted to its original color, the color of the earth from which it has come and to which it must return. "It [the black blood] seemed to rush out of his pale body like the rush of sparks from a rising rocket; upon that black blast the man seemed to rise soaring into their memories forever and ever" (LIA, 440; CT, 513). Thus the apotheosis is followed by the consecration: memory here is made into the altar where humanity—thanks to its poets—can praise its own chronicle and share in the cult of "names and faces of heroes," as Reynolds Price put it.[13]

Just as in *As I Lay Dying,* Cash the conscientious craftsman and Darl the mad seer represent two aspects of writing which Faulkner esteemed; it seems as if the two aspects are expressed in this "grand finale": "They are not to lose it, in whatever peaceful valleys, beside whatever placid and reassuring streams of old age, in the mirroring faces of whatever children they will contemplate old disasters and newer hopes" (LIA, 440; CT, 513). This is the professional writer who speaks here. It is his world he is writing about. Out of the world which has been his ever since "The Hill," he is now making exactly what he wants to make—as he wrote in one of the two versions of the 1933 introduction to *The Sound and the Fury:*

> then I began Light in August, knowing no more about it than a young woman, pregnant, walking along a strange country road. I thought, I will recapture it [the "ecstasy" that had attended the writing of The Sound and the Fury] now, since I know no more

about this book than I did about The Sound and the Fury when I sat down before the first blank page.

It did not return. The written pages grew in number. The story was going pretty well: I would sit down to it each morning without reluctance yet still without that anticipation and that joy which alone ever made writing pleasure to me. The book was already finished before I acquiesced to the fact that it would not recur, since I was now aware before each word was written down just what the people would do, since now I was deliberately choosing among possibilities and probabilities of behavior and weighing and measuring each choice by the scale of the Jameses and Conrads and Balzacs.[14]

But there is the prophet, too: "It will be there, musing, quiet, steadfast, not fading and not particularly threatful, but of itself alone serene, of itself alone triumphant" (LIA, 440; CT, 513). There is a good deal of poignancy in these few lines coming at the end of a 440-page narrative, just as there is faith in writing—an affirmation of the existence and importance of an imaginary world. Nor is this faith less fervent than the one Keats placed in a certain Grecian urn. Here perhaps more clearly than anywhere else, were it only because it has taken him these 440 pages to shape his own urn, Faulkner declares himself to be a Keatsian: "Again from the town, deadened a little by the walls, the scream of the siren mounted toward its unbelievable crescendo, *passing out of the realm of hearing*" (my emphasis).[15] It is through sound and through the suggestion of the limits of sound that we return from the symbolic world of the novel to the "real" world. These walls may no longer be those of Jefferson, but of a holy city like Jerusalem. Nonetheless, they are what circumscribes, limits—and therefore constitutes—the real world we construct through our senses.

It is indeed by way of a vision that Joe Christmas encounters what lies beyond the pale of the senses. Here one can speak unambiguously of an epiphany. Thus, whereas Sanctuary, a "black" novel of evil surprises, ends in the grey, wet autumn of the old world, Light in August, the solar narration of Lena Grove's innocent astonishments, virtually ends in the pure (and therefore abstract) realm of ultimate knowledge. In one novel Faulkner addresses the power of blackness, in the other the grace of light: Dark House/Light in August.

PART FIVE

The Absolute Relationship

chapter eleven

Outrage

As I Lay Dying

> It begins to rain . . . Pa lifts his face, slack-mouthed . . . from
> behind his slack-faced astonishment he muses as though from
> beyond time, upon the ultimate outrage.
>
> .   .   .   .
>
> . . . again he looks up at the sky with that expression of dumb
> and brooding outrage and yet of vindication, as though he had
> expected no less.—*As I Lay Dying*

Outrage is undoubtedly one of the most recurrent and one of the most idiosyncratic phenomena in Faulkner's fiction. It results almost without exception from some visual provocation; it seems suddenly to loom up on the horizon and is usually associated with a glance, which alerts the reader to the fact that something is being acted out. It is not even necessary that the acting out be human: a natural setting, a simple landscape, the falling of rain may embody the gestures of the dramatic moment. Under these conditions the "tieless casual" once more appears as an archetypal figure. His very lack of connections elsewhere makes him the perfect observer of life here and now. From both a topological and a symbolical point of view, the sentence from "The Hill," "before him lay the hamlet which was home to him, the tieless casual," asssumes an essential significance.

The word *outrage* is associated with the notion of scandal and is in a sense a synonym. The etymology of both words is revealing. Outrage comes from the French *outre*, an adverb that comes from the Latin *ultra*, meaning across or beyond. Webster lists three meanings: "1. An act of violence. 2. An injury or insult to a person or a thing. 3. A feeling of anger and resentment aroused by something regarded as an injustice or insult." Thus the word covers a spectrum of meanings that range from the physical to the ethical. On the other hand, both the Latin *scandalum* and the Greek *skandalon* mean "a stumbling block." Webster's first three definitions for *scandal* are: "1. Discredit brought upon religion by unseemly conduct in a religious person. 2. Offence, doubt, or bewilderment occasioned to a person's religious feelings by another's lapse in ethics or religion. 3. Something that prevents the reception of religion or other faith or serves as justification for a lapse in ethics or religion." Thus, the word *scandal* always conveys a sense of falling, a lapse or a tripping; the word's meanings range from the physical to the theological. Common to both *outrage* and *scandal*, then, is the notion of transgression; we shall bear this in mind throughout this chapter.

Outrage in Faulkner's fiction is an obstacle which thwarts a perfect kind of vision—the human equivalent of God's own objectless vision—therefore, an ideal vision. In other words whatever stands in the way of a project or a projection is susceptible of being felt as outrageous if it is perceived or conceived as being part of the natural scheme of things. It is relatively unimportant whether the obstacle is one revealed by perception or through some mental operation.

The title *As I Lay Dying* is itself a direct reference to a kind of nightmare of outrage. Faulkner borrowed it from one of the following translations of *The Odyssey* (11, 424–26):

> As I lay dying, the woman with the dog's eyes would not close
> my eyelids for me as I descended into Hades[1]

> I, as I lay dying / Upon the sword, raised up my hands to smite her;
> / And shamelessly she turned away and scorned / To draw my eyelids
> or close my mouth / Though I was on the road to Hades' house.[2]

If closing the eyes of a dying person is a duty which ritual ordains, then failing to close the eyes constitutes a scandal.

Darl's excessively privileged position in *As I Lay Dying*—nineteen of the fifty-nine "monologues"—makes him a sufficient example of the relationship between scandal, outrage, and vision. In eleven out of his nineteen sections Darl's entry into the novel is like a sudden eruption. For instance, he interrupts Tull's monologue during the flood; he does the same to his brother Vardaman during the fire in the barn. There is nearly always some kind of violence in Darl's relationship with others, including his own family. Whereas he does communicate verbally with Vardaman (their kinship is not merely biological), it is only by way of furious glances that he achieves some kind of communication with his sister Dewey Dell.

Darl's relationships with his two grown-up brothers, Cash and Jewel, are diametrically opposed. Because of a near total absence of spiritual kinship with Cash, Darl gets along rather well with him, even putting himself literally in his brother's place when he is wounded: "He opens his eyes, staring profoundly up at our inverted faces" (AILD, 154; CT, 148; my emphasis). Darl's problem is clearly with Jewel. Darl tells us that Jewel's eyes are "like pale wood" (14; CT, 16), "paler than ever" (126; CT, 121), "pale as two bleached chips in his face" (136; CT, 131), etc. They obsess him. If Darl comes across to the reader as "all glance," Jewel comes across as "all eyes." For Darl the scandal is associated with these eyes which his glance cannot reach, even less control or master. Both illustrate the problem raised by Sartre at the end of his analysis of the glance: "In short, the Other can exist for us in two forms: if it is experienced conspicuously, one fails to know it; if it is known, if it is acted upon, one reaches only its being-as-object and its probable existence in the midst of the world; no synthesis of these two forms is possible" (B&N, 302). Thus, for Darl Jewel is the Other. If his eyes are so often the object of Darl's comments, it is because they never look at him: "It is never when eyes look at you that you find them beautiful or ugly, or that you can tell their color. The glance of the other covers up the eyes and seems to go out in front of them" (B&N, 258). Jewel "only has eyes" for his mother, a fact which becomes perfectly clear in the scene where Jewel's nocturnal activities are revealed. This scene is important for understanding the structure of kinship in the novel—a structure based on Addie's *oikonomia*, or "house-keeping rules": as we know, Darl, Dewey Dell, and Vardaman are the children of her husband. Cash, her firstborn, and Jewel, the fruit of her adultery, are, on the contrary, her own and thus belong only to her. "One morning—it was November then, five months since it started—Jewel was not in bed and he didn't join us in the field" (AILD, 123; CT, 119). This is the morning of the *show*, the morning when the truth about Jewel is revealed: "But now it was like we had all—and by a kind of telepathic agreement of admitted fear—flung the whole thing back like covers on the bed and we all sitting bolt upright in our nakedness, staring at one another and saying 'Now is the truth. He hasn't come home. Something has happened to him. We let something happen to him'" (AILD, 123–24;

CT, 119). Jewel—Addie's "jewel"—occupies the center of the stage as well as the center of everyone's gaze. Sitting on his mount and magnified by it, as different from the rest of the family as a pilot is from those who stay behind on the ground, Jewel the horseman creates a focal point in the middle of the confusion: "Then we saw him. He came up along the ditch and then turned straight across the field, riding the horse. Its mane and tail were going, as though in motion they were carrying out the splotchy pattern of its coat: he looked like he was riding on a big pinwheel" (AILD, 124; CT, 119). This is a description worthy of Bernini's Constantine. How would the horse paint, if not by caracoling? "If a bird could paint, would it not be by letting his plumes fall off; a snake, by casting off his scales; a tree, by raining down its leaves?" (FFCP, 114).

This is also a scene of unabashed seduction, in which the sexual overtones are all the more unmistakable since the reader recalls Darl's equally glittering description of his brother's amorous struggle with his horse at the beginning of the novel (AILD, 9–10; CT, 11–12). Jewel's seduction scene is also a kind of revenge—the revenge of the alien against his kin, of the bastard against the legitimate children, of the shameful young man against his father. What is even more noteworthy, though, is that the later revenge derives much of its power from the fact that is staged in front of the mother's eyes: "'Jewel,' ma said, looking at him. 'I'll give—I'll give—give—' Then she began to cry. She cried hard, not hiding her face, standing there in her faded wrapper, looking at him and him on the horse, looking down at her, his face growing cold and a little sick looking, until he looked away quick and Cash came and touched her" (AILD, 125; CT, 120–21). This single meeting between Jewel and Addie, during which much more seems to be said through looking than through speaking, reminds one of a similar moment in *Pelléas et Mélisande*, when Pelléas complains "And I have not yet looked at her glance."

If Jewel's being is contained entirely in his eyes, Darl's is contained entirely in the way he looks at—and beyond—people. His sister Dewey Dell sees him sitting "at the supper table with his eyes gone further than the food and the lamp, full of the land dug out of his skull and the holes filled with distance beyond the land" (AILD, 23; CT, 23). Just as Jewel's eyes inform the reader that he is solid matter—a kind of walking sculpture—so Darl's look informs him that he is all dumb knowledge. Again, it is Dewey Dell who does the seeing for us: "It was then, and then I saw Darl and he knew. He said he knew without the words like he told me that ma is going to die without words, and I knew he knew because if he had said he knew with the words I would not have believed that he had been there and saw us" (AILD, 24; CT, 24). Thus Dewey Dell, through the scandal of her sexual fall or "tripping," which Darl has discovered by spying on her from "the secret shade" while she was with Lafe, has become the object of Darl's knowledge, which is to say, Darl's object. Just as Darl "possesses" his sister by the tyranny of an insidious glance, so he also possesses his little brother Vardaman through the complicity of a protecting gaze. The three ill-loved siblings are all united in this way. It is as if Darl brought to them an identity which they never had—because of the nonexistence of their mother's glance.

The fate of the three brothers at the end of the narrative is instructive. During the incident with the Negroes on the road, as the Bundrens draw near Jefferson, Darl observes that "Jewel has never looked at me"—indeed, he observes, "it is as though Jewel had gone blind for the moment" (AILD, 219; CT, 212). Jewel's blindness is no doubt an effect of anger—or rage at the insult he believes he has received. Yet did not also Oedipus, the archetype of the victim of scandal, also end up blind? There is a profound poetic justice in both of these endings.

Darl falls a victim to the tyranny of his own, divided glance: having become literally his own voyeur—the voyeur who spies on himself—he ends as a victim of schizophrenia (his last monologue). The eldest child, Cash, also changes, but for the better. His limited craftsman's glance, his shortsighted, obdurate vision seems to give way to a remarkable capacity for distance-taking. In the end he understands many things, perhaps not "in the heaven," but "in the earth"[3]—including Darl. In spite of a limited vocabulary, he is capable of thinking intelligently about his brother's madness: "But I aint so sho that ere a man has the right to say what is crazy and what aint. It's like there was a fellow in every man that's done a-past the sanity and the insanity, that watches the sane and the insane doings of that man with the same horror and the same astonishment" (228; CT, 221). It is indeed through these extreme states of horror and astonishment (both different from surprise) that outrage manifests itself.

Horror ("a painful emotion of intense fear, dread, dismay"—Webster) and astonishment (which, in its diluted, modern sense, is all too often confused with surprise) are quite different reactions to some "shocking" aspect of reality. Both are emotions distinct from terror, which, according to Edgar Allan Poe, "is not of Germany, but of the soul."[4] Reality in *As I Lay Dying* is not so much the death of the mother but the "living" presence of the dead mother. The dead mother *is*: this is demonstrated by the reactions her death provokes in each member of her family as well as in a number of her neighbors.

In an often quoted passage, Doctor Peabody, called to Addie's bedside, diagnoses not her illness—she is beyond recovery—but the conditions that prevail in their country: "That's the one trouble with this country: everything, weather, all, hangs on too long. Like our rivers, our land: opaque, slow, violent: shaping and creating the life of man in its implacable and brooding image" (AILD, 41; CT, 40–41). In the manuscript the end of the sentence reads "in its implacable and oblivious image"; the latter adjective was deleted and replaced by the more typically Faulknerian word *brooding*—a word already encountered and which later crowns the description of the wilderness in *Go Down, Moses*. In the author's imagination, brooding is clearly the essential attribute of the obscure, inscrutable womb or matrix in which he locates the organic origin of all events. Here, as seen through Peabody's eyes, this original womb seems to breed a kind of outrage that he identifies as a symptom of surfeit, of an excess of everything—space, time, nature in general. These remarks are prophetic at least in dramatic terms since the funeral procession lasts no less than nine days and a flood, a fire, and a few more incidents turn the trip into a virtual epic.[5] Yet Peabody's prophecy also foreshadows some of the themes in the later novels, like the flood in *The Wild Palms* and the wilderness in *Go Down, Moses*. The description of both of these conveys the same image of nature's unruly autonomy, which is what seems to outrage Peabody. Anse also shares this feeling, which Darl translates for us in one of the most important monologues in the book:

> The air smells like sulphur. . . . Below the sky sheet-lightning slumbers lightly; against it the trees, motionless, are ruffled out to the last twig, swollen, increased as though quick with young.
>
> It begins to rain. The first harsh, sparse, swift drops rush through the leaves and across the ground in a long sigh, as though of relief from intolerable suspense. . . . Pa lifts his face, slack-mouthed, the wet black rim of snuff plastered close along the base

of his gums; from behind his slack-faced astonishment he muses as though from beyond time, upon the ultimate outrage. (AILD, 71; CT, 69–70)

Astonishment ("slack-mouthed," "slack-faced") is literally painted on Anse's face. The "ultimate outrage" is what passes understanding. The everyday rules of reality seem to be suspended. Not only does Anse's wife die, but drops of rain begin to fall, "big as buckshot, warm as though fired from a gun"! "Good things of day begin to droop and drowse"[6]—the long night of the Bundrens has begun: ". . . again he looks up at the sky with that expression of dumb and brooding outrage and yet of vindication, as though he had expected no less" (AILD, 72; CT, 69). The Bundrens are alone as few human beings can be. They live in a kind of Third World.[7] What is striking, however, is the fact that they are all alone with *something:* Addie is alone with her death. Anse thinks he is alone with his wife's dead body. Darl is alone with everyone he looks at. Jewel is alone with his horse, and Cash with "his" coffin. Dewey Dell is alone with her embryo. Vardaman is alone with his fish.

Just as Addie intimates to him that he should leave the room where she lies dying, Peabody thinks aloud again: "That's what they mean by the love that passeth understanding: that pride, that furious desire to hide that abject nakedness which we bring here with us, carry with us into operating rooms, stubbornly and furiously with us into the earth again" (AILD, 42; CT, 41–42). No sociological explanation is possible for this phenomenon. Again, a check of the manuscript reveals an important alteration of words: "abject" has replaced the simpler "helpless." Judgment replaces pity. It is a meaningful change because abjection conveys the idea of separation and forlornness as well as the idea of debasement and dejection. Indeed, being thrown into abjection is not very different from being overwhelmed by what Faulkner would later call "the immemorial attitude." Probably the best example of this is found in the "Old Man" section of The Wild Palms.

The first example of an "immemorial attitude" appears at the very moment when the hemophiliac convict has a hemorrhage. This has the effect of associating him with the flood of the river (providing an ironic counterpoint to Charlotte's hemorrhage in "Wild Palms"): "he sat bent forward, elbows on knees in the immemorial attitude, watching his own bright crimson staining the mud-trodden deck" (TWP, 242–43). How else indeed could the tall convict react—the heroic antihero, the poor prince of the outraged, the Pierrot of contingency's whim—when confronted with two equally improbable organic discharges?

At the end of the "Wild Palms" section of the novel the reader is struck by something he thinks he has already read. In his prison Harry Wilbourne adopts the same attitude because, like Horace in *Sanctuary,* he experiences a typically Faulknerian nausea, one that is induced by "weak, oversweet and hot coffee": "So he set the cup on his stool and sat on the cot's edge above it; without realising it he had assumed the immemorial attitude of all misery, crouching, hovering not in grief but in complete guttish concentration" (TWP, 308). The word "immemorial," as with Poe, literally signifies what lies beyond memory, or what extends beyond the reach of record or tradition. However, Faulkner adds the anthropological meaning of indefinitely ancient, which sends us back to the idea of some first origin. Later, in *Go Down, Moses,* the word is used in conjunction with "brooding." In brief, the uses of the notion of the immemorial show how for Faulkner outrage leads characters to seek to return to the matrix of all things, to some earth-mother or, as in "Delta Autumn," to "the wilderness' flank . . . the brooding and immemorial tangle" (GDM, 342).

Addie, in this scheme of things, is at once the hub and the circumference of the Bundrens' world. All paths in the novel lead to her. No member of the family is unaffected by the "outrage" of her being dead, although Darl, as the expert narrator, is the one with whom the reader most associates the sentiment.

The episode of the log, in which the wagon capsizes, is both the dramatic and the symbolic climax of the whole river scene. This episode is also the climax of one of the most important and most beautiful of Darl's monologues, in which one finds one of Faulkner's celebrated similes—a simile which was added after the manuscript stage:

> *It surged up out of the water and stood for an instant upright upon*
> *that surging and heaving desolation like Christ*
> (AILD, 138; CT, 134)

In this looming up of things and people—in the constant exchange of qualities between objects and beings within a universe dominated by instability and metamorphosis,[8] there is always some opaque immanence, some obstacle like the log. This obstacle is both a stumbling block and something with a volition of its own, which seems to cause one to fall, which actually "trips" one. As Cora comments sanctimoniously: "Log, fiddlesticks . . . It was the hand of God." Her husband's reply is as saucy as it is wry: "Then how can you say it was foolish?" (AILD, 143; CT, 138).

Since the log—and what has just been said about it—are bound to make one think of the no less famous root in Sartre's *Nausea,* one turns with interest to the comments made by Georges Poulet in his "Sartre's *Nausea* and Descartes' *Cogito.*" Sartre, says Poulet, has laid down the basic idea of an "existential *cogito*": "At the centre of consciousness," in fact, there is not " 'a positive and active thought,' as with Descartes; nor is there 'a passive feeling' as in Rousseau's *Rêveries.*" But neither is there in Faulkner exactly what Poulet says he finds in Sartre, "a vertigo whose name is nausea."[9] Rather, at the center of consciousness is an emptiness, a gazing/gaping state, literally a stupidity. This is precisely what is implicit in the glance which Faulkner's characters project again and again.

In the imaginary world of Faulkner's fiction, nothing important happens outside the field of vision circumscribed by a glance. An object looms up, imposes itself, becomes obvious, without warning or preparation. By virtue simply of being there, this object immediately raises, for whomever looks at it, the problem of his or her own existence. Because it raises this problem, the "strange" object can be taken as immediate proof of one's existence, and the recognition is acknowledged through astonishment or, in the most radical cases, through a kind of stupor, for example, the tall convict's "expression of aghast and incredulous amazement" (TWP, 156) when confronted with the tidal wave. This is also true of "the long mournful heads of mules . . . which seemed to glare reproachfully back at him with sightless eyes, in limber-lipped and incredulous amazement" (TWP, 158). The tidal wave is an outrage to all of God's creatures—it is Faulkner's version of the original Flood. The crossing of the flooded river in *As I Lay Dying* can be seen as an adumbration of this universal contact with outrage. If, therefore, there is a Faulknerian cogito, to borrow Poulet's term, it lies in the sense of outrage. Faulkner's characters come into existence by virtue of this outrage.

The relationships between the sons and their mother in *As I Lay Dying* lead one to the same conclusion. However, if a whole community, expressing itself through the mouth of its (witch) doctor, experiences what might be called generalized outrage, it is because the Bundrens, in their collective acting out of the death of their mother, constitute, in turn, an outrage in the eyes of this community. They are, in fact, a socioethnological scandal in their own right. One need only trace the reactions of the Bundrens' more vocal female neighbors who, under the direction of Cora Tull, make up a kind of subgroup or chorus. These reactions are clearly manifestations of their solidarity with the dead one. Rachel, Samson's wife, sets the tone at the moment when the Bundrens arrive at their farm after a three-day journey. "It's a outrage," she declares (AILD, 107; CT, 103). Lula, Armstid's wife, says the same thing (AILD, 179; CT, 174). Even the Negroes are struck by "that expression of shock and instinctive outrage" (AILD, 219; CT, 212) as the Bundrens reach Jefferson at last.

To this collective dimension of outrage, one should add an individual, private, even intimate dimension. One sees this in Dewey Dell—a character so marginalized by her sexual faux pas as to have become an introvert:

> I heard that my mother is dead. I wish I had time to let her die. I wish I had time to wish I had. It is because in the wild and outraged earth too soon too soon too soon. It's not that I wouldn't and will not it's that it is too soon too soon too soon.
>
> Now it begins to say it. New Hope three miles. New Hope three miles. *That's what they mean by the womb of time: the agony and the despair of spreading bones, the hard girdle in which lie the outraged entrails of events.* (AILD, 110; CT, 106)

As for Vardaman, the day he became acquainted with outrage was the day he first associated his mother's death and the dead glance of the half-buried fish whose eyes he tried to gouge. Later, by boring into his mother's casket so that she could breathe (AILD, 68; CT, 66), Vardaman symbolically liberated the imaginary glance of the absent eye that he no longer could see but which he compulsively associated with the real but empty glance of the fish he had actually seen in the dust. Vardaman illustrates perfectly my thesis that every mise-en-scène is also a mise-en-acte, that every staging is also an acting out and vice versa.

However, the public and the private aspects of outrage converge in Darl alone. What Darl embodies in the overall structure of the novel as a work of fiction is the symbolic function of the glance in any literary text. Without this, there would be no "fiction" in Faulkner's work. Whether it is Darl the voyeur or Darl the *voyant*[10] who is given a privileged place is relatively unimportant. Technically, Darl is both, because his role is essentially that of an onlooker—a kind of *Ur-anschauer* or primordial peeping Tom. This does not make him the bearer of the author's glance—as is arguably the case for both Gavin Stevens and Ratliff in the later novels. Both quantitatively and qualitatively, Darl's visual involvement is greater than that of the six other Bundrens and their eight neighbors.

At the center of all this looking, glancing, and peeping lies the body of the mother. Read in this light, the novel is indeed the tour de force that Faulkner himself said it was,[11] that is, the story (the unfolding, the opening out in time and space) of a ritual, "a devotional service," "a religious ceremony," a practice with "a symbolic or quasi-symbolic significance" (Webster). In depth, the theme of the novel is that of the Eucharist, both in its pre-Christian sense of recognition or grace ("*thanksgiving*"), and in the Christian sense of a sacrament to commemorate Christ's sacrifice, during which his flesh and blood are consumed. Addie's death can be seen as an occasion for a communion, both in the Christian sacramental sense and in the ethnological sense of cannibalism. What Faulkner once called the "esoteric"[12] quality of the novel becomes comprehensible if one realizes that the physical accomplishment of the mother's death wish is also the occasion of a symbolic consumption of the mother's body. The ritual sacrifice of her body by the family—to which the ostentatious, grammatically incomplete title of the book may well refer—allows one to think of the novel in terms of an evening meal during which the body of the mother is offered like a host to the kinfolk. It can hardly be an accident if her dying coincides with the actual preparation of an evening meal, the main dish of which, the fish, is said to be as "full of blood and guts as a hog" (AILD, 34; CT, 34). This reminds us of Dewey Dell's fertile womb, which is described by her as "a little tub of guts" (AILD, 54; CT, 53), and of Addie's monologue itself, which is full of blood. Seen as "primitive theatre,"[13] *As I Lay Dying* can indeed be interpreted as the mother's death scene turned into a last supper.

For Darl the drama takes root in what Faulkner calls elsewhere "the tragic complexity of motherless childhood" (GDM, 130–31). Darl says, in fact, "I cannot love my mother because I have no mother" (AILD, 89; CT, 84). This has tragic consequences for him and even puts his ontological status in jeopardy. Some of his monologues reveal him to be literally haunted by ontological doubts: "In a strange room you must empty yourself for sleep. And before you are emptied for sleep, what are you. And when you are emptied for sleep, you are not. And when you are filled with sleep, you never were. I dont know what I am. I dont know if I am or not. Jewel knows he is, because he does not know that he does not know whether he is or not (AILD, 75; CT, 72).

First, Darl searches for the ideal glance, the perfectly clear or uncorrupted vision, in his father—then, by substitution, in his brothers. The reader is struck by the frequency of Darl's minute portraits of his father in the first monologues: "Pa stands over the bed, dangle-armed, humped, motionless" (AILD, 48; CT, 48). Thus, even at his dying wife's bedside, the father—himself the first victim of the "generalized outrage"—becomes, in the jealous eye of his son, an outrageous object. Peabody confirms this vision of the incapable father with "his arms dangling, the hair pushed and matted up on his head like a dipped rooster" (AILD, 40; CT, 40).

Insofar as Faulkner's fiction seems to obey what one could call a "law of exchange," according to which humans acquire the qualities of animals and vice versa, it is particularly interesting to note that the vignette of Anse just quoted is later retold by Samson but in reversed order: "When I walked into the hallway I saw something. It kind of hunkered up when I first come in and I thought at first it was one of them got left, then I saw what it was. It was a buzzard. It looked around and saw me and went down the hall, spraddle-legged, with its wings kind of hunkered out, watching me over one shoulder and then over the other, *like a old baldheaded man* (AILD, 109; CT, 105; my emphasis). In fact, the association of Anse with a rather unpleasant bird is underscored by Addie herself: "And so I took Anse. I saw him pass the school house three or four times before I learned that he was driving four miles out of his way to do it. I noticed then how he was beginning to hump—a tall man and young—so that he looked already like a tall bird hunched in the cold weather" (AILD, 161; CT, 156). The repeated association of the father with a carrion-eating bird is all the more interesting since the buzzard, as we know, incarnated for Faulkner the exemplary glance, lofty and indeed disinterested.[14]

Time and again, Darl casts oblique, jealous (in Sartre's sense) glances at Jewel (for example, in monologues 1, 3, 10) and at Cash the craftsman, the *homo faber* (monologues 5, 12, 17). Moreover, insofar as Jewel is primarily an *eye,* Cash a *hand,* and Darl a *voice,* one can say that Addie Bundren's three sons symbolize the organs of the missing master, the ideal of the self, the father. As Giliane Morell writes: "In *As I Lay Dying,* Cash, Jewel and Darl are moved by a force which they can neither control nor understand.

All three throw themselves into a mad race of desire, which takes them as far as the verge of the abyss of loss, so as to be the one who shall succeed in tearing death away, in resuscitating the object of their original passion."[15]

If the stakes are so high, what can the ludicrous figure of the father count for? He is only a caricature (AILD, 72–73; CT, 68) compared with the symbolic Mother, the lost object of Darl's desire, whose glance is capable of turning his own into an ideal glance. To quote again from Giliane Morell, "Because he was never 'seen' by his mother, [Darl] doubts his own identity, he experiences in himself the anguish of separation, until the final explosion, when he literally bursts into mad laughter and addresses his lost identity in order to ask the question of his own laughter: 'What are you laughing at?' "[16]

Before Darl's eye turns back upon itself at the end of the novel, one witnesses in his sixth monologue a demonstration of how he obeys the symbolic law of the novel—indeed how he himself sets this law. The monologue begins with six words that summarize the way imagination works here: "The lantern sits on a stump" (AILD, 70; CT, 67). In the night of Darl's frustrated desire, a smothered glance shines. It is like a light at sea, both a beacon that guides one to land and a marker that indicates a danger. The reader is struck by the use of assonance and alliteration in this phrase as well as by a verb which reminds him of the intransitive verb in the title. The passive verb is nonetheless active, deliberate, perverse—almost vicious. The position of the sentence at the very beginning of the monologue and the "power of blackness" that the six words call forth make the reader sense that some uncanny force is looming. Images by Goya, Füssli, or Bosch come to mind.

The end of the monologue is also worth looking at. The well-known and highly disturbing meditation by Darl on being and nothingness is framed by two sentences which, one feels, foreshadow the character of Joe Christmas, the outcast: "In a strange room you must empty yourself for sleep. . . . How often have I lain beneath rain on a strange roof, thinking of home" (AILD, 76; CT, 72). "Home" can only refer to the Mother, just as "strange" alludes to life outside the field of her vision; "room," associated with emptiness and sleep, and "roof," associated with rain, call to mind the interior and the exterior, the inside and the outside of a dialectic of identity. The words also make one think of some forbidden place coveted by desire, where the glance cannot reach. One may even sense a kind of dereliction which, for Darl, represents a solipsistic pleasure. Both the dereliction and the pleasure are clearly alluded to in Darl's second monologue:

> And at night it is better still. I used to lie on the pallet in the hall, waiting till I could hear them all asleep, so I could get up and go back to the bucket. It would be black, the shelf black, the still surface of the water a round orifice into nothingness, where before I stirred it awake with the dipper I could see maybe in the dipper a star or two before I drank. After that I was bigger, older. Then I would wait until they all went to sleep so I could lie with my shirt-tail up, hearing them asleep, feeling myself without touching myself, feeling the cool silence blow upon my parts. (AILD, 7; CT, 9)

Vardaman follows almost completely in Darl's steps. His very first monologue, however, introduces us to the most notable—and ignoble—aspect of outrage in Faulkner's fiction. In the manuscript version Faulkner identified this aspect in the second sentence, but he deleted it from the typescript: "Then I begin to run. [I can feel something hot and salt sickness beginning to come up from inside me.] I run toward the back door because that is the way I came in and I try to run back into where it hadn't been. I run to the edge of the porch and stop because beyond is where it is and the edge of the porch is the edge of the is-not. Then I begin to cry" (AL, manuscript version of AILD, 49; CT, 49). In both the typescript and the published version, Vardaman announces three times that he is going to "vomit the crying." He thus exemplifies the organic nature of grief. He shows moreover how vomiting is the ultimate effect of outrage in Faulkner's fiction.

chapter twelve

Failure

"Landing in Luck," *Sanctuary*

Only those who induce failing deserve being listened to.

—E. M. Cioran

The relationship between outrage and vomiting is easy to establish: vomiting is less a consequence than a sign (or a symptom) of outrage. In the case of Vardaman Bundren it is clear that the relationship is not understood. The same is true for many other characters; the meaning of the violent physical reaction is obscure, as though it were part of a code which the reader has to decipher in lieu of the characters because they do not see into it. In this chapter I wish to consider the semeiology of the typically Faulknerian motif of vomiting and physical revulsion.

Vomiting appears very early in Faulkner's work, as early, in fact, as his first published prose, "Landing in Luck," in 1919. In this sketch, as with Vardaman, vomiting is a "pure" physiological reaction to a visual phenomenon. One could almost speak of a momentary interruption of the brain's control over the eyes:

> For Thompson's nerve was going as he neared the earth. The temptation was strong to kick his rudder over and close his eyes. The machine descended, barely retaining headway. He watched the approaching ground utterly unable to make any pretence of levelling off, paralyzed; his brain had ceased to function, he was all staring eyes watching the remorseless earth. He did not know his height, the ground rushed past too swiftly to judge, but he expected to crash any second. Thompson's fate was on the lap of the Gods. (EP&P, 48)

The failure of the brain to control visual perception is followed by the "inverted vision," which also appears for the first time in this first sketch: "Hanging face downward from the cockpit, Cadet Thompson looked at Bessing, surprised at the words of this cold, short tempered officer. He forgot the days of tribulation and insult in this man's company, and his recent experience, and his eyes filled with utter adoration. *Then he became violently ill*" (EP&P, 49; my emphasis). Failure, or the sequence sight-fascination-vomiting, is directly related here to the physiological symptom of nausea. Vomiting is the symptom of a "sickness beginning to come up from inside me," as Vardaman Bundren observes with more than literal accuracy.

In *Sanctuary* Gowan Stevens vomits after drinking too much. Uncle Bud throws up after downing too much beer. Like Vardaman, these characters are young boys, and it is precisely their youthfulness that renders Horace's repeated feelings of nausea so ironic—because Horace is forty-three years old. For Horace, as later for Harry Wilbourne in *The Wild Palms,* coffee—not alcohol—sparks off a violent physiological reaction. The circumstances of the reaction are also interesting. Horace sees a photograph of Little Belle, whom he associates with his fantasy about Temple Drake. Thus, through a series of images, recollections, and fantasies, Horace arrives at a recognition of truth, which is, as it were, embedded in the world of appearances:

> Then he knew what that sensation in his stomach meant. He put the photograph down hurriedly and went to the bathroom. He opened the door running and fumbled at the light. But he had not time to find it and he gave over and plunged forward and struck the lavatory and leaned upon his braced arms while the shucks set up a terrific uproar beneath her thighs. Lying with her head lifted slightly, her chin depressed like a figure lifted down from a crucifix, she watched something black and furious go roaring out of her pale body. She was bound naked on her back on a flat car moving at speed through a black tunnel, the blackness streaming in rigid threads overhead, a roar of iron wheels in her ears. The car shot bodily from the tunnel in a long upward slant, the darkness overhead now shredded with parallel attenuations of living fire, toward a crescendo like a held breath, an interval in which she would swing faintly and lazily in nothingness filled with

> pale, myriad points of light. Far beneath her she could hear the
> faint, furious uproar of the shucks. (SAN, 268; CT, 234–35)

Whatever Horace's degree of consciousness (or of unconsciousness) at the moment of having such a blatantly symbolic hallucination, there can be no doubt that it follows on from vomiting.

Toward the end of the first version of the novel, Horace best illustrates the meaning of vomiting in Faulkner's fiction: " 'I ran. Once I had not the courage to admit it; now I have not the courage to deny it. *I found more reality than I could stomach, I suppose*' " (STOT, 281; my emphasis). It is worth noting that both Horace and Vardaman react to outrage by vomiting and running. Their use of the verb "to stomach" reveals clearly how their reactions challenge an individual to deal with reality; swallowing and ingesting, then, here as elsewhere in Faulkner's fiction, become metaphors for the perception of reality. Time and again Faulkner stresses a young character's difficulty in taking in reality: a failure to do so constitutes the ultimate failure in a human being.

Just as there is hardly a novel by Faulkner without a literal or figurative voyeur, so there is hardly one in which at least one character does not literally or figuratively vomit. The best known example is perhaps Joe Christmas, who acts in a way that sheds light on Faulkner's fundamental way of reasoning, his cogito. Indeed, one may go so far as to say that, at a certain crucial stage of Joe's education, the relationship of being to experience could be summarized as *vomito ergo sum:* "At once the paste which he had already swallowed lifted inside him, trying to get back out, into the air where it was cool. It was no longer sweet. In the rife, pinkwomansmelling obscurity behind the curtain he squatted, pinkfoamed, listening to his insides, waiting with the astonished fatalism for what was about to happen to him. Then it happened. He had said to himself with complete and passive surrender: 'Well, here I am' " (LIA, 114; CT, 134).

Another characteristic instance of vomiting and another aspect of the failure of the glance when confronted with an outrageous spectacle can be found in *Absalom, Absalom!,* when Henry Sutpen is forced by his father to watch his own wild wrestling with the blacks. The boy's reaction differs crucially from that of his sister Judith. First, here is the scene as viewed— that is, as imagined—by Mr. Compson: "And Judith . . . who while Henry screamed and vomited, looked down from the loft that night on the spectacle of Sutpen fighting halfnaked with one of his halfnaked niggers with the same cold and attentive interest with which Sutpen would have watched Henry fighting with a negro boy of his own age and weight" (AA, 120; CT, 149). The same episode, as reconstructed by the implacable and hysterical Miss Rosa, is slanted out of a sympathy for her sister Ellen's point of view:

> "Yes. That is what Ellen saw: her husband and father of her children standing there naked and panting and bloody to the waist and the negro just fallen evidently, lying at his feet and bloody too save that on the negro it merely looked like grease or sweat— Ellen running down the hill from the house, bareheaded, in time to hear the sound, the screaming, hearing it while she still ran in the darkness and before the spectators knew that she was there . . . and the spectators falling back to permit her to see Henry plunge out from among the negroes who had been holding him, screaming and vomiting." (AA, 29; CT, 31)

In observing that Henry vomits and Judith does not, one must also emphasize the fact that in *Sanctuary* Temple Drake does not vomit after listening to her friend's story about sex and the snake.[1] The snake that creeps into *Absalom, Absalom!* comes to mind: ". . . and Ellen not watching them now either but kneeling in the dirt while Henry clung to her, crying, and *he* standing there while a third nigger prodded his shirt or coat at him as though the coat were a stick *and he a caged snake*" (AA, 30; CT, 32; last five words my emphasis). The son's point of view—"Henry clung to her, crying"—is reminiscent of Horace's childhood memory, upon seeing the Jewish lawyer in court at the end of the first version of *Sanctuary:* "Once when he was a boy he had two possums in a barrel. A negro told him to put a cat in with them if he wanted to see something, and he had done so. When he could move at all he ran to his mother in a passion of crying that sent him staggering and vomiting toward the house" (STOT, 272). There are many more examples of vomiting in Faulkner's fiction. Indeed, Mark Van Doren wrote in 1935: "*Pylon* probably establishes the record among contemporary novels for the amount of vomiting it records, there being at least one major upheaval in each of the seven chapters, and many minor landslides."[2] And no wonder: in this respect, as the following chapter will show, *Pylon* is undoubtedly the *nec plus ultra* of Faulknerian cosmology.

But what exactly is Faulknerian cosmology? It could be described as a radical version of idealism and defined in terms of those things that cannot be endured—of what lies beyond the capacity of the individual to cope with reality. In the final analysis only those characters vomit who find the confrontation between innocence and experience both a shock and an impossible ordeal. But the role played by such notions in Faulkner's fiction varies considerably.

In the early stories "innocent" is a strictly descriptive term. It means being stripped of something that could or should have been there: either trees in a street or a razor on a chin. As for the ethical meaning of the word, there is hardly any similarity, at least apparently, between Quentin Compson's interpretation of Thomas Sutpen's "trouble" as "innocence" in *Absalom, Absalom!* and the following definition of innocence in *The Town:* "Innocence is innocent not because it rejects, but because it accepts" (TOWN, 203).[3] Is this to say that the only thing these versions of innocence have in common is their antonym, experience?

But the meaning of experience is hardly more stable in Faulkner's fiction. A disillusioned Elmer can ask "But who wants experience, when he can get any kind of substitute? To hell with experience, Elmer thinks, since all reality is unbearable" (US, 612). His attitude is more a brash and youthful gesture of rejection than real Nietzscheanism and is echoed by this remark in *Mosquitoes:* "'Experience: why should we be expected to learn wisdom from experience?'" (MOS, 233).

In *Soldiers' Pay* experience is a part of the glamour of the femme fatale, a notion often associated with something that females inherit by birth and from which males are virtually barred. In *The Hamlet,* for instance, Eula Varner possesses "a weary knowledge which he [Labove] would never attain, a surfeit, a glut of all perverse experience" (HAM, 120). Many of Faulkner's early characters seem to illustrate such a dichotomy, particularly Horace Benbow in *Sanctuary.* One needs to note, however, that experience is often (traditionally, in fact) closely associated with such activities as war and hunting—so much so, in fact, that some of the stories and certain novels could be described as initiations.

In the final analysis what is typical of Faulkner, and what makes him—from this point of view—different from the English or American Romantics,[4] is not an interest in either innocence (like Hawthorne) or experience (like Melville), but an interest in the dramatic confrontation of innocence and experience. One may well describe his favorite topic as the *failure* of the capacity to pass smoothly on from one to the other.

However, there is another way of looking at the symptom of vomiting. If we stop asking what it means and ask rather what part it plays in the development of the generic hero or the Faulknerian idealist, there appear to be two possibilities. One can, as Gilles Deleuze suggests, turn one's back on representation, consider the event as a "pure" repetition in the structural fabric of the work, and interpret not the vomiting, but the repetition of it— not *vomo,* but *vomito.* In this case we abolish all notions of linear evolution, of progress, in order to highlight the structural circularity or the compulsion of repetition. Indeed, there are no differences among Cadet Thompson, Horace Benbow, and Henry Sutpen in the nature of their vomiting.

If, on the other hand, we choose no longer to interpret vomiting as a pure event in a novelistic sequence, but as a function in character-drawing, is it conceivable that a reader would perceive the two following scenes in the same novel as being the same? The one involves a male character: Horace Benbow meets Belle's sister, Joan Heppleton, and associates her with a yawning tiger he remembers seeing in a circus.[5] The other scene involves a female character, Narcissa Benbow, at the moment of confronting the reality of hunting for the first time:

> Narcissa saw the creature in the pool of the flash light, lying on its side in a grinning curve, its eyes closed and its pink babylike hands doubled against its breast. She looked at the motionless thing with pity and distinct loathing—such a paradox, its vulpine, skull-like grin and those tiny, human-looking hands, and the long ratlike tail of it. . . . and while Narcissa watched in shrinking curiosity, he [Caspey] laid the axe across the thing's neck and put his foot on either end of the helve, and grasped the animal's tail. . . . She turned and fled, her hand to her mouth. (SAR, 285; a different version in *Flags,* 273)

Even without analyzing Faulkner's highly idiosyncratic bestiary, what reader would recognize these two vignettes as being the same? Structurally, Horace and Narcissa are brother and sister; the nature of their reactions is part and parcel of their incestuous relationship in *Sartoris* but not in

Sanctuary, where the incestuous tendency gives way to belligerence. This is another way of saying that each individual novel has its roots in an imaginary structure or a central fantasy. Thus, even though Horace and Narcissa Benbow are common to both *Sartoris* and *Sanctuary,* they are not quite the same people in each. In the former incest is the central fantasy; in the latter rape. Faulkner's recurring characters, in other words, are fundamentally different from Balzac's.

Why does Faulkner repeat the motif of vomiting? As can be expected, Faulkner has nothing—and Freud a great deal—to say about this. Yet there still seems to be disagreement among psychoanalysts about the theory of vomiting. Is it a psychopathological symptom, "an incoercible process of unconscious origin, by which the subject puts himself into unpleasant situations, thus repeating former experiences without recalling the prototype, and with the vivid impression of something which is powerfully motivated in the present?" Or is it "an autonomous factor, which ultimately cannot be reduced to a mere conflict between the principle of reality and the principle of pleasure?"[6] Whether Faulkner the man was unconsciously pleased by fantasizing about vomiting (or whether he even had an actual tendency to vomit), one will probably never know. If one sees in the act a deep reaction to alcoholism, one only raises another problem rather than solving the present one.

Problems arise for the characters in Faulkner's fiction, therefore, because of transitions from one state to another. The transition is not a transfer of one setting into another nor a psychological change nor even a question of will. The transition is related to a kind of mutation, or a metamorphosis, which is reflected for example in the writer's penchant for a word such as *avatar* and in his interest in polymorphism in general.[7]

What is certain is that there is no analytical way into Faulkner's fiction without recourse to the notions of failure and of difference/repetition. From this point of view one can look again at the symmetrical relation in which Horace and Narcissa find themselves in *Sanctuary.* It is a novel of such extremism as to point directly toward *Pylon.*[8]

Horace could be called the idealist and Temple, according to Baudelaire, the bitch. Horace is fascinated by Temple via Little Belle (the photograph), and Temple can be said to be fascinated by herself (the mirror). As in Hogarth's "Rake's Progress," one could call progress here their career, the process by which both end up as they do at the close of the novel.

The failure of Horace's progress is due to the fact that in his interpretation, the whole masculine kind (the Latin *vir*) is excluded from what he calls "the old ferment," "the green-snared promise of unease," as if Adam had never fallen. Thus, Horace's innocence has theological overtones.[9] It also has—as always—a psychological justification: Horace is making himself a cover so as to protect his (de)fault—his most vulnerable spot.

This is what the initial scene of the published novel dramatizes so effectively, as does its repetition in those scenes in which a glance is trapped by appearances. In the course of the novel the mirrors, photographs, and reflections in which Horace, as an idealist, seeks reality are either shattered or insulting, literally. And there is no doubt that his "progress" leaves Horace undone. At novel's end his illusions are gone, his ideals broken. He has no reason for living. Stripped of his panoply of fictions, Horace is a man without qualities. His revulsions have uncovered an ambiguous longing for the impure. His failure dooms him to unsatisfied desire, to reflexiveness, to frozen introspection instead of action.

Temple's progress is the reverse of Horace's. As Ruby Lamar points out, Temple refuses to be trapped by a glance. Her failure lies in the belief that only other people are so trapped. Unlike Horace, Temple has a kind of innocence. She does not exclude herself, as a woman, from the Old Frenchman's Place, but does exclude herself as a class, as a sheltered "Daddy's little girl." This is, moreover, precisely the kind of exclusion that Horace diagnoses in his sister's case. There is, however, something almost physiological in the way Temple plays at being a "maiden," untouched and therefore untouchable; she remains untouchable until the end, when, like a robot, she passes symbolically through the old Luxembourg garden, at the center of the old world, where "dead tranquil queens in stained marble" muse, undaunted and inviolate, "in the embrace of the season of rain and death." Lee Goodwin's trial develops around the confusion between Horace's and Temple's kinds of innocence. The one is the myth that the district attorney knows the jury will want to believe. The other is the reality that the same man does not even need to appeal to: Temple's relatives can take care of it. Thus Temple's progress is the opposite of Horace's: whereas all of his illusions are shattered, Temple, by contrast, passes through the novel like an apparition which nothing can violate—not even her own glance, which, at least in front of her mirror, remains just as serene as that of the well-named Narcissa in front of her brother. Since Temple does not feel sick when her youngest friend in the dorm, hearing the facts of sex, runs out of the room in revulsion (SAN, 181–82; CT, 159), one can say that she never falls into the trap set for her—the trap of seeing herself as degraded by experience, as *fallen*. Temple's imperviousness is confirmed by the innocent *and* perverse way in which she relates her experience to Horace. This is what pushes Horace to the limit. After this he experiences the typical Faulknerian nausea: "He did not even return to his hotel. He went to the station. He could get a train at midnight. He had a cup of coffee and wished immediately that he had not, for it lay in a hot ball on his stomach. Three hours later, when he got off at Jefferson, it was still there, unassimilated" (SAN, 266; CT, 232–33).

From the perfect symmetry of these two kinds of progress, the first genetic, the other structural, one can draw the following conclusions:

(1) Symmetry results from the exact similarity of parts relative to a dividing point or line. In Faulkner's fiction the dividing line is a glance or a gaze. The dividing point, the basic unit of the symmetry, is none else than a glance trapped by fascination.

(2) On opposite sides of the line Horace and Temple do indeed form reversed images: the former flees repetition into difference, whereas the latter flees difference into repetition. That is to say, Horace associates and ultimately superimposes the images of his sister, of Little Belle, of Temple, and, finally, of the college girls in chapter 19 with each other. In other words Horace may unconsciously regret that "Byron never had his wish" (TSATF, 115; CT, 107) (that all women had one pink mouth). But he runs away from his repetitious and ambiguous experience with women and takes up another attitude. When, at Miss Jenny's window he peeps at his sister walking in the garden holding the arm of Gowan Stevens, he does not associate himself with the suitor; moreover, he is outraged when Ruby Lamar makes it clear that she expects him to wish to be paid in kind. In other words, he turns into a defense and a value what is only his failed relations with women. This value falls apart at the end, along with all other values. It is easy to see what shaky foundations they were laid upon.

(3) One may say that Temple is more or less assaulted with difference—at first because she enters a world in which different social codes prevail. Her failure reveals an interesting ambiguity: at the Old Frenchman's Place, her mouth speaks one language while her body speaks another;[10] fallen in this trap, she seeks refuge, so to speak, in repetition. Not only does she accustom

herself to the perversion of Popeye's sexual play-acting, she falls abjectly in love with Red, thus pushing the repetition to the limit. To be in love is to be trapped. The amorous relationship brings about a total loss, because it is defined strictly by glances—that is, by a kind of sustained peeping wherein (almost by definition, since he is deprived of liberty) the subject collapses, passes out—or "fails."[11]

In Faulkner's symbolic world, there is no discontinuity between the physical and the metaphysical or between the erotic and the ontological: sex—even sex—is always under the eyes of God. One can only hide away from His sight or confront it: there is no other alternative. This is the "choice" that the fated lovers in *The Wild Palms* encounter, even though, in their case, it appears to be society's sight, or even their own, that they must hide from or confront. The mechanism, however, is the same: love is their *fatum*.

Is there a place for liberty in all this? As opposed to the "problematic heroes" of the nineteenth-century novel,[12] Faulkner's main characters exercise liberty only in the inevitable choice between transformation and collapse, between passing and failing to pass. In other words each of his novels is basically concerned with a rite of passage, whether it be a simple linear evolution (as in Lena Grove) or a dramatic transgression (as in Joe Christmas).

But this is also true of the whole oeuvre. Its only truly problematic hero may well be Faulkner himself, at once the origin and the product of his own literary creation. It is true that the chrysalis is fed in the dark fabric of the imaginary, but only the flight of the full-fledged butterfly can charm our eyes. Or, to use another, better-known metaphor: "I like to think of the world I created as being a kind of keystone in the Universe; that, as small as that keystone is, if it were taken away, the universe itself would collapse" (LITG, 255). It is interesting that Faulkner should conceive of his work as something which locks everything together. What is striking in this statement is not so much an author's *hubris* as the literally phantasmic/fantastic choice between "hold together" and "collapse."

Exactly how a psychic necessity becomes a law in the game of fiction remains to be seen. *Pylon* is the best possible case in point.

chapter thirteen

Dead End

Pylon

Because we are not meant to "understand" them. The three of
them are the literal center of the novel; but our geographical or
spatial relation to them is the same as that of the nameless
reporter—the relation of circumference to center. The subject of
Pylon is that relationship—and a picture of it, at that (however
murky), not an investigation.—*Reynolds Price,* "The Posture of
Worship"

Pylon is a paradigm. From the first lines, which paint the scenery, the text
strikes out aggressively at the reader. The typography itself (especially in the
first edition)[1] conveys this strategy: traffic in New Valois calls for direction
signs, billboards, timetables, and bus fare. Numerous insets, which imitate
the posters on display, announce the other main setting, the air show: the
program for "Thursday (Dedication Day)" (PYL, 27; CT, 24) which is
described as "heavy, blacksplotched, staccato" (14; 10), the list of participants (60; 58), the program for "Friday" (142; 143). One is also confronted
with a series of titles and headlines printed in boldface or italic characters,
such as: "*Airport Dedication Special*" (14; 10). The local newspaper is
"with a thick heavy typesplattered front page filled with ejaculations and
pictures" (13; 9), and at the exact center of the hangar entrance is "a big
board lettered heavily by hand and possessing a quality cryptic and peremp-
tory and for the time incomprehensible as though the amplifier had spoken
the words": a "*NOTICE*" posted for the pilots' use (129; 130). This
constant aggression is aimed not only at the reader outside the text, but at
the main, though nameless, character within the text:

when he began to see it was as if the letters were beginning to emerge from the back of his skull . . .

AVIATOR'S BODY RESIGNED TO LAKE GRAVE

Then he quit seeing it. He had not moved; his pupils would still have repeated the page in inverted miniature, but he was not seeing it at all, shaking quietly and steadily in the bright warm sun until he turned and looked into the window with an expression of quiet and bemused despair—the notflies or wereflies, the two grapefruit halves, the printed names of food like the printed stations in a train schedule and set on an easel like a family portrait—and experienced not only that profound and unshakable reluctance but actual absolute refusal of his entire organism (298–99; 307).

The situation here brings us back to the very beginning of the novel, when Jiggs, utterly fascinated, stands "for a full minute" in front of the shopwindow, "looking at the boots." More even than *Sanctuary, Pylon* is structured around gazes and glances. One could even say that in the passage above, Faulkner is writing about the physiology of vision.

The story begins with a headline: Colonel Feinman, the "fine man" and chairman of the Sewage Board, is heralded with a caption so bombastic as to make one suspicious of a hidden allusion to the author himself:

Through Whose Undeviating Vision and Unflagging Effort This Airport was Raised Up and Created out of the Waste Land at the Bottom of Lake Rambaud at a Cost of One Million Dollars (14; 11)

These are the motifs, indeed the leitmotifs, of Faulkner's remarks about his art: the presence of an original "vision," the necessity of effort, the cost of the operation consisting in drawing a literary work from the limbo of imagination. If one adds that the word "dedication," the title of the first chapter, is thoroughly ambiguous—since it has a literary meaning—and that it serves to disguise Faulkner's own relation to the city of New Orleans,[2] it becomes clear that *Pylon* is an even more self-conscious work than the preceding ones. The question is whether the novel is not also the most devastatingly self-critical of Faulkner's whole career.

To return to the text: the forced pairings, concatenations, and repeated dislocations in the first paragraph of the text have the effect of making the referential world unreal. This effect is both immediate and lasting since it continues until the accident. The autonomy of the language is most palpable at the beginning of chapter three, which describes the Walpurgis "Night in the Vieux Carré": "Now they would cross Grandlieu Street; there was traffic in it now; to clash and clang of light and bell trolley and automobile crashed and glared across the intersection, rushing in a light curbchanneled spindrift of tortured and draggled serpentine and trodden confetti pending the dawn's whitewings—spent tinseldung of Momus' Nilebarge clatterfalque" (77; 76). This is not an exercise in onomatopoeia nor (merely) an IOU to James Joyce; it would be all too obvious, if it were. The writing makes itself deliberately din and chaos, thus hinting at self-destruction since it tends to abrogate meaning and deny reason.

In addition, the first paragraph of the book has a structure that is important for the book as a whole: after describing the fetishist's glance at the boots on the wooden pedestal in the shopwindow, it introduces the double motif of words and pictures ("the same lettering, the same photographs"), which one sees everywhere in the city. Such a microstructure corresponds to the repetitive nature of the book's topic (stunt flying) as well as to its symbolism and reflexiveness. The story comes to us repeatedly through the double channel of image (whatever is shown through description) and letter (whatever is told in print). The end point of this double channel is, however, a single organ, the eye, which belongs to an underdog, to a wandering mechanic looking for a job. He is the latest avatar of the familiar "tieless casual." For the reader the spectacle of flying is the obvious focal point of the novel, whether one perceives the spectacle as an image (following the example of the mechanic looking at the boots) or as words to be read (whatever the text "advertises"). Yet this focal point is duplicated: the motif of Jiggs's eyes glued on the object of his desire recurs, duplicated as it were ad infinitum, near the end, when Laverne is shown being stared at by a crowd of newspapermen through the window of a restaurant; this scene occurs just before we are told their true identity in the title of the epilogue: "The Scavengers."

Both the theme of the novel, fascination, and its motifs of fetishism are forcefully conveyed through a sustained comparison with staging. Consider the following:

". . . the scene began to resemble that comic stage one where the entire army enters one taxicab and drives away" (15; 11).

"As they stood side by side and looked at one another they resembled the tall and the short man of the orthodox and unfailing comic team" (56; 54).

". . . a room apparently exhumed from a theatrical morgue . . ." (91; 90).

". . . speaking apparently in soliloquy to an empty room . . ." (103; 102).

". . . the reporter had brought into the house, the room, with him that atmosphere of a fifteenth century Florentine stage scene" (167–68; 170).

On the other hand, the idea that the air show is nothing but a kind of gratuitous exhibitionism on the part of the stunt flyers was corroborated by Faulkner himself:

"Q. Mr. Faulkner, do you regard *Pylon* as a serious novel, and what were you driving at in this novel?

A. To me they were a fantastic and bizarre phenomenon on the face of a contemporary scene, of our culture at a particular time. I wrote that book because I'd got in trouble with *Absalom, Absalom!* and I had to get away from it for a while so I thought a good way to get away from it was to write another book, so I wrote *Pylon.* They were ephemera and phenomena on the face of a contemporary scene. That is, there was really no place for them in the culture, in the economy, yet they were there, at that time, and everyone knew that they wouldn't last very long, which they didn't. That time of those frantic little aeroplanes which dashed around the country and people wanted just enough money to live, to get to the next place to race again. Something frenetic and in a way almost immoral about it. That they were outside the range of God, not only of respectability, of love, but of God too. That they had escaped the compulsion of accepting a past and a future, that they were—they had no past. They were as ephemeral as the butterfly that's born this morning with no stomach and will be gone tomorrow. It seemed to me interesting enough to make a story about, but that was just to get away from a book that wasn't going too well, till I could get back at it. (FITU, 36)

These remarks, associated as they are with a reminder of how *Pylon* came to be written ("I wrote that book because I'd got in trouble with *Absalom, Absalom!*"), merit our attention. Perhaps the most striking simile above is that of the airmen being like insects without stomachs, mere ephemeral phenomena on the face of the contemporary scene. This image underscores all the more the sense of show—the flyers are doomed to disappear, not by divine decree nor because of a fundamental transgression, but because of the inadequacy of their bodies. "Tragedy begins when the sky empties itself," Jean Duvignaud wrote.[3] There is no god in *Pylon,* and Roger Shumann's sacrifice takes place far away from any altar. The only "god" in the book might be the pylon itself, the phallic object that perversely transforms the flight into racing and reinforces the stunning visual aspect of the show. One could say that the two pylons are the grand priests of the god for whom Roger dies, that is, the God of the Gaze or, in Jean Duvignaud's words, "the leader-god of the marionette-hero."[4]

There are two main aspects of the show in *Pylon:* the suspense of the story and, therefore, a linear continuity, and the brilliant moments of the show that captivate the reader and in fact isolate him from the story. One might extend this comparison by juxtaposing the word "pylon" as signifier, with the phallic object and focal point as signified. The air show takes place against the backdrop of a ground show: the Mardi Gras parade, Grandlieu Street, the whole tawdry pageant of the (dreary) city festival, with streets littered with rubbish and confetti, without mirth, without even a crowd. The earthly, horizontal show is not part of a festival but part of the bitter aftermath of a festival. This is especially true of chapter three, "Night in the Vieux Carré."

Verticality is the other spatial dimension. From the beginning we are struck by phrases such as "the upgazing motionless bodies" (38; 36) or the description of the four machines flying in a circle just before the accident: "The noise was faint now and disseminated; the drowsy afternoon was domed with it and the four machines seemed to hover like dragonflies silently in vacuum, in various distance softened shades of pastel against the ineffable blue, with now a quality trivial, random, almost like notes of music—a harp, say—as the sun glinted and lost them" (233; 238). The correspondence between the sky and the hangar is quite explicit:

> Now the first starting bomb went—a jarring thud followed by a vicious light repercussion as if the bomb had set off another smaller one in the now empty hangar and in the rotunda too. Within the domed steel vacuum the single report became myriad, high and everywhere about the concave ceiling like invisible unearthly winged creatures of that yet unvisioned tomorrow, mechanical instead of blood bone and meat, speaking to one another in vicious highpitched ejaculations as though concerting an attack on something below. (25; 22)

This is not so very different from what is commonly called a hallucination. Looking forward one feels that the description contains the germ of the apocalyptic vision of a mechanical future that Faulkner was to develop, fifteen years later, in his celebrated Nobel Prize acceptance speech and, again, in *A Fable:*

> . . . when the last ding-dong of doom has clanged and faded from the last worthless rock hanging tideless in the last red and dying evening, that even then there will still be one more sound: that of his puny inexhaustible voice, still talking (ESPL, 120).
> . . . to watch the final two of them engaged in the last gigantic wrestling against the final and dying sky robbed even of darkness and filled with the inflectionless uproar of the two mechanical voices bellowing at each other polysyllabic and verbless patriotic nonsense. (FAB, 354)

If the sky in *Pylon* is one of the two settings of the narrative, it also occupies an exalted place in Faulkner's imagination. Two observations follow from this fact. In *Pylon* is to be found the apotheosis of the erotic ideal that is now familiar to us, from the early poems to *The Sound and the Fury* by way of *Soldiers' Pay*. Usually associated in Faulkner's fiction with the earth and even with a perversion of the pastoral—where every copse conceals a peeping Tom—the sexual act, now airborne, takes on the dazzling though paradoxical character of having escaped from the fall. However, if this is true, then it is equally logical that this novel should be the one in which we find the dramatic climax of the "dying fall": it is as if this literary theory now has become literally true.[5]

These conclusions serve to illustrate, again, that there are two Faulkners: one is Baudelaire-like, a writer who cannot tolerate—but dwells on—the "ludicrous posturings" of sexual intercourse, the other is Mallarméan, a writer stricken with the "*maladie d'idéalité*," who feels compelled to stage his ideal love scene in the azure sky.

The story can be divided into two parts: before Shumann's mortal accident (chapters 1–4) and after the accident (chapters 5–7). In the first part the motif of sight virtually replaces psychology. Jiggs, for example, is not fascinated by airplanes but by boots. The latter are associated with images of airplanes from the very first page. But because of the boots' "unblemished and inviolate implication of horse and spur," that is, their association with objects of male fetishism (also corroborated by the name Shu-mann), one can say that they correspond, albeit in diametrical opposition, to the central object-fetish, the airplane: "Waspwaisted, wasplight, still, trim, vicious, small and immobile, they seemed to poise without weight, as though made of paper for the sole purpose of resting upon the shoulders of the dungareeclad men about them" (18–19; 15). "The six aeroplanes rested like six motionless wasps, the slanting sun glinting on their soft bright paint and on the faint propellerblurs" (30; 27).

In the reporter's mouth the imagery is explicit: "Around the home pylon on one wingtip *and the fabric trembling like a bride*" (47; 44; my emphasis). This comparison is decisive, especially as it is followed by an evocation of "the rest of them, the wives and children and mechanics, standing on the apron and watching like they might have been stole out of a department store window" (47; 44–45).

Thus, the structure of the glance has come full circle: Jiggs, who looks like a horse, is clearly the latest avatar of the centaur, and the reporter's relationship with the airplanes recalls no less clearly the early male heroes' relationship with whatever is epicene. Both are associated, as perverts, by their fetish. According to Jean Baudrillard, "it is not the passion of substances which is expressed [in fetishism], but the passion of the code"; it is not the fascination of a force which is exerted, but that of a form: "Something like a desire, like a perverse desire, the desire of the code, shows itself here."[6] Joyce McDougal adds: "Fetishism is the prototype of all perverse formations, because it shows in an exemplary way the manner in which the emptiness left by the denial and negation of the truth is filled afterwards. In a way, it is an act of great lucidity."[7]

Can one speak of the lucidity acquired by Faulkner in *Pylon,* a lucidity that might thus become the key to the enigma of why the novel was—had to be—written as a break from the composition of *Absalom, Absalom!?* I have already noted the peculiar tone Faulkner employed when, on 7 March 1957, he answered one of the rare questions about the novel—as if, in evoking both the stunt flyers and their machines, he had been speaking about insects (which is the final comparison).

But who is the one "who never did tell [Faulkner] who he was" (LITG, 132)—this uncouth character, who has no other name but the nickname of "Lazarus" (33; 30), whose face is like "a Halloween mask on a boy's stick being slowly withdrawn" (50; 47), whose eyes "look like holes burned with a poker in a parchment diploma, some postgraduate certificate of excess" (134; 135), and are "like two spots of dying daylight caught by water at the bottom of abandoned wells" (135; 136)? Who is he, indeed, if not the archetypal victim of fascination? (The same could be said of Quentin Compson in *Absalom, Absalom!* In his case, however, the hall of mirrors is replaced by a hall of voices. One may indeed imagine that the writing of *Pylon* had purged Faulkner of the hell of fascination, thus allowing him to concentrate on language—particularly on the spoken word.)

The way in which each character in *Pylon* uses his sight is described by an adjective: *hot* for Jiggs, *pale* or *cold* for Laverne (like Charlotte in *The Wild Palms*), *bleak* for both the parachutist and Shumann (like Bayard in *Sartoris*). In this respect the reporter, however, has no eyes (much like Darl in *As I Lay Dying*): he is a sustained glance. The reporter's "curious glazed expression like that of one who has not slept much lately" (78; 77) conveys to Jiggs a "shocked immobility." Later, the reporter is seen "lying sprawled in the door with his eyes open and quiet and profoundly empty—that vision without contact with mind or thought, like two dead electric bulbs set into his skull" (122; 123). Even Popeye in *Sanctuary* has more expression in his eyes than this, although Popeye, too, has something "electric" about him.

Just as *The Sound and the Fury* can be thought of as an "ordeal of consciousness,"[8] so *Pylon,* as it develops through the reporter's narrative, can be thought of as an "ordeal of sight." The theme runs parallel to the Lazarus theme of premature burial and resurrection. "Hell," for the fascinated reporter, begins at the end of the chapter entitled "Tomorrow": "that face which the few hours of violent excess had altered from that of one brightly and peacefully dead to that of one coming back from, or looking out of, hell itself" (138–39).

For the reporter, the surprise, the outrage, and the failure, already noted in previous chapters, take the form of a betrayal of the sense of sight itself. Here is the optical nightmare of a fascinated person:

> He held the key in his hand now while the door clicked behind him, standing for a moment longer with his eyes shut against the impact of light, of the thin sun, and then opening them, steadying himself against the doorframe where he had slept, remembering the coffee which the negress had made and he had forgot about until now, while the alley swam away into mirageshapes, tilting like the sea or say the lake surface, against which the ordeal of destination, of hope and dread, shaped among the outraged nerves of vision the bright vague pavilion glitter beneath the whipping purple-and-gold pennons. (139; 140)

When he comes to the airport, everything is a "mirage" (141); he stares at the program of the show in a stupor: "He continued to look at the page long after the initial impact of optical surprise had faded" (142; 143). In the restaurant "he seemed to watch himself creeping slowly and terrifically across the plate like a mole, blind to all else and deaf now even to the amplifyer" (143; 145). With "cringing eyeballs" or "while his eyeballs still throbbed" (145; 146) he at last confronts his opposite, Jiggs, with his "hot impenetrable eyes, the membrane and fiber netting and webbing the unrecking and the undismayed" (148; 149).

This is where the author gives what I take to be the clue to the ultimate meaning of *Pylon*—the play on the word *organ* (organ of sight, organ as a synonym for newspaper) that could have been expected from the beginning. Just before the accident, when we learn that Shumann is in trouble, the reporter begins to run:

> . . . it was as though all the faces, all the past twenty-four hours' victories and defeats and hopes and renunciations and despairs, had been blasted completely out of his life as if they had actually been the random sheets of that organ to which he dedicated his

days, caught momentarily upon one senseless member of the
scarecrow which he resembled, and then blown away. A moment
later . . . he saw the aeroplane lying on its back, the undercarriage
projecting into the air rigid and delicate and motionless as the legs
of a dead bird. (163–64; 165–66)

In other words, the reporter now finds himself in the same relationship of
fascination as that which binds Popeye and Horace at the beginning of
Sanctuary. The comparison of the wrecked plane with a dead bird—which
may recall the lovebird which Popeye cut alive with scissors—implies that
the glance is like an act of murder.

The first person to attract the reporter's eye, Laverne is the embodiment
of desire. It is perfectly logical, in both psychological and symbolic terms,
that Faulkner's Venus should be born from the sky just as Botticelli's is born
from the sea. When the reporter, "like a scarecrow in a gale," runs toward
the wreck after Laverne, Faulkner uses four words that readers of *The
Sound and the Fury* will remember as being associated with Benjy's desire
for his sister Caddy: "the bright plain shape of love" (235; 240).[9]

The second person the reporter notices is Shumann. He is the eternal rival
as well as the father figure, who also cultivates a fetishistic relationship with
his epicene airplane. The airplane is opposed to the "bright plain shape of
love," just as Patricia was opposed to Jenny in *Mosquitoes*.

Between the hellish chapter "Tomorrow" and the chapter entitled "Lovesong of J. A. Prufrock," the reporter's gaze is gradually emptied of everything: at the beginning of "And Tomorrow," as he looks at the two heroes,
Shumann and Ord, "his eyes seemed to watch them without looking at
either, as though they actually were armed invaders" (168; 170); as he
walks along with Ord, we are told how different they are ("the one volatile,
irrational, with his ghostlike quality . . . the other singlepurposed, fatally
and grimly without any trace of introversion" (171; 174). And yet "Walking, they seemed to communicate by some means or agency the purpose, the
disaster, toward which without yet being conscious of it apparently, they
moved" (172; 174).

From this point of view the climax of the novel occurs on the eve of the
fatal day, during the reporter's "absence." After lending his apartment to
the outrageous trio, the reporter is described in an unforgettable way:

The cab moved on. Through the back window Shumann saw the reporter standing at the curb in the glare of the two unmistakable pariah-green globes on either side of the entrance, still, gaunt, the garments which hung from the skeleton frame seeming to stir faintly and steadily even when and where there was no wind, as though having chosen that one spot out of the entire sprawled and myriad city he stood there without impatience or design: patron (even if no guardian) saint of all waifs, all the homeless the desperate and the starved. (183; 186)[10]

Laverne and Shumann sleep together, for the last time, at the reporter's place, in his very bed. Next comes the flashback—eight crucial pages at the center of the onionlike structure of the novel[11]—which the reader cannot but interpret as the reporter's hallucination. To "see"—as a double voyeur peeping at his own hallucination—the sublime and grotesque scene in which Laverne actually makes love to Shumann in full flight is to undergo the most exquisite torture imaginable in Faulkner's hell. It is also a "vision" that symbolically sentences Shumann to death. This night of passion takes place in the same mental theater as that which served for Oedipus's blinding, the murky theater of the unconscious, lit up by the imaginary gratification of repressed desires. This is the only known occasion when Faulkner described the male sexual organ: "the bereaved, the upthrust, the stalk: the annealed rapacious heartshaped crimson bud" (196; 199).

After being abandoned by his "friends," the reporter, cadaverous, spectral, disembodied, goes to his newspaper. There, he falls back, as he must, into the infernal circle of professional voyeurs, of journalists who work at night under green lampshades—much as did Byron Snopes, old Bayard Sartoris's accountant, at his stool in the bank.[12] Now, "wildfaced, gaunt and sunkeneyed from lack of sleep and from strain" (217; 221), the reporter only has to wait for the fatal event, while repeating what he has already told his editor: " 'That's it,' he thought quietly, with that faint quiet grimace almost like smiling; 'they aint human. It aint adultery; you can't anymore imagine two of them making love than you can two of them airplanes back in the corner of the hangar, coupled' " (231; 236). A second instance of the metonymic exchange, already noted, occurs here: if the airplane wings tremble like a bride, the pilot's bones are only "little rockerarms and connecting rods," and his blood is "cylinder oil" (231; 236). In fact, the death of Roger Shumann will only leave a spot of oil on the lake—and a spot of ink in the newspapers. But has the reporter understood that if oil runs in Shumann's veins, ink runs in his own? Contrary to all of Faulkner's former novels, no blood actually runs in *Pylon,* which may be why it feels like an "evil," inhuman novel—one that hardly pleased anybody in America. And yet *Pylon* may well provide us with the key to Faulkner's imagination.

The obsessive voyeurism of the first part of the novel ends with the death of the pilot. It gives way, in "Lovesong of J. A. Prufrock," to a slow, laborious reconstruction of the world, which is achieved through the use of artificial eyes (flashlights and electric projectors), of the sinister, imperturbable, omnipresent yellow, lidless eye of the lighthouse, of eyes spying into the automobiles, and, finally, of the sun itself, now shining for the first time in four days. With the sunlight life comes back and eyes begin to function again. I have already pointed out how the novel ends on the same kind of image as it began with. What one witnesses in the interim is the exhumation of Lazarus as the reporter returns to the light and to his "savagely bright" lodgings:

> In the corridor he quit blinking, and on the stairs too: but no sooner had he entered the room with the sun coming into the windows . . . he began to blink again, with that intent myopic bemusement. He seemed to await the office of something outside himself before he moved and closed the jalousies before the window. It was better then because for a while he could not see at all; he just stood there in some ultimate distillation of the savage bright neartropical day, not knowing now whether he was still blinking or not, in an implacable infiltration which not even walls could stop. (262; 269)

Later, heading toward the airport, still ignoring Jiggs's pertinent advice to get "some shuteye," (282; 289)[13] the reporter looks behind him through the back window of his taxi and perceives "the city, the glare of it, no further away" than "the sense of being suspended in a small airtight glass box clinging by two puny fingers of light in the silent and rushing immensity of space" (283; 291)—an "illusion" reminiscent of Horace Benbow's hallucination at the end of chapter twenty-three of *Sanctuary.* He cannot rid himself of this image: "It [the city] would be there—the eternal smell of the coffee the sugar the hemp sweating slow among the plates . . .—tomorrow and tomorrow and tomorrow; not only not to hope, not even to wait: just to endure" (284; 292). What the reporter runs away from is home, in Faulkner's fiction something always equivalent to a womb, a place which seldom connotes happiness, but that is a symbol of stability and endurance, a "horizontal" virtue which later became an antidote to the tragic verticality of man.

In the epilogue, which is again set at night, the scavengers (or the four evangelists, "four in overcoats with upturned collars")[14] seem to switch from seeing to saying (they are professionals of the Word). The motionless reporter even declines to drink: is this a watch before the resurrection or just a wake for Shumann? In the morning, blinking beneath the sun, the reporter seems to be about to come to terms with the whole airborne spectacle, just as Jiggs did with his own fetish by pawning his boots in order to leave a present for Laverne and her son. The change can be explained by a key word which appears after the drunken reporter arrives at the newspaper and cries: " 'Oh God, I feel better! I feel better! I feel! I feel!' until he quit that too and said quietly, looking at the familiar wall, the familiar twin door through which he was about to pass, with tragic and passive clairvoyance: 'Something is going to happen to me. I have got myself stretched out too far and too thin and something is going to bust' " (300; 309). He is still trying to see: " 'I see so little of it,' he said. 'I dont know the family's habits yet' " (301; 309). Is this grim humor? Only if the phrase is taken out of context. As long as the words are understood as belonging to a sequence of actions, we are justified in reading them as part of the process which leads the reporter back to humanity.

The reporter undergoes a kind of fantasy agony, by imagining himself in the place of Shumann, "having to lie there too and look up at the wreath dissolving, faintly rocking and stared at by gulls" (301; 309). But he slips again from guilt to desire, this time in a ludicrously bourgeois way: he imagines himself holding Laverne by her arm, some fourteen years later. Then he has his second vision.

Laverne arrives at Dr. Shumann's, where she leaves her son so that he will have a home, she herself being pregnant with another child who is not the doctor's grandson; the scene of Laverne's visit to the Shumanns seems to be opposed thematically to the erotic hallucination of chapter 5. If one admits, as one can hardly fail to do, that this scene (302–13; 310–22) is perceived, indeed "written," by the reporter himself, thanks to the clairvoyance he has recently acquired, then one must admit that the central character of this novel, devoid of any other psychology, ends up by acquiring compassion. Thus, the novel concludes with a scene in which Shumann's parents, whose only wish is for "peace"—not for "equity" or "justice," not even for "happiness," just for "peace"—suddenly see destiny intrude in the form of a young pregnant woman. The same happens when Byron Bunch intrudes on Hightower in *Light in August* or when Harry Wilbourne barges in on the old doctor in *The Wild Palms*. There *is* something fantastic about pregnancy in Faulkner.

The reporter thus triumphs over a merely optical illusion, which is the focus of a desire whose frightening "purity" verges on inhumanity and leads him to fantasy murder. He triumphs over this thanks to a comprehensive vision of the human condition. One might even say that, after having tried very hard to escape his own home, he understands the necessity of a home through imagining Laverne's return to Roger's hometown in Ohio. He experiences most, if not all, of the Faulknerian ills: frustration, impotence, alcoholism, the tyranny of the sight, and, finally, the catastrophe that leads to suffering and enables him to rediscover his humanity. He thus acquires in extremis the capacity to write "the sentences and paragraphs which he believed to be not only news but the beginning of literature" (314; 323).

By a final "savage" irony this first version of the reporter's account of Roger Shumann's "Last Pylon" only finds one reader, the copyboy who, while salvaging what lies in the wastebasket, looks with eyes "big with excitement and exultation through downright triumph" (314; 323). Hagood, the editor, is simply not interested in "the beginning of literature." What will probably be printed is the much more matter-of-fact second version of the reporter's account, which the editor finds on his desk, and which contains a glaring lie: "Mrs Shumann departed with her husband and children for Ohio, where it is understood that their six year old son will spend an indefinite time with some of his grandparents and where any and all finders of Roger Shumann are kindly requested to forward any and all of same" (315; 324). In the meantime, with the hero of the reporter's worship thus relegated to the rank of a lost object, the reporter can leave a note written "savagely in pencil," in which he tells his superior (Ha-*God?*) that he is going on a drinking binge which François Pitavy is probably right in interpreting as a "mock suicide" ("*un simulacre de suicide*"). The last words of the novel, in the reporter's hand, are loaded with as many possible meanings as the final dots make possible: "*I am on a credit. . . .*"

Reynolds Price, who even doubts whether *Pylon* is a novel, is certainly right when he asks, at the end of a remarkably perceptive essay: "Why do Orators (even the reporter) adore the Heroes (even these three, so tawdry and small)?"[15] But Pitavy is even more persuasive when he relates the harsh nature of *Pylon* to the difficulty Faulkner had in writing *Absalom, Absalom!:* "Perhaps *Pylon* is not a novel, but a question that Faulkner had to raise in order to legitimate the extraordinary ambition displayed in *Absalom, Absalom!. Pylon* is not an answer but a questioning of literature. Or rather, it is the question which answers the problems raised by *Absalom, Absalom!:* this is why the book remains as it were suspended, without a final period."[16]

chapter fourteen

The Metaphor of
the Subject

The most desirable mode of existence might be that of a
spiritualized Paul Pry, hovering invisible round man and
woman, witnessing their deeds, searching into their hearts,
borrowing brightness from their felicity, and shade from their
sorrow, and retaining no emotion peculiar to himself.

—*Nathaniel Hawthorne*, "Sights from a Steeple"

The preceding analyses tend to demonstrate the existence in Faulkner's oeuvre of a veritable anthropology of the effects of the glance. It would certainly be plausible to infer from them a basically evil central fantasy, the Eye of God. But to do so would consist only in drawing a kind of mathematical—or even statistical—conclusion out of the series of examples. In fact, the central fantasy in itself possesses the primordial attributes of necessity and identity. It is what gives Faulkner's greatest works their imaginative convulsiveness. However, saying this does not mean that the central fantasy is not *also* a construction, controlled by a consummate artist.

The diptych *Sartoris/Sanctuary* suffices to demonstrate the intolerable presence of a hidden but watchful God in Faulkner's fiction. The two works reveal two kinds of forces, one active and the other passive, which characterize what could be called the Metaphor of the Subject, that is, the symbolic projection of one of the writer's most recurrent fantasies in his fiction. This is what I want to examine by way of closing.

Recalling the introductory remarks on Faulkner's choice, we can perhaps now reintroduce the category of the "actual" in its simplest (particularly biographical) sense, next to the Lacanian categories of the "imagi-

nary" and the "symbolic." I will, therefore, begin with a set of three
"theses."

    1. In Oxford, from 1925 to 1950, Faulkner was immobile (the actual).

    2. Popeye at the spring is always immobile (the imaginary).

    3. In Faulkner's fiction God is equally immobile (the symbolic).

A phrase from Sartre's analysis of idealism reads: "Perpetually, wherever I
may be, I am being looked at" (B&N, 282). "Even as I want Evil for Evil's
sake, I try to comtemplate divine transcendence, whose own possibility is
Good, as a purely given transcendence which I transcend towards Evil.
Thus I make God 'suffer,' I 'irritate' Him, etc. These attempts, which imply
the absolute *recognition* of God as a subject who cannot be an object, are
pregnant with contradictions, and can only prove to be a continuous
failure" (B&N, 290).

How does the subject, that is, the symbolic projection of the writer's
consciousness in his fiction, manifest itself in Faulkner's work? Essentially
through a metaphor that is repeated from novel to novel, sometimes alive,
sometimes "dead," sometimes explicit, sometimes concealed, and often
varying according to the representation of God in a given work. For example, one cannot expect the same manifestation of God in a "pagan" novel
like *The Hamlet* as in a novel like *Light in August,* in which Faulkner makes
explicit use of institutionalized religion. But there is a general tendency
toward the association of the syllable "God" with whatever is found to be
intolerable in the artist's representation of life.

Consider the following attributes of the authority that serves as "God" in
Faulkner's fiction: it is sinister, implacable, unforeseeable; above all, it is
impersonal, ubiquitous and entirely impervious. Faulkner's God is not
essentially an aspect of time; it is not a philosophical God. In Faulkner's
fiction God is always more or less an effect of man's imagination; therefore,
it is first and foremost a category of space. The world is like Keats's urn,
offered for man's perusal by an authority that remains unseen, but whose
presence is always implied in the act of human perusal. Here we are at the
very center of the paradox of the "absolute relationship" that characterizes
Faulkner's very peculiar mode of dramatization. This is the quality that
Mayoux called his "intensity."

As Jean Paris has pointed out, "the nostalgia for an absolute Gaze
embracing all space, encircling all ages, subjugating all beings, does not

only illuminate innumerable legends, it forces us to reconsider the design of every painting."[1] Faulkner said as much, albeit innocently, when he said: "To me, a proof of God is in the firmament, the stars" (LITG, 103). What is the firmament—"the vault or arch of the sky, the orb of the fixed stars" (Webster)—if not a canvas, a painting? Does it not imply the point of view of an onlooker from below? One need only recall the recurrence of the image of the star in both his poetry and early fiction to realize how personal this remark in 1955 actually was.

Indeed, what are the names given to God in Faulkner's fiction? The Supreme Player (*Sartoris*); the Judge or Umpire (*Absalom, Absalom!*); the cosmic Joker, the supreme Manipulator (*The Wild Palms*), the maniacal Laugher (*The Hamlet*), the immortal Arbiter (*Go Down, Moses*)—in short, the Stage Manager (*Absalom, Absalom!*).[2] If everything on the Faulknerian stage appears as a déjà vu, it is because everything there, including the pleasures of the earth and of the flesh, is and has always been stolen by human glances from the lidless eye of the universal voyeur.

Let us now look at the two aspects of the metaphor of the subject introduced in the diptych *Sartoris/Sanctuary*. The first is the passive aspect, as found in old Bayard's meditation over his trunk of memories: "Fatality; the augury of a man's destiny peeping out at him from the roadside hedge, if he but recognize it." The reminiscence of the panting child's escape from the Yankee cavalry patrol and his hiding by "a spring he knew flowed from the roots of a beech tree" follow immediately: "and as he leaned his mouth to it the final light of day was reflected onto his face, bringing into sharp relief forehead and nose above the cavernous sockets of his eye and the panting animal snarl of his teeth, and from the still water there stared back at him for a sudden moment, a skull" (*Flags*, 82; slightly different version in SAR, 93). "What is this strange, suspended, oblique object in the foreground. . . . What? A skull" (FFCP, 88): one might think he has been reading Lacan's analysis of Hans Holbein's famous anamorphosis in *The Ambassadors*.[3] The symbolism is thrust down our throats. There is no ambiguity or subtlety—the author "objectifies" the symbols as an event in the narrative—so that life is identified as a stroll along a safe stretch of road until the stroller stumbles upon what has always been lying in wait for him, behind the hedge. We sense here the anticipation of some unknown, always lurking power: the unknown comes by definition as a surprise. With Faulkner the surprise is always fatal, or at least loaded with portents. One can understand why Malraux felt that this was the world of the "irremediable."[4]

Faulkner's world is also, however, the world of imminent disaster: Everything seems to be threatened by something as irremediably ancient as Greek tragedy or of something impending like nuclear catastrophe.[5] Why? The question has no answer outside the work in which it is posed. But the question, once posed, casts a new light on Malraux's overrepeated, bombastic final formula: "*Sanctuary* is the intrusion of Greek tragedy into the detective novel." In fact, the statement has a meaning even outside the genres to which it seems limited. What strikes me as important is to recognize what Faulkner gained by his obsession with what I have called the ambush motif, the image of "the augury of man's destiny peeping out at him from the roadside hedge." This haunting, ghostlike image can even be said to lie at the origin of an intensely personal, not to say eccentric, understanding of the history—and mythology—of the Western world. In particular, Faulkner must have detected a deep continuity in moral, physical, and psychological *vision* from Sophocles's Oedipus to, say, Alfred Hitchcock's *Rear Window*.[6]

Although such an awareness of threat gave rise, especially in *Sanctuary*, to a kind of exhibitionist impulse that Faulkner later censured, it is probably not enough to say that *Sanctuary* differs from earlier novels to the extent that Faulkner decided to make a decisive gesture toward his public.[7] What he did, in fact, was to go one step further in expressing his fantasy nightmare.[8] In *Sanctuary*, he later wrote in the Modern Library introduction, he "invented the most horrific tale [he] could imagine." By this he meant the rape with a corncob. What role does this rape play imaginatively, if not that of the gratification of the most perverted desire? However, Jason Compson and Flem Snopes share with Popeye what Faulkner admitted to be their inhumanity (FITU, 132). At least in Popeye's and Flem's cases (if not also in Jason's), this has clearly something to do with substituting eyes for sexual organs.

The overriding obsession in Faulkner's fiction is the presence of a lidless, ubiquitous eye. To emulate this eye is certainly to partake of evil. As Horace Benbow says to Aunt Jenny, "Dammit, say what you want to, but there's a corruption about even looking upon evil, even by accident; you cannot haggle, traffic, with putrefaction—" (SAN, 152; CT, 134). With Faulkner, Captain Ahab's celebrated curse ("the inscrutable thing is chiefly what I hate") is still frightening even when placed in a psychological rather than cosmic context. In his fiction the intuition of evil comes from the awareness that one cannot see the eye that looks at one. What infuriates Horace Benbow is the mechanism of corruption, the way it operates passively, independent of whether one acts or does not act.

This clarifies why Faulkner liked the fable of "the trinity of conscience" that he extracted from Ahab's three lieutenants on the *Pequod*. He spoke of this for the first time in an interview in 1954, the year when *A Fable* was published. A year later, Faulkner returned to this "parable," still with reference to *A Fable*, but citing this time its origin in *Moby-Dick*. What he meant was that there were three possible attitudes before evil: "knowing nothing, knowing but not caring, knowing and caring" (LITG, 247). For our purpose "knowing" can be replaced by "seeing." The problem had already been clearly posed in this exchange between Horace and Miss Jenny—

> "I cannot stand idly by and see injustice—"
> "You wont ever catch up with injustice, Horace," Miss Jenny said.
> "Well, that irony which lurks in events, then." (SAN, 141; CT 123)

—in which Horace repeatedly strikes the visual metaphor.

One cannot be the spectator of Evil—whether it is called injustice or corruption—without being an accomplice. There is a faltering, a "haggling" or equivocation in the act of sight. To look is neither to participate nor not to participate. It is participation inchoate, desire satisfied only by proxy. Leaving Miss Reba's brothel, where he has just heard Temple's confession, before returning home where he hallucinates about the picture of Little Belle, Horace gives a kind of summary of Faulkner's perception of evil down to *Pylon* (references to earlier works are included between brackets):

> Better for her [Temple Drake] if she were dead tonight, Horace thought, walking on. For me, too. He thought of her, Popeye, the woman, the child, Goodwin, all put into a single chamber, bare, lethal, immediate and profound: a single blotting instant between the indignation and the surprise [Quentin in *The Sound and the Fury*]. And I too; thinking how that were the only solution. Removed, cauterised out of the old and tragic flank of the world.

And I, too, now that we're all isolated; thinking of a gentle dark wind blowing in the long corridors of sleep [*A Green Bough*]; of lying beneath a low cozy roof under the long sound of the rain [Darl in *As I Lay Dying*]: the evil, the injustice, the tears. In an alley-mouth two figures stood, face to face, not touching; the man speaking in a low tone unprintable epithet after epithet in a caressing whisper, the woman motionless before him as though in a musing swoon of voluptuous ecstasy [*Mosquitoes*, Epilogue, 9]. Perhaps it is upon the instant that we realise, admit, that there is a logical pattern to evil, that we die, he thought, thinking of the expression he had once seen in the eyes of a dead child, and of other dead: the cooling indignation, the shocked despair fading, leaving two empty globes in which the motionless world lurked profoundly in miniature. (SAN, 265–66; CT, 232)

This can be called a description of passive evil. The evil in *Sanctuary*, though, is an active kind, which is illustrated by the other metaphor. One finds it in chapter 2 of the original version, just before Horace reaches the spring: "The night before he told her [his sister Narcissa]: 'There's no hurry. You cant break into ten years like a footpad in an alley crashing into the fatuous moment of an oblivious pedestrian'" (STOT, 20–21). Miss Jenny is right, of course: there is "an irony which lurks in events," since, a minute later, Popeye does indeed intrude on Horace as he drinks at the spring. It is this image of intrusion, this subtle act of agression, that is not so very different from the first, rather static image of someone peeping at someone from behind a hedge. In both cases, whether by a glance or by a gesture, the unsuspecting innocent individual is violated. Moreover, the person who cannot recognize the voyeur in the hedge is no less to blame than the person who thinks that only other people suffer such acts of agression. Most of Faulkner's male heroes are innocent because none of them is ever ready for the encounter with evil.

It is in this sense that many of his characters are "doomed" when they are not, like Caddy, "damned." They are incapable of winning a struggle because they have lost it in advance. They are always taken by surprise, even though they expect to be surprised. Faulkner's characters parade in front of the subject in the same way as Caesar's prisoners were made to march in front of him, and cry out: *Morituri te salutant*.

That Faulkner's supreme authority is this universal voyeur can be demonstrated by one more argument, this time outside his fiction. It is to be found in one of his most powerful essays, written during the years after the Nobel Prize, when he became a public figure. In the first of the two chapters he wrote for a projected but unfinished book called *The American Dream*, it is clear that one topic more than any other puts him in a righteous frenzy, and this is privacy: to him, pure, unadulterated evil lies in the violation of the individual's privacy: "This was the American Dream: a sanctuary on the earth for individual man: a condition in which he could be free not only of the old established closed-corporation hierarchies of arbitrary power which had oppressed him as a mass, but free of that mass into which the hierarchies of church and state had compressed and held him individually thralled and individually impotent" ("On Privacy," ESPL, 62). The polarization as regards the individual is clear enough: at one extreme is the country which gave the individual a "sanctuary" by protecting his rights as nowhere else in history, and by safeguarding him from all kinds of totalitarianism, and at the other are the two great institutions of the Old World: the church and the state, the tyrannical authorities that are magnified when combined instead of being separated. Note how the inevitable corollary of collective, institutional power is, for Faulkner, individual impotence.

Next Faulkner analyzes the decline of the dream. One might quote the whole of this essay, so completely does it illuminate the fiction. But what brings about the decline, what is the "something which upset the dream"? Boldly, Faulkner attributes the vast continental decline he has just described to a cause, "a symptom," which was in reality only a minor episode in his life, that is, the interview that *Life* magazine finally obtained from him. After opposing "good taste" and "bad taste" (that is, watered-down or polite ways of expressing the categories of good and evil), Faulkner writes:

> The point is that in America today any organization or group, simply by functioning under a phrase like Freedom of the Press or National Security or League Against Subversion, can postulate to itself complete immunity to violate the individualness—the individual privacy lacking which he cannot be an individual and lacking which individuality he is not anything at all worth the having or the keeping—of anyone who is not himself a member of

some organization or group numerous enough or rich enough to frighten them off. (ESPL, 70)

Faulkner gives three examples of the intrusiveness of publicity and of the aggressiveness of public curiosity—of the violation of the private by the public: the kidnapping of the Lindbergh child, the trial of Dr. Oppenheimer, and the case of a doctor from Cleveland who was charged with killing his wife.

One need not pursue the specific points raised here nor what is so typically American about them. What is more important is the fact that, behind their resentful rhetoric, they provide us with yet another illustration of what can now be called—without any obscurity, I hope—the tyranny of the gaze according to William Faulkner. Indeed, the words that might be used to paraphrase this indignant diatribe could well be those used in the analyses above: the jealously guarded right to privacy; the horror of theft, blackmail, voyeurism, and rape—all of which come from the same impulse to negate the other's privacy; outrage (unbelief); surprise (*Life* magazine's insistence upon the interview), pained astonishment (the end of the dream); failure of a sort, too, insofar as Faulkner does not conceal that he loses his equanimity when confronted by the *organs* of public life—newspapers, magazines, and the like. In brief, we are still in *Pylon,* with its dehumanized world of "scavengers," where only oil flows—and ink. *Pylon* was indeed the expression of Faulkner's hell.

At the stage at which we are leaving the analysis of sight and vision in Faulkner's fiction, we have to note that certain things still remain obscure. Among these, there is one problem that provokes the most contradictory opinions. This is the problem of how one evaluates Faulkner's own remarks about his work. For some Faulkner is, by definition, always the best judge of his own work. For others, who believe that the meaning of a work of art, once it has entered history, lies beyond the writer, Faulkner is not necessarily a good judge. To me the truth of the matter seems to lie not so much between these two extremes as on a different level. A good example is offered by his well-known statement, from the 1955 interview with Jean Stein Vanden Heuvel, about "life is motion"—a statement all too often quoted out of context:

> Life is not interested in good and evil. . . . Since people exist only in life, they must devote their time simply to being alive. Life is motion and motion is concerned with what makes man move—which are ambition, power, pleasure. What time man can devote to morality, he must take by force from the motion of which he is a part. He is compelled to make choices between good and evil sooner or later. Because that moral conscience demands from him in order that he can live with himself tomorrow. His moral conscience is the curse he had to accept from the Gods in order to gain from them the right to dream. (LITG, 252–53)

What is Faulkner talking about—now, from a "pinnacle" raised up by thirty years' work—if not, once more, about the triangle of evil, the glance, and immobility? By this time he had shaken off the obsession with fascination and was speaking from a point of view outside of the oeuvre. He had acquired a distance from his own material, and he had finally accepted the facts of his own life: to write is to condemn oneself to immobility. He had accepted the fact that literary discourse is not life. Life is indeed movement, if only because stasis is death. This attitude demonstrated the realization he had come to, not through some Bergsonian revelation, but through reflection on the story of his own life—and work: if to write is to die to life, then there is a dangerous, an evil potential in writing. This potential could take two forms, both tragic: one is suicidal; the other is what Clément Rosset has called the logic of the worst.[9]

What Faulkner refers to in this truly autobiographical passage, then, is not so much the problems raised in literature as the problems writing poses to the writer as a person. And yet he does not talk as a moralist. He only expresses an idea as banal as the analogy between immobility and death: morality is always something imposed, something that goes against movement. What Faulkner is proposing here, after all, is as much an ethic as an aesthetic. Taken in isolation, all of these propositions are truisms or banalities—except the last one, which depends on the context, just as "life is motion" does. To the sound principle of the radical difference between art and life, Faulkner adds the no less sound principle of conduct as a kind of economy: in his own, simple words, "What time man can devote to morality, he must take by force from the motion of which he is a part." If one pushes the argument far enough, there appears to be a contradiction in terms between living and being moral. Writing is something else again: who would dream, Faulkner seems on the point of asking, of questioning the morality of an immobile being like the marble faun, for instance? It would be like asking whether God (or the writer) is a moral being. This is a question that interests theologians, on the one hand, and gossip columnists, on the other, both of whom are improbable readers of Faulkner's fiction.

As for the last observation: "His moral conscience is the curse he had to accept from the Gods in order to gain . . . *the right to dream.*" The perfect construction of the sentence, and even its rhythm, conveys a sense of balance which is part of its meaning, the balance or trade-off between the curse and man's right to dream. As I have already suggested, barring suicide, Faulkner had to end his life *negotiating the intolerable.* Moral conscience is the price paid to "the gods" for our liberty and for the right to dream.[10] Moral conscience can also be seen as the part of their divinity which "the gods" force upon us in exchange for this right which they alone can confer. Or must we commit a crime and steal it from them like Prometheus? Faulkner's last words on literature were not without wisdom nor without beauty. They certainly draw on years of experience and practice. The theory behind the words is almost impalpable. The writer's right to speak is not basically different from his right to dream: it consists in making the Subject close His Eye.

Focal Point,
Vanishing Point

> Reality is the vanishing point of all languages.
> —Interview with Paul Ricoeur

Let us imagine being in the center of a room where paintings are exhibited like panels belonging to one large, folding work. One attempts to form an impression of the whole before passing on to the next room. Yet one has noted, at the end of the great folding piece, a much smaller work, itself a polyptych, set in the middle of the space between the two rooms. This is how one might describe *The Unvanquished,* a minor work linking the two main periods of Faulkner's production.

But Faulkner's work could be divided just as legitimately into three rooms, the one in the center housing not just one pivotal work, but three, from the years 1936–39: *Absalom, Absalom!, The Unvanquished, The Wild Palms*—or even six: all the major works from *Pylon* to *Go Down, Moses.* It is, after all, only a question of curatorial perspective. Like a curator, the critic may organize his exhibition as he understands the oeuvre. In Faulkner's case the essential thing is that the whole oeuvre be put together, so that his career is not thought to begin in 1929 and to end in 1942—as was the case at one time.

One point needs to be emphasized: what is true of *Pylon* is also true of most of the other novels in which one finds both narrative movement and arrested scenes or, in my terms, a linearity of reading and a polarity of fascination. Faulkner kept telling *stories* until the end. Often, his stories stretched from one book to another, though not necessarily to the next book: Horace Benbow appears in *Sartoris* and *Sanctuary;* Caddy Compson, in *The Sound and the Fury* and the "Compson Appendix"; Temple Drake in *Sanctuary* and *Requiem for a Nun;* the Snopeses in *The Hamlet,*

The Town, and *The Mansion. The Reivers* was meant to be a grand re-capitulation of the Yoknapatawpha novels. Furthermore, beginning with the map of Yoknapatawpha at the end of *Absalom, Absalom!,* Faulkner made it clear that his future writings would capitalize on what had already been published.

At the middle of Faulkner's career, however, the dynamic impulse to project his fantasies into literature was still far stronger than the later, economical need to organize this impulse. There is no lack of memorable, indeed unforgettable scenes in the work of the first half of Faulkner's career: Horace's encounter with Popeye at the spring in *Sanctuary,* Lena's walk along the road in *Light in August,* Laverne's parachute jump in *Pylon,* Sutpen's children watching their father fight Negroes in the barn in *Ab-salom, Absalom!,* the "wild" birth of the child in *The Wild Palms,* etc. One might even wonder whether most of these scenes do not imply sexuality, directly or indirectly—and even whether, in Faulkner's fiction, the fact of pregnancy is not first and foremost an effect of the gaze: consider Dewey Dell, Lena Grove, Laverne, Eula Varner . . . and Everbe Corinthia Hoggan-beck.

In *The Sound and the Fury* the most visual scenes are probably those involving Caddy and her daughter Quentin: particularly, the latter's flight from the Compson house down the pear tree or the rain pipe.[1] The most un-forgettable scenes of the novel, however, may well be far less visual, though infinitely more nostalgic: Quentin Compson's walk along the Charles River—and his meditation over the bridge as he watches the trout—and the scene on the bank of the branch where, as he played with his sister Caddy as a child, his entire future was already at stake.

I would like to devote the first part of this conclusion to some observa-tions about another, less well-known, though no less remarkable passage in *The Sound and the Fury,* a passage I have already quoted in chapter two without, however, analyzing it. It involves Quentin Compson, perhaps Faulkner's archetypal hero. Because the tone is low-key, the characteristics of Faulkner's fiction reverberate all the better. Moreover, the passage in-duces a feeling that is typical of the Faulknerian encounter: the feeling of something *unheimlich.* This feeling is somewhat paradoxical, since in this particular case, at least from Quentin's point of view, there is nothing secret, stolen, or stealthy in the scene, which is, on the contrary, remarkably open, even public:

The train was stopped when I waked and I raised the shade and looked out. The car was blocking a road crossing, *where two white fences came down a hill and then sprayed outward and downward like part of the skeleton of a horn,* and there was a nigger on a mule in the middle of the stiff ruts, waiting for the train to move. How long he had been there I didn't know, but he sat straddle of the mule, his head wrapped in a piece of blanket, *as if they had been built there with the fence and the road, or with the hill, carved out of the hill itself, like a sign put there saying You are home again.* He didn't have a saddle and his feet dangled almost to the ground. The mule looked like a rabbit. I raised the window. (TSATF, 106–7; CT, 98; my emphasis)

I have italicized the two manuscript passages added by the author in the typescript—that is, after the manuscript stage—because they help to understand how Faulkner worked. First, there is, as Malraux said, a (dramatic) "situation." This encounter begins as the archetypal hero "looks out" at his absolute opposite in social terms, a Negro. (In terms of the inner logic of Faulkner's literary creation, however, this Negro is nothing but another avatar of the tieless casual.) As far as the character and his surroundings make up a "situation" in the sense given to the word by Sartre, the situation seems to have always been there: "How long he had been there I didn't know." It is typical of Faulkner to make a character "materialize" in the midst of a déjà vu—one might even say a *toujours* déjà vu. As if to materialize the fact of the gaze as the medium of the scene, the subject and the object are separated by a window. This window plays a similar role when Jason shows Caddy her daughter from the back of a taxi. Likewise, in *Pylon* Shumann moves off in a taxi in the back window of which he sees for the last time the cadaverous-looking reporter. And in *Requiem for a Nun* Cecilia Farmer inscribes her name upon the pane of her window. These recurrent windows can be seen as the objective correlatives of writing as both an obstacle and a transparency.[2]

The familiar scene takes on an additional significance when one examines the effect of the two manuscript passages added in the typescript. The first addendum structures the scene like two brushstrokes of paint designed to draw the eye toward the visual center or focal point of a painting, here, the level crossing, which Quentin's gaze identifies as resembling "part of the skeleton of a horn." The analogy, although mainly concerned with a spatial description, is typical of an *unheimlich* feeling since it conveys an image of death. And the second manuscript addendum integrates the dimension of time, which is implicit in the notion of home no less than that of space: "How long he had been there I didn't know . . . as if they had been built there . . . carved out of the hill itself." What or rather who is involved by the repeated use of the passive mode, especially in the transition from "built there" to "carved out"? Would this not be the artist himself, here no longer a painter but a sculptor or even an architect, the architect/author of the scene itself?

Now Quentin understands the meaning of the scene for him. It becomes "like a sign put there saying *You are home again.*" Embedded here in the monologue of a character who, more than any other, is looking for himself, this message (for it is truly a message) would seem to be about literature and literature's purpose. Literature should help the reader to find himself, to feel as though in it he were "home again." At this point, however, let us not underestimate the nostalgic quality implied in the word "again." As he recalls the Southern episode in Cambridge, Massachusetts, it would seem only natural that the scene be loaded in Quentin's mind with an intolerable burden of nostalgia. Many other recollections torture him in this way. If this is not the case here, it is because Quentin makes himself the author of the scene. Particularly, the second addition, beginning as it does with the metaphoric operator "as if," expresses what is only latent in the first part of the passage: we shall say that it accomplishes the feeling of nostalgia. Quentin is thus made to articulate what he sees with his eyes into language: *You are home again.*

This is precisely what Darl cannot say in *As I Lay Dying,* he who "sits at the supper table with his eyes gone further than the food and the lamp, full of the land dug out of his skull and the holes filled with distance beyond the land" (AILD, 22; CT, 23). In this respect he differs from his brother Cash, who, by dint of language (particularly in his remarkable last but one monologue), manages to make sense out of the ordeal he and his family have just gone through. Darl is only—though superbly—capable of expressing a simple fact like *The lantern sits on a stump,* in which the words suggest a painting—an expressionist still life.

Darl's statement and Quentin's realization constitute respectively the physical and the spiritual poles of the gaze in Faulkner's fiction. In other words, the reader perceives these as respectively the *focal point* ("The lantern sits on a stump") and the *vanishing point* ("You are home again") within the same field, the *field of vision,* which is the matrix of Faulkner's fiction.

Let me now return to the three-term proposition about the actual, the imaginary, and the symbolic at the beginning of chapter fourteen.

First, there was an actual or "biographical" setting: to be in Oxford was to write. To write was to be, in a sense, immobilized. This fact was later corroborated in Faulkner's life.[3]

Second, there is the imaginary setting that the writer compulsively offers us again and again. Among the many scenes which can be called fascinating because life in them has been arrested, I shall mention once more the opening scene of *Sanctuary.* Popeye has been at the spring for an interminable moment before Horace arrives and brings with him an awareness of time. For a while, they are both immobile, like "the dead tranquil queens in stained marble" at the end of the novel. But there are many more examples of this: one of them is the scene at the end of the seventh chapter of *The Wild Palms,* in which Harry is seen sitting quite still on a bench in Audubon Park in New Orleans, as he imagines the ultimate meeting between Charlotte and her husband.

Third, there is the symbolic significance of the scene. This is where we encounter the "God" of Faulkner's fiction, the Subject brought into being by the writing itself. This Subject is also immobile.

Does this mean that Faulkner's world is just a series of frozen tableaux or that it tends to immobilize everything under a stare? As we saw in the first chapters, such a temptation existed in the early works. Indeed, the reader catches glimpses of it now and again in the later fiction: for instance, the description of the cemetery in *Absalom, Absalom!,* with its explicit references to both Oscar Wilde and Audrey Beardsley. Like Faulkner himself, some characters seem to be attracted to such "still scenes." And it may well be that if Faulkner was so fond of the leitmotif "life is motion," it was only because he was never quite free of a fascination for stasis and death. And yet, as Mayoux pointed out, his characters do retain a degree of liberty.[4] But what kind of liberty?

The best way to describe liberty in Faulkner is probably to use a theatrical analogy once again and to return to André Malraux's suggestion that

Faulkner's art, like all great tragic art, is rooted in fascination. In our terms the protagonist is doomed by what Faulkner called man's "follies"—clowning, poses and postures, attitudes—only because they inspired him both with fascination and repulsion. In other words, these "follies" exist by virtue of the intolerable, always open, ubiquitous and immobile eye. Calling them "follies" even presupposes this eye, which is not that of a moralist, but of a visionary idealist. Indeed he who says *posture* also says *imposture,* in so far as the attitude is measured against the ideal justice, the equanimous gaze common to both the Torah and the Protestant Bible. In Faulkner's fiction this ideal is embodied by characters twice removed from the various avatars of the hero, the young writer. These characters are mostly old women (Aunt Jenny, Mrs. Millard, even Rosa Coldfield, etc.) through whom the past survives in the form of the spoken word. This, I would suggest, is the symbolic reason that Faulkner chose to stay behind in Oxford, with such spokesmen and spokeswomen to back him. The back country was also a chorus of such witnesses, a landscape of mouths opened to speak.

To return to my other proposition—that there is no other hell in Faulkner's fiction than that of the author's fantasies—let me now ask the final question: can one negotiate with the intolerable? Can writing circumvent one's own worst nightmares? By the time he sent his publisher the last, typewritten chapter of *Pylon,* entitled "The Scavengers," Faulkner knew that, like the reporter who was incapable of explaining his feelings to the four newspapermen, he could never make the Subject close his eye by staring at it. *Pylon* was in this way quite conclusive: it was a dead end.

When, twenty years later, Faulkner mentioned "the right to dream" in his essay "On Privacy," he certainly no longer had in mind the searing visions and visual nightmares of the great novels from the 1920s and 1930s. He used the word "dream" in the pastoral sense, very much as it was used by Gaston Bachelard when he expressed the wish that "each of our senses may have its character and each character its scenery. In literature, the description of the setting is entirely psychological."[5]

Many plots of ground still remain to be broken in Faulknerland. We need a study of the evolution of Faulkner's landscapes—and of his descriptive techniques—from "The Hill" to *The Reivers;* another of the highly cultural, even literary Mediterranean "dream" that is often found to be superimposed on the Mississippi scenery, for instance in *Light in August.*[6] But by far the most important task, more abstract perhaps but also more encompassing, would be to analyze the progressive substitution of what I have called a vanishing point for a focal point as the aesthetic goal of the writer. My conviction is now that Faulkner's career actually developed around the pivot of this changing emphasis, from the fixity of fascination to what Flannery O'Connor was later to call superbly "the realism of distances."[7] This is true not only of Faulkner's work, but even of his career.

On 7 May 1958 at the end of a rather unexciting interview with the psychiatrists of the University of Virginia, and after evading the inescapable question about why he wrote by saying, with tongue in cheek: "The demon lit on my shoulders. I dont know why he came, why he picked up me. That's the only explanation I have," Faulkner volunteered the following statement after a somewhat meaningful pause: "It may be that I took up writing as— what do you call it?—*a protest to being—against being small and insignificant,* that I wanted to be big and brave and handsome and rich, it could be that, I dont know" (my emphasis).[8] This statement is extremely interesting. For one thing, this was the only time when Faulkner gave a hint as to the existence of what Roland Barthes would certainly have called a biographeme—in this case his small size (five feet five inches). There are two ways of dealing with this, one structural, the other genetic, though neither shall be my preoccupation in this final chapter. I am not going to be concerned here with the structural relationship between this biographeme and the work—particularly with the recurrence of characters who could be called "great small characters," for example, Popeye, Flem or Mink Snopes, Ratliff and the old general in *A Fable*—or of characters who "elongate" or magnify themselves by riding horses, flying aeroplanes, or having tall statues or monuments erected on their tombstones. Nor am I going to discuss the genetic interest of this admission. This would be quite another topic, and a somewhat hypothetical one on theoretical grounds—as much, say, as the part played by Jean-Paul Sartre's squint in his chapter on the glance in *Being and Nothingness*. In the same way as Jean Brun suggested it about Sartre,[9] however, it can be asked whether there are not "some powerful biographical influences" in the remarkable part played by the distortions of the human body in Faulkner's fiction and why his work evinces such a need for "elongation" or magnification.

My interest in this chapter rather lies in a second biographeme, which is revealed not in but by Faulkner's statement, as well as by almost any other of his many spoken and recorded statements. As those who have had an opportunity to hear Faulkner alive know, and as anybody can verify by listening to the tapes of the University of Virginia or to the records he made, Faulkner's voice was characteristically so extremely thin and flat and soft and quiet as to merit either of two sets of epithets.

One of these two sets is precisely the pair of adjectives "small and insignificant" which he used, as it were privately, to answer the Charlottesville psychiatrists' question about why he wrote at all. The other is the diptych he used in his highly public and eloquent, and yet reportedly almost inaudible, Nobel Prize speech, immediately after the all too well known statement "I decline to accept the end of man." Here is the full sentence, which is carefully built into a crescendo and then immediately undercut by the final anticlimax: "It is easy enough to say that man is immortal simply because he will endure: that when the last ding-dong of doom has clanged and faded from the last worthless rock hanging tideless in the last red and dying evening, *that even then there will still be one more sound: that of his puny inexhaustible voice, still talking*" (ESPL, 120; my emphasis).

Faulkner's imaginative representation of "the end of man," in this speech and in his fiction, is a striking structure involving both visual and aural elements. I do not hesitate to call it a structure of Faulkner's imagination, not unlike the scene at the spring or the climbing of a hill, because it emerged as a poetical feature in his fiction long before it became the main rhetorical device in his celebrated Nobel Prize speech.

In its Stockholm version the structure is given a particularly powerful effect by the remarkable economy of the speech and by the hammering effect of its wording. The syllable "doom" calls for the alliterative "ding-dong," and only after this has "clanged and faded" like a bell can the remarkably anticlimactic "puny inexhaustible voice" be heard. When he takes this motif up again in *A Fable,* however, one notices the addition of the copula: "his puny and inexhaustible voice still talking, still planning" (FAB, 354). The question might be: is it puny and yet inexhaustible, or is it inexhaustible because it is puny?

Whatever may be the case, Faulkner's use of voice in his fiction is clearly individual: the best, indeed the exemplary expression of it is to be found nowhere else but in the Nobel Prize speech. As one reads it now, almost forty years after the event, how could one doubt that this was a speech delivered not to humanity, but directly to his fellow writers, and that the "pinnacle" Faulkner was speaking from was only physically the Stockholm podium; how could it not be clear to everybody, *beginning with himself*, that the reason why he was there was none else but his *work*?

Indeed, Faulkner's Nobel Prize speech makes no effort to conceal the "I" trying to reach "the young men and women already dedicated to the same anguish and travail" (ESPL, 119). In fact, one cannot help being struck by the mirror effect of what he said in Stockholm on 10 December 1950 and what he said in Charlottesville on 7 May 1958. There is an unmistakably reflexive quality in Faulkner's Nobel Prize final statement about the poet's voice. Faulkner seemed to be saying, in substance: even when the last blood-red sun sets in the Western sky, Faulkner's voice shall still be heard: however "small and insignificant" it may be/have been, it can be counted on because by definition, being a writer's voice, it is inexhaustible, even beyond the disappearance of the body of which it was the emanation, because it can be duplicated by reading forever. Indeed, the third sentence after this, which is the last sentence of the speech, runs: "the poet's *voice* need not merely be the record of man, it can be one of the props, the pillars to help him endure and prevail" (my emphasis). By the end of his inaudible and yet nonetheless "eloquent" speech, voice had thus become the central metaphor of Faulkner's message, both as tenor and as vehicle.

On 30 March 1935, when he resumed work on *Absalom, Absalom!*, Faulkner resorted to a plan quite different from the disastrous direct confrontation with the Subject in *Pylon*. This time, he confronted the Word. *Absalom, Absalom!* took Faulkner to "the limits of metaphor," to the furthermost capacity of language to evoke reality. *Absalom, Absalom!* is a work that belongs to what Maurice Blanchot later characterized as "the literature of absence." It does more, though—it is the apotheosis of voice in literature. Not only is Quentin's "very body" described from the beginning as "an empty hall echoing with sonorous defeated names" (AA, 12; CT, 9), which is a far cry from the hall of mirrors in, say, *Sanctuary*, but the novel goes through what is probably the most extraordinary effect of echoing duplication in the history of literature: "two, four, now two again, according to Quentin and Shreve, the two four the two still talking" (AA, 346; CT, 432), so that Henry Sutpen is finally evoked by what Robert Knox has so aptly called "the blended voice"—the apotheosis of evocation indeed.

Voice thus takes on the characteristic of an asymptote, as it tends to become the objective correlative of the impersonality of art: it is bloodless, dimensionless, disembodied, impalpable, etc. Is this the reason why Faulkner chose to end so many of his novels not only with sound, but with a vocal sound? *Mosquitoes, Light in August, Absalom, Absalom!, The Wild Palms, The Hamlet, Go Down, Moses, Intruder in the Dust, Knight's Gambit, A Fable,* and *The Reivers* all end on a final utterance by one of the characters.

However, the case of *Soldiers' Pay, Sartoris,* and *Sanctuary* is, in a way, even more interesting, as the three of them end on a musical "dying fall": the Negroes chanting in *Soldiers' Pay,* Narcissa playing the piano in *Sartoris,* and the celebrated "waves of music" played by "the dying brasses" of the band in the Luxembourg Gardens in *Sanctuary.* Even *As I Lay Dying* can be considered as ending on the promise of mail-order music being played on the new Mrs. Bundren's remarkable "graphophone."[10]

But of course the truth of these endings must be sought in the aesthetics of symbolism more than anywhere else. The best proof is given by two novels which do not end in music at all and yet have the same "dying fall" effect as if they did. One of them is *The Sound and the Fury,* with Benjy's voice roaring "above" "post and tree, window and doorway, and signboard, each in its ordered place," much in the same way the bird's "idiotic reiteration" hovers above the slowly creeping lorries in *A Fable.* Another, more symbolic (even symbolist) ending is that of *The Unvanquished,* with "the single sprig" of verbena "filling the room, the dusk, the evening with that odor which she said you could smell alone above the smell of horses."[11]

From this point of view, however, the most interesting ending must be that of the third narrative section of *Requiem for a Nun:* "*Listen, stranger. This was myself; this was I*" (REQ, 262). There is no doubt that in the story of Cecilia Farmer, Faulkner found the perfect, seamless symbol of individual voice disembodied to the point of surviving only in a graph—and a hard, imperishable, indeed "inexhaustible" graph at that.

Against the individual voice, Faulkner seldom sets the voice of the multitude, as other writers have; one looks in vain for evocations of the voice of the crowd, even in *Intruder in the Dust* or in *A Fable.* What one finds instead are the familiar words like *seething* and *moiling*—which do not evoke voice nor sound, but movement—and mark the return of an intensely *visual* fascination. For instance, as Hightower is dying (literally or metaphorically), he sees "... a halo ... full of faces. The faces are not shaped with suffering, not shaped with anything: not horror, pain, not even reproach. They are peaceful, as though they have escaped into an apotheosis; his own is among them. In fact, they all look a little alike, composite of all the faces which he has ever seen" (LIA, 465; CT, 542). The well-known passage in *Intruder in the Dust* is even more to the point here, in which the mob is described as having "not faces but a Face: not a mass nor even a mosaic of them but a Face: not even ravening nor uninsatiate but just in motion, insensate, vacant of thought or even passion: an Expression significantless and without past" (INT, 182).

Paradoxically, what best evokes a collective voice in Faulkner's fiction is not the lynching mob in *Intruder in the Dust,* which is like a voiceless face nor the humble crowd in *A Fable* ("The mass made no sound" [FAB, 51]), but something nondescript, hybrid, neither human nor inhuman, which partakes in the "sourcelessness" of the bird song. This, it seems to me, is what is conveyed in the vexing word "myriad" (perhaps the arch-Faulknerian word) as in "the hushed myriad life of night things" (SP, 275) or when one reads about old Isaac McCaslin in "Delta Autumn": "He lay on his back, his eyes closed, his breathing quiet and peaceful as a child's, listening to it—that silence which was never silence but was myriad" (GDM, 353). There seems to be no doubt left: the one way to fight the hopeless immanence of visual fascination in Faulkner's fiction is through voice.

Voice is a quality that Faulkner clearly identifies with transcendence. This is unambiguously the message left by both Cecilia Farmer in "The Jail" and by William Faulkner at the end of his Nobel Prize speech.

With *Absalom, Absalom!,* then, Faulkner began a new phase of his career, a phase characterized by a revision of the aims of fiction: voice now predominated over sight. This new phase led him in turn to a true ontology of discourse. To the compulsively idealistic function originally assigned to literature by the writer's need to express his visual fantasies was now substituted an ambitiously idealistic conception of literature as something fulfilling an ontological function. This function has probably never been so well described as in this comment: "I like to think of the world I created as being a kind of keystone in the Universe: that, as small as that keystone is, if it were ever taken away, the universe itself would collapse" (LITG, 255).

At the same time there were other transitions, for instance, the transition from a single subject to the community at large. Within the Snopes trilogy, for example, from *The Hamlet* to *The Town* and *The Mansion,* it is very clear that the earlier (and very individual) theme of perverted desire was now toned down, as it were "socialized," and treated in more sublimated ways—for example in the typically comic motif of dodging or shirking. One has even argued that Jefferson, the hub of the whole system, became truly a "collective subject" only in *Requiem for a Nun.*[12]

To the degree that the dynamic or libidinal forces gradually gave way to the "economic" or organizational forces, one might even be tempted to infer a law of literary creation from Faulkner's example: not only does a writer constantly reinvest in his writing whatever problems his life and preceding work have not solved, but he reinvests even the solutions he has found, because the subject's desire cannot have been gratified in the world of the "apocryphal."[13] Indeed, as John T. Matthews puts it, fiction even "produces the very insufficiencies it seeks to overcome."[14] In Faulkner's case it is likely that literature soon became a means of survival. At any rate his work was as concerned with telling how exacting writing was as was Hemingway's, for example, with keeping such reflexiveness under control.

At this point it is also necessary to discard the all too glib theory of Faulkner's "puritanism." Its place should be taken by the more inclusive idea of a drama—in the manner of Mallarmé's *Igitur:* a fictional staging of the act of writing. And indeed, one can witness a formal theatricalization of writing in Faulkner's later work. The grandiose, indeed the sometimes grandiloquent unfurlings of rhetoric became indistinguishable from the message—particularly in *A Fable.* Faulkner's later work did not just cease to conceal an ontological meaning, it clamored *urbi et orbi* for one. The best possible example lies in the proud, indeed the hubristic *"from Jefferson to the world"* to be found in *The Town.* Thus, one cannot but take seriously the fact that, once "Nobelized," Faulkner saw himself as the archetypal serious writer.

What happened during the five or six-year-long "turning point" (1936–42, roughly) was that Faulkner discovered a set of "antidotes" to his own obsessions. The best illustration of this transition was the emerging notion of "endurance." This celebrated value appeared for the first time in *Pylon,* was consecrated ten years later in the final, laconic line of the "Compson Appendix," and led on to epochal predictions in the Nobel Prize speech, later to be orchestrated in *A Fable.*

Again, one should be careful not to interpret this too hastily as a simple or glib ideological return to the pen of Christian humanism (especially as endurance can hardly be called a Christian virtue!). In reality the evolution was as much an appeal against personal obsessions as an overtly (and probably over-) advertised decision to get rid of the hell of his own, private (or *heimlich*) fantasies. Love, compassion, courage, hope, pride, honor, pity, and sacrifice became potions for a writer who had unwittingly become his own doctor, a *médecin malgré lui* of his own fantasies. In other words, his list of virtues was endowed by him with a magic power against what Sartre called the evil of pure vision. Faulkner may even have dreamed of using a set of allegorical characters based on these qualities. In 1925 he wrote a brief allegorical story called *Mayday* in which, as Carvel Collins has cogently shown, one finds the blueprint of the Faulknerian idealist, later to be called Quentin Compson. To put values on stage, as once he had put fantasies, may well have been the mad dream which guided Faulkner during and after the Second World War, particularly during the nine long, painful years in which *A Fable* was thought through.

This—the possibility that Faulkner became quixotic about his fiction—may well be the reason why he, at least for a while, cherished the idea (which he may well have known was an illusion) that *A Fable* was what he called his "magnum opus." This impressive work contains, however, the third and last of Faulkner's grand operatic duets between father and son, realist and idealist, authority and revolt, compromise and radicalism, etc. In many ways the exchange of ideas, both extremely tense and extremely noble, between the general and the corporal in *A Fable* is more accomplished than the imaginary dialogue between Quentin and his father in *The Sound and the Fury* and even than the commissary scene in *Go Down, Moses*. The study of the transition from the focal point to the vanishing point should also include an attentive reading of these three "ideo-logical" highlights of Faulkner's work.[15]

From the immediate, indeed the urgent, dramatization of the illusions that enthrall the eye to a generous and self-assured mastery of verbal technique—this is the way, it seems to me, one should describe Faulkner's evolution. Once the tragedy inherent in vision had been explored, once it became clear that there was no way to "endure" without negotiating with evil, the solution for Faulkner was to use words as a kind of countermagic: This is what lies behind the grandiloquence of *A Fable*.

However, Faulkner's main resource, the one from which he drew most inspiration and which made him a more versatile writer than most of his contemporaries, was the invention of the Snopeses and his departure into the comic vein. That most readers still consider him a tragic writer, as did his three great heralds in France (Malraux, Sartre, and Camus), does not prove that he is a lesser writer in *The Hamlet* than in *Go Down, Moses*. Both are masterpieces of his mature period. In recounting the resistible rise of Flem Snopes and, more generally, in inventing what is now called "Snopeslore," he treated himself to the gratifying spectacle of his own capacity for almost endless renewal.

Yet the new "vanishing point" could never prevent the occasional return of the old, focal—or nodal—points of sheer visual intensity that were so much part of Faulkner's imaginative power. The best example lies in the ultimate resurgence of the nightmare of unadulterated voyeurism in the loathsome character of Otis in *The Reivers*. And yet it was no doubt as a consummate artist (one could even risk the phrase: an old hand at fiction writing) that Faulkner finally assembled in the same character (Lucius Priest as aged narrator/child actor) the gift of double sight that allowed him at last *both* to glance at the focal point and to gaze at the vanishing point.

Exit Faulkner, not without panache—with a flourish, in fact. He had failed in his entrance upon the stage of the world. In leaving the theater of writing, however, he gave us a book which is not only a wonderful summary of his art; it is undoubtedly one of the most successful literary farewells since Shakespeare's *The Tempest*.

NOTES

Foreword

1 Le Maistre de Saci, *La Sainte Bible* (Bruxelles: Eugène-Henri Frick, 1704), 1.

2 Anatole Bailly, *Dictionnaire Grec-Français* (Paris: Hachette, 1950; 26th ed., 1963).

3 *Webster's Third International Dictionary* (Springfield, Mass.: G. & C. Merriam, 1965).

4 See Jean Rousset, *Circé et le paon: la littérature de l'âge baroque en France* (Paris: Corti, 1954).

5 "If idealism is the temptation of the West, it is because the West keeps *looking*, in spite of fruitless efforts, at least until recently, in order to rehabilitate the other senses." Alain Roger, *Nus et paysages: essai sur la fonction de l'art* (Paris: Aubier, 1978), 31.

6 *The Holy Bible* (London and New York: Collins' Clear-Type Press, no date), 8.

7 Félix Gaffiot, *Dictionnaire illustré Latin Français* (Paris: Hachette, 1934).

8 Paul Robert, *Dictionnaire alphabétique et analogique de la langue française* (Paris, 1967; new, revised edition, 1983).

9 André Breton, *L'Amour fou* (Paris: Gallimard, 1937), 105.

10 See Jean Brun, *Les Conquêtes de l'homme et la séparation ontologique* (Paris: Presses universitaires de France, 1961).

Introduction

1 *Selected Letters of William Faulkner,* ed. Joseph Blotner (New York: Random House, 1977), 352. Hereinafter SL.

2 James B. Meriwether, *The Literary Career of William Faulkner: A Bibliographical Study* (Princeton University Library, 1961). Hereinafter *Career*.

3 Michael Millgate, *The Achievement of William Faulkner* (New York: Random House, 1965). Hereinafter *Achievement*.

4 The names are given in the chronological order of their published comments on Faulkner's work; the real pioneers were Maurice Edgar Coindreau and Valery Larbaud. See my "Valery Larbaud et les débuts de Faulkner en France," *Preuves* 184 (1966), 26–28.

5 "Ecrire nécessite une exorbitante écoute à soi." Jacqueline Rousseau-Dujardin, *Couché par écrit: de la situation psychanalytique* (Paris: Galilée, 1980), 183.

6   *Independent* (Oxford, Mississippi), 9 April 1917, III, 15.

7   Murry C. Falkner, *The Falkners of Mississippi: A Memoir* (Baton Rouge: Louisiana State University Press, 1967), 9–10.

8   For an example of the writer's remarkable lucidity concerning the problem of influences, see his "Verse Old and Nascent: A Pilgrimage" in *William Faulkner: Early Prose and Poetry,* ed. Carvel Collins (Boston: Little, Brown, 1962), 114–18. Hereinafter EP&P.

9   Henry F. May, *The End of American Innocence: A Study of the First Years of Our Own Time, 1912–1917* (Chicago: Quadrangle, 1959), 393. Hereinafter *The End.*

10   Joseph Blotner, *Faulkner: A Biography,* 2 vols. (New York: Random House, 1974). Hereinafter FAB. Blotner calls these poses personas (e.g., FAB, 1772), whereas I reserve the use of this word for the literary impersonations of the figures of the ego.

11   See my "Home and Homelessness in Faulkner's Works and Life," *William Faulkner: Materials, Studies, Criticism* (Tokyo) 5 (May 1983), 26–42.

12   "Faulkner is a small man (5 ft. 5, I should judge)," according to Malcolm Cowley, *The Faulkner-Cowley File: Letters and Memories, 1944–1962* (New York: Viking, 1966), 103. Hereinafter *File.* On the part played by his size in Faulkner's work, see my "Faulkner's Self-Portraits," *The Faulkner Journal* 2 (Fall 1986): 2–13, and p. 270 of this book.

13   William Faulkner, *As I Lay Dying* (New York: Cape and Smith, 1930), 160, 167; *As I Lay Dying,* the corrected text, ed. Noel Polk (New York: Vintage, 1987), 155, 162. Hereinafter, respectively, AILD and AILD, CT.

14   ". . . there was a gap of almost twenty-five years during which I had almost no acquaintance whatever with contemporary literature." *Faulkner in the University: Class Conferences at the University of Virginia, 1957–1958,* ed. Frederick L. Gwynn and Joseph L. Blotner (New York: Random House, 1965), 243. Hereinafter FITU.

15   See in particular Carvel Collins, *Biographical Background for Faulkner's "Helen"* (Tulane University and Yoknapatawpha Press, 1981). Hereinafter *Background.*

16   Jean-Paul Sartre, *Les Mots* (Paris: Gallimard, 1964).

17   James B. Meriwether, "An Introduction to *The Sound and the Fury,*" in *A Faulkner Miscellany* (Jackson: University Press of Mississippi, 1974), 160. Hereinafter *Miscellany.*

18   H. E. Richardson, *William Faulkner: The Journey to Self-Discovery* (Columbia: University of Missouri Press, 1969), 167. Hereinafter *Journey.*

19   "Interview with Jean Stein vanden Heuvel" in *Lion in the Garden: Interviews with William Faulkner, 1926–1962,* ed. James B. Meriwether and Michael Millgate (New York: Random House, 1968), 255. Hereinafter LITG.

20   "Afternoon of a Cow" in *Uncollected Stories of William Faulkner,* ed. J. Blotner (New York: Random House, 1979), 426, 431. Hereinafter US. See also my "Faulkner's Self-Portraits."

21   See his letter of submission and the one he wrote after the novel was rejected by Horace Liveright in SL, 38–39.

22   See chapters 3 and 4 of this book.

23   William Faulkner, *Mosquitoes* (New York: Boni & Liveright, 1927), 144. Hereinafter MOS. See also my "Faulkner's Self-Portraits," 4.

24   Even as late as September 1955, when asked by Cynthia Grenier whether he had "any

special advice for young writers," Faulkner answered characteristically: "What counts is that you have done *something*" (LITG, 227).

25 Robert Penn Warren, "Faulkner: Past and Present" in *Faulkner: A Collection of Critical Essays* (Englewood Cliffs, N.J.: Prentice-Hall, 1966), 6. Hereinafter FACCE.

26 The facsimile of the typescript was published in *"Man Working," 1919–1962: A Catalogue of the William Faulkner Collections at the University of Virginia,* comp. Linton Massey (Charlottesville: Bibliographical Society of the University of Virginia, 1968), 76. See also FAB, 373.

27 Yves Bonnefoy, *L'Arrière-pays* (Geneva: Skira, 1972).

28 Gary Snyder, *The Back Country* (New York: New Directions, 1967).

29 In this short form the poem was printed first, under the title "My Epitaph," in *Contempo* 1 (1 February 1932), then in *An Anthology of Younger Poets,* ed. Oliver Wells (Philadelphia: Centaur Press, 1932), and with no title, under number XLIV, in *A Green Bough* (New York: Smith & Haas, 1933), 67. Hereinafter AGB. For a list of the typescript versions extant, see Keen Butterworth, "A Census of Manuscripts and Typescripts of William Faulkner's Poetry," *Miscellany,* 81.

30 William Faulkner, "Carcassonne," *These 13* (Cape and Smith, 1931), 352, and *Collected Stories* (New York: Random House, 1950), 895. Hereinafter cited, respectively, as T13 and CS.

31 Isaac MacCaslin in *Go Down, Moses* and David Levine in *A Fable* are other avatars of what I call the "generic hero" in *Faulkner: ontologie du discours, Delta* 25 (November 1987), passim.

32 I am borrowing this notion from John Hagopian, "Nihilism in Faulkner's *The Sound and the Fury,*" *Modern Fiction Studies* (hereinafter MFS) 13 (Spring 1967): 55.

33 "The figure of Lena Grove, in *Light in August,* monumentally serene in this violent landscape, is a force that no disaster, natural or unnatural, will wash away. She would seem to be the only convincing anchor that Faulkner would allow to drag in the present. She is the great mother, the abiding earth, the patient and enduring force of life that speaks out in him again, somewhat disembodied, in his belief in the indestructibility of man. But she is a woman as well as an abstraction, and we claim her as one of us." Wright Morris, "The Function of Rage," in *The Territory Ahead* (New York: Harcourt, Brace, 1958), 181.

Chapter One: Cold Pastoral

1 *New Republic* 20 (6 August 1919): 24; *Mississippian,* 29 October 1919, 4; EP&P, 39–40.

2 "Fantoches," "Clair de Lune," "Streets," and "A Clymène," all in EP&P. On Faulkner's "translations" see Martin Kreiswirth, "Faulkner as Translator: His Versions of Verlaine," *Mississippi Quarterly* (hereinafter MQ) 30 (Summer 1977): 429–32.

3 Faulkner's relationship with Phil Stone seems to have begun in the summer of 1914: see my *Faulkner: A Chronology* (Jackson: University Press of Mississippi, 1985), 10ff.

4　For Jules Laforgue's influence on Faulkner's generation, see Arthur Symons, *The Symbolist Movement in Literature*, rev. ed. (New York: E. P. Dutton, 1958), 56–62; F. O. Matthiessen, *The Achievement of T. S. Eliot* (Boston: Houghton, Mifflin, 1935), passim; and Stéphane Mallarmé's "Crisis in Verse" in Thomas G. West, *Symbolism: An Anthology* (New York: Methuen, 1980), 4.

5　Mallarmé was thirty when he published his poem in 1872, but he had been working at it since 1865, when he was twenty-three—the same age as Faulkner by the end of 1919.

6　Arthur Mizener, *The Sense of Life in the Modern Novel* (London: Heinemann, 1965), 142–43.

7　Pierre Leyris, "Translator's Foreword," T. S. Eliot, *Poèmes 1910–1930* (Paris: Seuil, 1947), 10.

8　See chapter 8 for a comparison of the two writers' "puritan" attitudes to young girls.

9　Faulkner's allusion to the French poet was even limited to his ceasing to write altogether: Loïc Bouvard, "Interview avec William Faulkner," *Bulletin de l'Association amicale France-Amérique* (January 1954), 27. Translated in LITG, 71.

10　Arthur Symons, *The Symbolist Movement in Literature* (New York: E. P. Dutton, 1954), 44.

11　"On Arthur Symons's Translation of Baudelaire," in *The Symbolist Poem,* ed. Edward Engelberg (New York: E. P. Dutton, 1967), 310.

12　William Faulkner, *Absalom, Absalom!* (New York: Random House, 1936), 193; *Absalom, Absalom!,* the corrected text, ed. Noel Polk (New York: Vintage, 1987), 241–42. Hereinafter AA and AA, CT.

13　William Faulkner, *Soldiers' Pay* (New York: Boni & Liveright, 1926), 31. Hereinafter SP.

14　William B. Yeats, "On Modern Poetry," in *The Symbolist Poem,* 343.

15　*Double Dealer* 7 (June 1925): 185–87; reprinted as poem I of *A Green Bough* (New York: Smith & Haas, 1933), 7–11. Hereinafter AGB.

16　William Faulkner, *The Marionettes,* ed. Noel Polk (Charlottesville: University Press of Virginia, 1977). Hereinafter MAR.

17　Lucy Somerville Howorth, "The Bill Faulkner I Knew," *Delta Review* 2 (July–August 1965): 38–39.

18　Laurette Veza, *La Poésie américaine de 1910 à 1940* (Paris: Didier, 1972), 84.

19　Arthur Symons, *The Art of Aubrey Beardsley* (New York, 1925), 8.

20　Jean Starobinski, *Portrait de l'artiste en acrobate* (Geneva: Skira, 1970).

21　See US, 526–74 and 707–8.

22　William Faulkner, *Go Down, Moses* (New York: Random House, 1942), 249. Hereinafter GDM.

23　William Faulkner, *Flags in the Dust,* ed. Douglas Day (New York: Random House, 1973), 160. Hereinafter *Flags.*

24　Even though it is unlikely that Faulkner was acquainted with the poem under this title by Marie Emile Albert Kayenbergh Giraud, alias Albert Giraud (1860–1929), which inspired Arnold Schoenberg with his Opus 21 (1912), he, like Eliot, discovered Symbolism by reading Arthur Symons, and it is not unlikely that he read about the "myth of the clown."

25   Melvin Backman, *Faulkner: The Major Years—A Critical Study* (Bloomington: Indiana University Press, 1966). Hereinafter *Major Years.*

26   Karl Shapiro, "Classicists All," *New York Times Book Review*, 9 January 1966, 12.

27   William Faulkner, *Helen: A Courtship and Mississippi Poems*, introductory essays by Carvel Collins and Joseph Blotner (Oxford, Miss., and New Orleans: Tulane University and Yoknapatawpha Press, 1981). Like his introductions to *Early Prose and Poetry* and to *New Orleans Sketches*, Carvel Collins's long biographical introduction to "Helen: A Courtship" is extremely useful.

28   William Faulkner, *Vision in Spring*, with an introduction by Judith L. Sensibar (Austin: University of Texas Press, 1984). I am not sure that Ms. Sensibar does not exaggerate the importance of "her" publication when she writes that "*Vision in Spring* [is] the pivotal work in Faulkner's self-apprenticeship," but I certainly agree with her that "he evolved as a writer of fiction not from short stories to novels as most novelists do, but rather from short poems to poem sequences . . . to novels." "Introduction," ix, xii.

29   Even though there is no proof of the Danish philosopher's influence on Faulkner, I am attributing to Faulkner himself, via the faun's persona, the (aesthetic) "stage" that preceded the (ethical) "choice." George C. Bedell's approach in *Kierkegaard and Faulkner: Modalities of Existence* (Baton Rouge: Louisiana State University Press, 1972) is quite different, as it illustrates the three stages of Kierkegaard's philosophy with characters taken from the novels (the aesthetic with Horace Benbow, the ethical with Charlotte Rittenmeyer and Harry Wilbourne, and the religious with Dilsey Gibson).

30   George Garrett, "An Examination of the Poetry of William Faulkner," *Princeton University Library Chronicle* 18 (Spring 1957): 125–26.

31   Henri Thomas, "Faulkner à dix-huit ans," in William Faulkner, *Proses, poésies et essais critiques de jeunesse* (Paris: Gallimard, 1966), 9.

32   On this subject, besides the indispensable *Faulkner's Library—A Catalogue*, ed. Joseph Blotner (Charlottesville: University Press of Virginia, 1964), see Richard P. Adams's "The Apprenticeship of William Faulkner," *Tulane Studies in English* 12 (1962): 113–56, or chapter 1 of his *Faulkner: Myth and Motion* (Princeton, N.J.: Princeton University Press, 1968); Mick Gidley's "Some Notes on Faulkner's Reading," *Journal of American Studies* 4 (July 1970): 91–102, and "One Continuous Force: Notes on Faulkner's Extra-Literary Reading," MQ 23 (Summer 1970): 299–314; and Michael Millgate's "Faulkner's Masters," *Tulane Studies in English* 22 (1978): 143–55.

33   "Once by the Pacific," *Selected Poems of Robert Frost*, introduction by Robert Graves (New York: Holt, Rinehart & Winston, 1963), 156–57.

Chapter Two: Locus Solus

1   Jean Laplanche and J.-B. Pontalis, *Vocabulaire de la psychanalyse*, 2d ed. (Paris: Presses universitaires de France, 1968), 263. Hereinafter *Vocabulaire.*

2   Joan Rivière, "La Haine, le désir de possession et l'agressivité," in Mélanie Klein and Joan Rivière, *L'Amour et la haine* (Paris: Payot, 1968), 9.

3 William Faulkner, "Sherwood Anderson," in *New Orleans Sketches,* ed. Carvel Collins, 2d ed. (New York: Random House, 1968), 134–35. Hereinafter NOS.

4 I am quoting from p. 2 of the typescript located in AL as this story was not published by Blotner because it was left unfinished (see US, xii).

5 James B. Meriwether, "Early Notices of Faulkner by Phil Stone and Louis Cochran," MQ 17 (Summer 1964): 163–64.

6 William Faulkner, *The Sound and the Fury* (New York: Cape & Smith, 1929), 106; *The Sound and the Fury,* the corrected text, ed. Noel Polk (New York: Vintage, 1987), 98. Hereinafter, respectively, TSATF and TSATF, CT.

7 William Faulkner, *Sanctuary* (New York: Cape & Smith, 1931), 16; *Santuary,* the corrected text, ed. Noel Polk (New York: Vintage, 1987), 16. Hereinafter, respectively, SAN and SAN, CT.

8 "Beneath it all one feels the incessant struggle of Benbow against his own impotence and powerlessness." Lawrence S. Kubie, "William Faulkner's *Sanctuary,*" *Saturday Review of Literature,* 20 October 1934, 224; reprinted in FACCE, 137–46.

9 "Now the bus, the road, ran out of the swamp though without mounting, with no hill to elevate it; it ran now upon a flat plain of sawgrass and of cypress and oak stumps." William Faulkner, *Pylon* (New York: Smith & Haas, 1935), 17; *Pylon,* the corrected text, ed. Noel Polk (New York: Vintage, 1987), 13. Hereinafter PYL and PYL, CT.

10 William Faulkner, *The Hamlet* (New York: Random House, 1940), 3. Hereinafter HAM.

11 Jean Piaget, *Problèmes de psychologie génétique* (Paris: Denoël/Gonthier, 1972).

12 The words between brackets were added by Faulkner between the manuscript and the typescript stages of his novel.

13 William Faulkner, *Light in August* (New York: Smith & Haas, 1932), 401–3; *Light in August,* the corrected text, ed. Noel Polk (New York: Vintage, 1987), 467–69. Hereinafter LIA and LIA, CT.

14 See my "Faulkner et l'océan," *Sud* 14/15 (1975): 185–89.

15 On the suggestion of an opposition between Melville's "poetics of departure" and Faulkner's "poetics of return," see Philippe Jaworski's ". . . M/F?," *Sud* 48/49 (1983): 201–5.

16 William Faulkner, *Father Abraham,* ed. James B. Meriwether (New York: Red Ozier Press, 1983), [71]. Hereinafter FA.

17 ". . . 2nd class poetry, which this is. But worse has been published." SL, 54.

18 William Rose Benét, "Round About Parnassus," *Saturday Review of Literature,* 19 April 1933, 565.

19 Eda Lou Walton, "Faulkner's First [*sic*] Book of Verse," *New York Herald Tribune,* 30 April 1933, 10, 3.

20 William Rose Benét, "Round About Parnassus," 565.

21 William Faulkner, *Mayday,* with an introduction by Carvel Collins (Notre Dame, Ind.: University of Notre Dame Press, 1976).

22 For a study of the symbolic part played by the snake in the pastoral, see Gérard Genette's introduction to Honoré d'Urfé's *L'Astrée* (Paris: Union Générale d'Edition, 1964), entitled "The Serpent in the Sheep-fold."

Chapter Three: La Ronde

1   The version published by Blotner in US, 495–503, is from a complete typescript of fourteen pages; the quotations I am giving are from the other, incomplete, typescript of sixteen pages (AL).

2   See Blotner's introduction to US (viii) for the reason why he did not include "Love." Like "Now What's To Do?," it was incomplete.

3   See the celebrated passage in "Sophistication" beginning: "There is a time in the life of every boy when he for the first time takes the backward view of life," *Winesburg, Ohio* (New York: Viking, 1964), 234.

4   See F. Scott Fitzgerald's letter to H. L. Mencken, dated 23 April 1934, concerning *Tender is the Night:* "That is what most critics fail to understand . . . that the motif of the 'dying fall' was absolutely deliberate and did not come from any diminution of vitality but from a definite plan." *The Letters of F. Scott Fitzgerald,* ed. Andrew Turnbull (London: Bodley Head, 1963), 510. See also his letter to John Peale Bishop dated 7 April 1934: "indeed I believe it was Ernest Hemingway who developed to me, in conversation, that the dying fall was preferable to the dramatic ending under certain conditions, and I think we both got the germ of the idea from Conrad" (363). Lastly, in a letter to John O'Hara dated 25 July 1936, Fitzgerald confirms that the idea of ending *Tender is the Night* "on a fade-away instead of a staccato" was the outcome of an exchange with Hemingway (538).

    Faulkner never seems to have used the phrase "dying fall" in the technical sense; it is nevertheless to be found here and there in his fiction, particularly at the end of *Sartoris,* in which it blends perfectly with the mood of the novel. Two years later, by substituting the Luxembourg scene to the original staccato ending of *Sanctuary,* he gave us what is probably the paradigm of all "dying falls." Concerning the strange similarity between the "dying falls" in *Sanctuary* and in *Murphy,* see my "Of Sailboats and Kites: The 'Dying Fall' in Faulkner's *Sanctuary* and Beckett's *Murphy,*" in *Intertextuality in Faulkner,* ed. Michel Gresset and Noel Polk (Jackson: University Press of Mississippi, 1985), 57–72.

5   See Giliane Morell's introduction to the new, revised edition of the French translation of the novel, *Monnaie de singe* (Paris: Flammarion, 1987), 7–25.

6   "Here was reason for being born into a fantastic world: discovering the splendor of fortitude, the beauty of being of the soil like a tree about which fools might howl and which winds of disillusion and death and despair might strip, leaving it bleak, without bitterness; beautiful in sadness" (EP&P, 117).

7   *Faulkner at West Point,* ed. Joseph L. Fant III and Robert Ashley (New York: Random House, 1964), 57.

8   See George K. Smart, *Religious Elements in Faulkner's Early Novels: A Selective Concordance* (Coral Gables, Fla.: University of Miami Press, 1965), passim.

9   The phrase, describing the year 1919, is taken from John Dos Passos's introduction to the Modern Library edition of *Three Soldiers* (1932).

10   Anonymous, "Soldier's [sic] Pay," *Times Literary Supplement* (London), 3 July 1930.

11   Olga Vickery, *The Novels of William Faulkner: A Critical Interpretation,* 2d ed. (Baton Rouge: Louisiana State University Press, 1964), 4. Hereinafter *Novels.*

12 The central place is the rector's drawing-room (and garden); there is even an allusion to "a French comedy" (74).

13 See Millgate's chapter on the novel in *Achievement*.

14 John Cowper Powys, "Finnegans Wake," *Obstinate Cymric: Essays 1935–1947* (Carmarthen, Wales: Druid Press, 1947), 21.

15 Cf. ". . . if Venus returned she would be a soiled man in a subway lavatory with a palm full of French postcards," William Faulkner, *The Wild Palms* (New York: Random House, 1939), 136. Hereinafter TWP.

16 See p. 70 of this book.

17 I have italicized the author's additions in ink in the margin of the typescript.

18 One inevitably thinks of the color yellow, which is common to both Charlotte Rittenmeyer's eyes and the Mississippi river flood in TWP; see Thomas McHaney, *William Faulkner's The Wild Palms: A Study* (Jackson: University Press of Mississippi, 1965). But the "evil" connotation of the color yellow in Faulkner's fiction is already present in the early fiction; see "The Liar" (NOS, 92–103).

19 Michel Gresset, "Le Regard et le désir chez Faulkner, 1919–1931," *Sud* 14/15 (1975): 39. Hereinafter "Le Regard."

20 F. G. Riedel, "Faulkner as Stylist," *South Atlantic Quarterly* 56 (Fall 1957): 472.

21 Cleanth Brooks, "People without a Past (*Pylon*)" in *Toward Yoknapatawpha and Beyond* (New Haven, Conn.: Yale University Press, 1978), 182.

22 T. S. Eliot, *Selected Poems* (London: Faber, 1955), 45.

23 I am using the French translation of the title of Arthur Schnitzler's play *Reigen* (1920), which was made into a well-known film by Max Ophüls (1950).

24 V. S. Pritchett, "Books in General," *New Statesman*, 2 June 1951, 626.

25 William Spratling, "Chronicle of a Friendship: William Faulkner in New Orleans," *Texas Quarterly* 9 (1966): 38.

26 See Thomas McHaney, "The Elmer Papers: Faulkner's Comic Portraits of the Artist" in *Miscellany*, 37–69.

27 Faulkner lived at number 26 of this small street near the Luxembourg Gardens during the fall of 1925.

28 "The great theme of art and literature at the end of the XIXth century was hermaphroditism . . . which symbolizes the overabundance of erotic possibilities." Armand Bitoun, "Aubrey Beardsley and Homosexual Estheticism," *Les Lettres nouvelles*, March–April 1967, 123.

29 " 'And Freud?'—'Everybody talked about Freud when I lived in New Orleans, but I have never read him.' " "Interview with Jean Stein vanden Heuvel" (1955), LITG, 251. In "American Drama: Inhibitions" (1922), Faulkner had stigmatized "the deadly fruit of the grafting of Sigmund Freud upon the dynamic chaos of a hodge-podge of nationalities" (EP&P, 93). At bottom, however, I agree with Noel Polk: "Whether Faulkner read Freud, no one knows for certain. I for one think it indisputable that he had at least a working knowledge of Freud's basic concepts." "The Law in Faulkner's *Sanctuary*," *Mississippi College Review* 4 (Spring 1984): 242.

30 Joseph Conrad, *Lord Jim* (New York: Doubleday, Doran, 1929), 214.

Chapter Four: Perversion

1 See David Minter, *William Faulkner: His Life and Works* (Baltimore: Johns Hopkins University Press, 1980), chapter 3, and Carvel Collins, *Background,* passim.

2 Raymond Queneau, Introduction to *Moustiques,* by William Faulkner (Paris: Minuit, 1948), 9.

3 Conrad Aiken, *A Reviewer's ABC* (New York: Meriden, 1958), 199.

4 Michel Mohrt, *Le Nouveau roman américain* (Paris: Gallimard, 1955), 81.

5 "Interview with Michel Tournier," France-Culture, July 1975. See also *Le Monde,* 28 March 1975.

6 The triad "wild and passionate and sad" occurs twice in Book 3, chapter 1 of *Elmer,* 80, 82.

7 "Trois choses me plaisent: l'or, le marbre et la pourpre, éclat, solidité, couleur." Théophile Gautier, *Mademoiselle de Maupin* (Paris: Garnier-Flammarion, 1966), 201. Millgate deserves credit for first writing about this borrowing in *Achievement,* 300.

8 The statue of Balzac was ordered from the sculptor in 1891, and the model, about ten feet high, was shown at the Salon in 1898, scandalizing the public. Faulkner could not see the statue where it has been for almost fifty years, at the corner of Boulevard Montparnasse and Boulevard Raspail (the setting of the present action of *Elmer*), but he did visit the Rodin Museum (SL, 24, and FAB, 465). Balzac was one of the writers most often quoted by Faulkner.

9 Quoted by James B. Meriwether, "Sartoris and Snopes: An Early Notice," *Library Chronicle of the University of Texas* 7, no. 2 (1962): 36–39, and by Michael Millgate, *Achievement,* 24.

10 Two of the hitherto unpublished contributions at the San Diego Faulkner Conference of 1–3 May 1986 were addressed to this theme: Patrick Samway, S. J., "Towards a Snopesian Bestiary: From *As I Lay Dying* to the Snopes trilogy," and Michel Gresset, "The Pastoral and the Poetics of Polymorphism."

11 James Hinkle, "Poor Labove," unpublished paper delivered at the San Diego Faulkner Conference, 1–3 May 1986.

12 Washington Irving, "The Legend of Sleepy Hollow," *History, Tales and Sketches* (New York: Library of America, 1983), 1065.

13 Cecil Eby, "Ichabod Crane in Yoknapatawpha," *Georgia Review* 16 (Winter 1962): 465–69.

14 The printing history of this sketch is peculiar: in 1937 Faulkner gave a typescript of it to Coindreau, who published it in his own translation in *Fontaine* (Alger, 1943); the original was published in the United States only in 1947 (reprinted in US, 424–34).

15 See Monique Pruvot, "Le Sacre de la vache," and Annick Chapdelaine, "Perversion as Comedy" in *Delta* 3 (November 1976), respectively, 105–23 and 95–104.

16 Maurice Edgar Coindreau, "Note," " 'L'Après-midi d'une vache' par Ernest V. Trueblood," in *Ecrivains et poètes des Etats-Unis d'Amérique, Fontaine,* 27–28 (1943), 67/187.

Chapter Five: Focusing

1 "Introduction," *The Portable Faulkner,* ed. Malcolm Cowley (New York: Viking, 1946), 1–2; revised edition, 1967, vii–viii. Hereinafter *Portable.*

2 Maurice Edgar Coindreau, "William Faulkner," *Apergus de littérature américaine* (Paris: Gallimard, 1946), 24.

3 See chapter nine of this book.

4 See my "Faulkner's 'The Hill,'" *Southern Literary Journal,* 6 (Spring 1974): 3–18.

5 The phrase was Melvin Backman's in "Faulkner's Sick Heroes: Bayard Sartoris and Quentin Compson," MFS 2 (Autumn 1956): 95–108.

6 This is the title of a story published in *Scribner's* in January 1932 after six failures to publish it in the year 1930–31 (*Career,* 171). It may therefore have been written not long after *Flags.*

7 In 1958 Faulkner himself used the words "psychotic injury" (FITU, 250).

8 This is provided one includes the epilogue, the "dying fall" mood of which adumbrates the title on the first page of the manuscript of the next novel, *The Sound and the Fury:* "Twilight."

9 *Flags,* 126; SAR, 141. Since this is a drinking scene, one may wonder whether there is not a pun on "still" intended.

10 This is the well-known thesis of Carlos Baker in *Hemingway: The Writer as Artist* (Princeton, N.J.: Princeton University Press, 1952).

11 Such a debt is almost precluded by the proximity of the dates of publication: 31 January 1929 for *Sartoris,* September of the same year for *A Farewell to Arms.*

12 See p. 99 of this book.

13 See Jean-Paul Sartre, "William Faulkner's *Sartoris,*" in *Literary Essays,* trans. Annette Michelson (New York: Philosophical Library, 1957), 73–78.

14 With the exception of Mandy, the (Negro, according to Kirk and Klotz) cook of the MacCallums, the clan is all male: old Virginius is a widower ("His wife was dead these many years, and her successor was dead" *Flags,* 305; SAR, 310), and none of his six sons seems to have a feminine relation. It is precisely because of this sterility that the ideal mood in which the episode is steeped is also tinged with an undeniable sadness.

15 See Michel Gresset, "Home and Homelessness in Faulkner's Works and Life," *William Faulkner: Materials, Studies and Criticism* (Tokyo) 5 (May 1983): 26–42.

16 This imperious need of a perspective is precisely what distorts all comparisons with Proust, in whose work remembrance is an end in itself, whereas with Faulkner it is only a means; this is particularly clear in *Absalom, Absalom!* in which Quentin is not so much after remembering as after understanding the past.

17 "*Sartoris* has an extraordinary depth because events widely separated in time, but spiritually akin, are made to seem simultaneous. In this respect it is an achievement, for it puts to new uses the discoveries of Proust, Joyce and Virginia Woolf." Willard Thorp, "Four Times and Out?," *Scrutiny* 1 (September 1932): 172.

18 John W. Corrington, "Escape into Myth," *Recherches Anglaises et Américaines* (hereinafter RANAM) 4 (1971): 31–47.

Chapter Six: Glamour

1 *Webster's Third New International Dictionary* (Springfield, Mass.: G. C. Merriam, 1965).

2 See Sartre's analysis of "the look" in *Being and Nothingness: An Essay on Phenomenological Ontology,* trans. Hazel E. Barnes (London: Methuen, 1958), 3, 1, iv, 252–302—particularly, "Thus in the look the death of my possibilities causes me to experience the Other's freedom" (271), and "it is never eyes which look at us; it is the Other-as-subject" (277).

3 "Legend of Roland," *Encyclopaedia Britannica* (Chicago: William Benton, 1962) 19: 389.

4 Edgar Morin, *Les Stars* (Paris: Seuil, 1957), 37.

5 Roland Barthes, *Mythologies* (Paris: Seuil, 1957), 234–41.

6 Douglas T. Miller, "Faulkner and the Civil War: Myth and Reality," *Arizona Quarterly* 15 (Summer 1963): 201.

7 Young Bayard thus reenters history. From this point of view, as Olga Vickery has noted, there is a relevant contrast between the Colonel's farewell in *Sartoris* ("And then he tole you to tell yo'aunt he wouldn't be home fo supper," 22)—a reported message that is meant to conceal the dramatic under the futile—and the version of the same farewell in *The Unvanquished,* in direct speech, and loaded with much graver connotations than just a dinner: "Take care of Miss Rosa and the chillen'" (84)—*Novels,* 252.

8 See Patrick Samway, S. J., "Searching for Jason Richmond Compson: A Question of Echolalia and a Problem of Palimpsest" in *Intertextuality,* 178–209.

9 Miss Jenny's immense merit is to be at once a language-maker and one who can see through language.

10 In November 1935 Faulkner had the same inscription carved on his brother Dean's tombstone (FAB, 916).

11 "It takes the protagonist five acts to erect his statue and to freeze forever the sublime gesture which eternalizes him in marble. . . . Tragedy is the restoration of statues, first among them the one which embodies the Law and Order, and which is often assimilated with the father archetype." My translation from C.-G. Dubois, *Le Baroque: les profondeurs de l'apparence* (Paris: Larousse, 1973), 233.

Chapter Seven: Shame

1 See chapter 13 of this book.

2 Robert C. Davis, "*Other Voices, Other Rooms* and the Ocularity of American Fiction," *Delta,* 11 (1980), 1–14.

3 See Monique Pruvot, "Le bestiaire," *L'Arc* 84/85 (1983): 144–56.

4 Her name is Minnie, to be found again as one of Miss Reba's girls in both *Sanctuary* and *The Reivers.*

5 The ending of Book 3 was thus reduced by half from *Flags* to *Sartoris.*

6   Compare "The next afternoon Virgil Beard killed a mockingbird. It was singing in the peach tree that grew in the corner of the chicken-yard" (SAR, 112), and "But Popeye was gone. On the floor lay a wicker cage in which two lovebirds lived; beside it lay the birds themselves, and the bloody scissors with which he had cut them up alive" (SAN, 369–70; CT, 324).

7   Jean-Paul Sartre, "Sartoris, par W. Faulkner," *Nouvelle Revue Française* 50 (February 1938): 323–28; reprinted in *Situations* 1 (Paris: Gallimard, 1947), 7–13; trans. Annette Michelson as "William Faulkner's *Sartoris*" in *Literary Essays* (New York: Philosophical Library, 1957), 73–78.

8   Joseph Blotner, "William Faulkner's Essay on the Composition of *Sartoris*," quoted in FAB (84), 222–23.

9   James B. Meriwether, "Introduction to *The Sound and the Fury, Southern Review* 8 (Autumn 1972): 706.

10 Simone de Beauvoir and others, *Que peut la littérature?* (Paris: U.G.E., 1965).

Chapter Eight: Fascination

1   See Erich Neumann, *The Great Mother: An Analysis of the Archetype* (Princeton, N.J.: Princeton University Press, 1955; Bollingen Paperback, 1972), passim.

2   Walker Percy, *The Moviegoer* (New York: Knopf, 1961; Noonday, 1967), 13.

3   See, for illustration, Virginia Woolf's "The Lady in the Looking-Glass," *A Haunted House and Other Stories* (Penguin, 1973); chapter 18 of *The House of the Seven Gables;* and the whole of *Absalom, Absalom!* I am referring to the part played by mirrors in imagination and in fiction (particularly in Anglo-American fiction) and to the belief that they are associated with death.

4   See chapter 12.

5   Jean Baudrillard, *De la séduction* (Paris: Galilée, 1979), "I'll be your mirror [in English]," 94–100, particularly: "Seduction is what cannot be represented, because it abolishes the distance between the real and its double, between the same and the Other."

6   Clément Rosset, *Le Réel: Traité de l'idiotie* (Paris: Minuit, 1977), particularly "La confusion des chemins," 14–23.

7   Jean Rousset, *Circé et le paon: la littérature de l'âge baroque en France* (Paris: Corti, 1954), chapter 7.

8   Jean-Jacques Mayoux, "The Creation of the Real in William Faulkner," *3 Decades*, 176, trans. F. J. Hoffman from "La Création du réel chez William Faulkner," *Etudes anglaises* 25 (February 1952): 25–39; reprinted as the second part of the chapter entitled "William Faulkner" in *Vivants Piliers: le roman anglo-saxon et les symboles* (Paris, Julliard, 1960; 2d ed., Maurice Nadeau, 1985).

9   Charles Baudelaire, *De l'amour* (Paris: Société anonyme d'édition et de librairie, 1919), 134.

10 André Bleikasten, "La Terreur et la nausée: le langage des corps dans *Sanctuaire*," *Sud* 14/15 (1975): 98–99.

11 Herman Melville, *Mardi and A Voyage Thither,* ed. Harrison Hayford, Hershell Parker, and G. T. Tanselle (Evanston and Chicago: Northwestern University Press and Newberry Library, 1970), 652.

12 E. W. Emerson and W. E. Forbes, eds., *The Journals of Ralph Waldo Emerson,* 10 vols. (Boston, 1909–14), vol. 6, 72–73.

13 The passage between brackets indicates the addition in the margin of the manuscript.

14 The exact quotation is: "*Il fallut soulever un peu la tête, et alors un flot de liquides noirs sortit, comme un vomissement, de sa bouche.*" Gustave Flaubert, *Madame Bovary* (Paris: Conard, 1902), 456–57. On this topic see André Bleikasten, " 'Cet affreux goût d'encre': Emma Bovary's Ghost in *Sanctuary,*" *Intertextuality,* 36–56.

15 John K. Simon, "Faulkner and Sartre: Metamorphosis and the Obscene," *Comparative Literature* 15 (Summer 1963): 216–25.

16 André Bleikasten, "La Terreur et la nausée," 113.

17 ". . . but our present investigation does not aim at constituting an anthropology" (B&N, 282).

18 Jean Brun, "Le Regard et l'existence," *Revue de métaphysique et de morale* 3 (July–September 1957): 286–302.

19 Georges Bataille, quoted by Jean Brun, ibid., 296.

20 Villiers de l'Isle Adam, quoted by Jean Brun, ibid., 302.

21 Roland Barthes (quoting Angelus Silesius), *Le Plaisir du texte* (Paris: Seuil, 1973), 29.

22 P. [sic] Bourdier, "Essai psychiatrique sur le regard," *La Fonction du regard/The Function of Gaze,* ed. A. Dubois-Poulsen et al. (Paris: INSERM, 1971), 417–18.

23 *Vocabulaire,* 106.

24 P. Bourdier, "Essai psychiatrique," 417.

25 Ibid.

26 Sigmund Freud, *Three Contributions to the Theory of Sex* (New York: Nervous and Mental Disease Publishing Co., 1925), 23–24.

27 *Vocabulaire,* 107.

28 P. Bourdier, "Essai psychiatrique," 430.

29 Jean Brun, "Le Regard et l'existence," 293, 294.

30 Jacques Lacan, *The Four Fundamental Concepts of Psycho-Analysis,* ed. Jacques-Alain Miller, trans. Alan Sheridan (New York: Norton, 1978), 65–119. Hereinafter FFCP.

Chapter Nine: Surprise

1 See p. 119, note 9 of this book.

2 The page numbers in the five following tables refer to the first editions only.

3 See my "Introduction: Faulkner between the Texts," *Intertextuality,* 3–8.

4 Melvin Backman, *The Major Years,* 25.

5 See in particular chapter 47 of *An American Tragedy,* by Theodore Dreiser (a novelist whose work Faulkner admired).

6 James Brown, "Shaping the World of Sanctuary," *University of Kansas City Review* 25 (December 1958), 137.

7 "Character is Fate, said Novalis, and Farfrae's character was just the reverse of Henchard's. . . ." Thomas Hardy, *The Mayor of Casterbridge* (London: Macmillan, 1912), 131.

Chapter Ten: Astonishment

1 In *The Time of William Faulkner* (Columbia: University of South Carolina Press, 1971), 88, Maurice Edgar Coindreau, the novel's translator, has dealt at length with the other interpretation, which he says was initiated by a reviewer named Isabel M. Paterson, in the Sunday book section of the *New York Herald Tribune* for 12 March 1933: "The *light* means the opposite of heavy; and Ben [Wasson, then Faulkner's agent] may get a glimmer of the idea by searching through English history till he learns what Queen Elizabeth said when she heard that Mary Queen of Scots had produced an heir to the throne of Scotland." "In 1946," Coindreau added, "Malcolm Cowley put forth an idea which seems to agree with that of Mrs. Paterson, but which gives to *Light in August* a much less aristocratic origin. 'Incidentally the title of the novel has nothing to do with August sunlight; it refers to Lena Grove and her baby. In the Mississippi backwoods, it is sometimes said of a pregnant woman, but more often of a mare or a cow, that she will *light* in August or September'" (*Portable*, 1946, 652; in the revised edition of 1967, the first sentence was amended to "Incidentally the title of the novel refers primarily to Lena Grove and her baby" [584]). Coindreau concludes: "In 1958, William Faulkner . . . settled the matter once for all: '*Light in August*,' said he, 'refers to the texture of the light in August in my country, in a spell of two or three cool days we call *Blackberry Winter*. It's the light. I had never heard that business of after the cow drops the calf she's light in August'" (FITU, 265). See also Brooks's *Yoknapatawpha*, 375.

2 Regina K. Fadiman, *Faulkner's "Light in August": A Description and Interpretation of the Revisions* (Charlottesville: University Press of Virginia, 1975), 40.

3 "A terrific figure on an urn": see the second quotation given in epigraph to chapter 2.

4 Alfred Kazin, "The Stillness of *Light in August*," *Partisan Review* 24 (Autumn 1957), 519–38.

5 A good example of the reverse (a "vertical" subject confronted with a "horizontal" spectacle) can be found in the tall convict and the flooded river in TWP.

6 Quoted by Jean Starobinski, *L'Oeil vivant* (Paris: Gallimard, 1961), 9.

7 Interviews taken place the summer 1931 and February 1932 (LITG, 8, 13, 32).

8 H. C. Nash, "Faulkner's 'Furniture Repairer and Dealer': Knitting Up *Light in August*," MFS 16 (Winter 1970–71): 529–31.

9 Particularly, but not merely, because of his bicycle, Percy Grimm can be seen in a burlesque light evoking both Jacques Tati's film *Les Vacances de Monsieur Hulot* and, of course, Bergson's well-known theory (the roots of the comic are in the mechanical) in *Le Rire*. Like Popeye, however, Percy Grimm is also a "pure" logician of the kind best represented by Adolf Eichmann as portrayed by Hannah Arendt.

10 There is the same difference in *As I Lay Dying,* a novel which is not simply the narrative of a death but of an entombment: Faulkner's fiction is always basically theatrical.

11 Quentin uses the same word in his fantasy of castration: see TSATF, 143.

12 Thus Faulkner's understanding of the way the community "makes" the Negro in *Light in August* can be said to anticipate by twenty-two years Sartre's *Réflexions sur la question juive* (1954).

13 Reynolds Price, *The Names and Faces of Heroes* (New York: Atheneum, 1963).

14 The text of this (shorter) version of the author's introduction to TSATF can be found in the *Southern Review,* n.s. 8 (Autumn 1972): 708–10; in André Bleikasten, William Faulkner's *"The Sound and the Fury": A Critical Casebook* (New York: Garland, 1982), 7–10; and in Arthur Kinney, *Critical Essays on William Faulkner: "The Sound and the Fury"* (Boston: G. K. Hall, 1982), 75–77.

15 For an interpretation of the reasons why Faulkner liked to end his novels with the evocation of a sound, see my conclusion.

Chapter Eleven: Outrage

1 Quoted (without reference) by Blotner, FAB, 634–35. Of the several translations of Homer's poem listed in *William Faulkner's Library—A Catalogue,* comp. with an introduction by Joseph Blotner (Charlottesville: University Press of Virginia, 1964), 80, only one, by S. H. Butcher and A. Lang, has the words of Faulkner's title, but it bears the inscription "1939" in Faulkner's hand (and the edition is dated 1935—too late for the author's use in this novel).

2 Trans. Sir William Marris, Oxford University Press, 1925.

3 "The Tell-Tale Heart" in *Edgar Allan Poe: Poetry and Tales,* ed. Patrick F. Quinn (New York, Library of America, 1984), 555.

4 "Preface, *Tales of the Grotesque and Arabesque*—1840," in *Edgar Allan Poe: Poetry and Tales,* 129.

5 The first to lay stress on the epic dimension of AILD was Valery Larbaud, whose preface to the French translation of the novel (Gallimard, 1934) is still untranslated into English; see also Carson McCullers, "The Russian Realists and Southern Literature," *Decision,* July 1941, reprinted in *The Mortgaged Heart* (Boston: Houghton Mifflin, 1971), 253–54; and Brooks's chapter, entitled "The Odyssey of the Bundrens," in *Yoknapatawpha,* 141–66.

6 *Macbeth,* 3, 2, 52.

7 Kateb Yacine, an Algerian novelist writing in French, has often said to me, in private conversations, that Faulkner meant a great deal for the third world writers, and there have been several dissertations comparing his best-known novel, *Nedjma* (Paris: Seuil, 1956), with Faulkner's work—particularly in AILD. The same can now be said of Latin American writers, Federico Garcia Marquéz first among them.

8 Two dominant features of baroque literature according to Jean Rousset.

9 Georges Poulet, "La *Nausée* de Sartre et le *Cogito* cartésien," *Studi Francesi,* 15 (September–December 1961): 452–62.

10 Michel Gresset, "Voyeur et voyant: essai sur les données et le mécanisme de l'imagination symboliste," *Nouvelle Revue Française* 14 (November 1966): 809–26.

11 FITU, 87, 113, 115, 207; LITG, 180, 222, 244.

12 In a letter to Harrison Smith dated October 1933, Faulkner writes that he has "another bee now, and a good title, I think: 'Requiem for a Nun.' It will be about a nigger woman. *It will be a little on the esoteric side, like* As I Lay Dying." SL, 75; my emphasis.

13 Jean-Louis Barrault, *Réflexions sur le théâtre* (Paris: Jacques Vautrain, 1949), 49.

14 See LITG, 243.

15 Giliane Morell, " 'Pourquoi ris-tu, Darl?'—ou le temps d'un regard," *Sud* 14/15 (1975): 132.

16 Ibid.

Chapter Twelve: Failure

1 See chapter 8 of this book.

2 Mark Van Doren, "A Story Written with Ether Not with Ink," *New York Herald Tribune Book Review,* 24 March 1935, 7, 3.

3 Compare with the last sentence of "Mississippi": "Loving all of it even while he had to hate some of it because he knows now that you dont love because: you love despite; not for the virtue, but despite of the faults." ESPL, 42–43.

4 See Robert Langbaum, *The Poetry of Experience* (New York: Norton, 1957), introduction: "Romanticism as a Modern Tradition."

5 *Flags,* chapter 4, 3. See chapter 8 of this book.

6 *Vocabulaire,* 86–89.

7 In an unpublished paper entitled "The Pastoral and the Poetics of Polymorphism," delivered at a Faulkner conference at San Diego State University, on 3 May 1986, I try to deal with the extraordinary exchanges of qualities between men and animals to be found in Faulkner's fiction.

8 Of particular interest here is the fact that *Sanctuary* and *Pylon* were Albert Camus' favorite Faulkner novels, according to his letter in the *Harvard Advocate* quoted in FACCE, 295.

9 In an unpublished study of the initial scene of the published version, a colleague of the university Paul Valéry of Montpellier, Claude Fleurdorge, arrives at the same conclusion.

10 See André Bleikasten, "La Terreur et la nausée," *Sud* 14/15 (1975).

11 Jean Paris's admirable analysis of Titian's "Allegory" in *L'Espace et le regard* (Paris: Seuil, 1965) might serve to study the triangular relationship between Temple, Popeye, and Red in *Sanctuary.*

12 See Lucien Goldmann, *Pour une sociologie du roman* (Paris: Gallimard, 1964) for a definition (after Georg Lukàcs) of the "problematic hero" as one "in quest of authentic values in a degraded world."

Chapter Thirteen: Dead End

1 The typography and punctuation of the quotations are those of the corrected text.

2 See Millgate's chapter on *Pylon* in *Achievement*.

3 Jean Duvignaud, *Spectacle et société* (Paris: Denoël/Gonthier, 1970), 43.

4 Duvignaud, 47.

5 See chapter 3, note 4, of this book.

6 Jean Baudrillard, "Fétichisme et idéologie: la réduction sémiologique," in "Objets du fétichisme," *Nouvelle revue de psychanalyse* 2 (Autumn 1970): 213–14.

7 Joyce McDougall, "Scène primitive et scénario pervers," *La Sexualité perverse* (Paris: Payot, 1972), 83–84.

8 Michel Gresset, "The Ordeal of Consciousness: Psychological Aspects of Evil in *The Sound and the Fury*," *Critical Essays on William Faulkner: The Compson Family*, ed. A. F. Kinney (Boston: G. K. Hall, 1982), 173–81.

9 In "An Odor of Verbena," Drusilla calls the two pistols "slender and invincible and fatal as the physical shape of love" (*The Unvanquished*, 273). I am indebted to Professor Polk for drawing my attention to this passage.

10 Yet another description of the "tieless casual."

11 *Pylon*, 194–201. In the restored text of the novel edited by Noel Polk for the Library of America, the whole passage occupies only one paragraph (907–12).

12 See chapter 7 of this book.

13 There could hardly be a more relevant piece of advice given to the reporter—or to any other Faulknerian idealist.

14 See how John Cowper Powys writes of the role played by the four Evangelists in *Finnegans Wake*: "the four old corpse-like Peeping Toms," *"Finnegans Wake," Obstinate Cymric* (Carmarthen, Wales: Druid Press, 1947), 20.

15 Reynolds Price, "The Posture of Worship," *Shenandoah* 19 (Spring 1968): 49–61; reprinted, slightly revised, as introduction to *Pylon* (New York: Signet, 1968), v–xvii.

16 François Pitavy, *"The Wild Palms*, ou la Jérusalem oubliée," chapter 6 of his unpublished dissertation, *William Faulkner romancier, 1929–1939* (Lille: Atelier de reproduction des thèses, 1981), p. 391.

Chapter Fourteen: The Metaphor of the Subject

1 Jean Paris, *L'Espace et le regard*, 40.

2 ". . . while he [Sutpen] was still playing the scene to the audience, behind him Fate, destiny, retribution, irony,—the stage manager, call him what you will—was already striking the set and dragging on the synthetic and spurious shadows and shapes of the next one" (AA, 72–73; CT, 87–88). This is by far the best quotation I can cite, since it

illustrates two of the things I have been trying to say: (a) that God has multiple, and relatively indifferent, names in Faulkner's fiction and (b) that the best name He can have is this, the stage manager, because it is perfectly true to the supreme law of Faulkner's imagination.

3 "In Holbein's picture I showed you at once . . . the singular object floating in the foreground, which is there to be looked at, in order to catch, I would almost say, *to catch in its trap,* the observer, that is to say, us. It is, in short, an obvious way, no doubt an exceptional one, and one due to some moment of reflection on the part of the painter, of showing us that, as subjects, we are literally called into the picture, and represented here as caught. . . . It reflects our own nothingness, in the figure of the death's head. It is a use, therefore, of the geometrical dimension of vision in order to capture the subject, an obvious relation with desire which, nevertheless, remains enigmatic." Jacques Lacan, FFCP, 92.

4 "Perhaps his one true subject is the irreparable; perhaps for him there is no question other than that of successfully crushing man" is the anonymous translator's version in FACCE, 273.

5 There is an imaginary quality, too, in Faulkner's assertion that "our tragedy today is a general and universal fear so long sustained. . . . There is only the question: When will I be blown up?" "Address upon Receiving the Nobel Prize for Literature," ESPL, 119.

6 Or from the blindness of Tiresias to the crippled *voyeur malgré lui* in *Rear Window.*

7 This is the starting point of Bleikasten in "La Terreur et la nausée."

8 "The Law in *Sanctuary* is an all-encompassing pair of eyes." Noel Polk, "Law in Faulkner's *Sanctuary*," *Mississippi College Law Review* 4 (Spring 1984): 243.

9 In his preface to *Logique du Pire* (Paris: Presses universitaires de France, 1971), Clément Rosset speaks of "anti-ecstasy."

10 Faulkner's phrase is also the title of a volume of posthumous essays by Gaston Bachelard, *Le Droit de rêver* (Paris: Presses universitaires de France, 1970). In the last of these essays the philosopher imagines that he is freed at last from the stings of the logical consciousness, and, writing what he dreams, he dreams what he writes: Is this not what, all told, Faulkner did, too?

Conclusion

1 Depending on whether one reads the episode in the novel or in the "Compson Appendix" as it was originally published by Malcolm Cowley in *The Portable Faulkner.*

2 I am using the title of Jean Starobinski's study of *Jean-Jacques Rousseau: la transparence et l'obstacle* (Paris: Gallimard, 1971).

3 Faulkner felt more and more restless and eager to travel in his late years: see Joseph Blotner, "Faulkner: Roving Ambassador," *International Educational and Cultural Exchange* (Summer 1966): 1–22.

4 See *Vivants Piliers,* 248–49. In this conclusion to the first part, entitled "Time and Destiny," of his two-part study of Faulkner, Mayoux distinguishes between three kinds of

liberty: the first is the possibility of liberty that lies in the denial of the fact of the irremediable, which is the idealist's choice; the second is, short of suicide, the withdrawal of the self and of the whole world, which is practically the liberty of despair; and last, there is a solution at once more noble and more typically Faulknerian, the author's favorite choice, that of the unvanquished.

5   Gaston Bachelard, *Le Droit de rêver* (Paris: P.U.F., 1970), 235.

6   See chapter 10 of this book, and my "Faulkner: Ontologie du discours," *Delta* 25 (November 1987).

7   Flannery O'Connor, "Some Aspects of the Grotesque in Southern Fiction," *Mystery and Manners,* ed. Sally and Robert Fitzgerald (New York: Farrar, Straus & Giroux, 1962), 44.

8   This is one of the many taped passages at the University of Virginia Library that the editors chose to leave out of FITU, where it would take place in session 32.

9   See chapter 8, note 18.

10 See John Matthews, "Faulkner and the Reproduction of History," in *Faulkner and History,* ed. Javier Coy and Michel Gresset (Salamanca: Ediciones Universidad de Salamanca, 1986), 51–62.

11 William Faulkner, *The Unvanquished* (New York: Random House, 1938), 293.

12 See Jacques Pothier, "Naissance d'un sujet collectif: Jefferson," RANAM 12 (1980): 48–63.

13 Interview with Jean Stein vanden Heuvel, LITG, 255.

14 John T. Matthews, *The Play of Faulkner's Language* (Ithaca, N.Y.: Cornell University Press, 1982), 9.

15 See my *Faulkner: Ontologie du discours.*

INDEX

Italic page numbers indicate full treatment of the topic.

About the Author

Michel Gresset is professor of American literature at the
Institut d'Anglais Charles V at the University of Paris VII.
He is editor of volume one of *William Faulkner: Oeuvres
romanesques* in the Bibliothèque de la Pléiade series and is
coeditor of *Faulkner and Idealism: Perspective from
Paris*,*Faulkner Between the Texts: Intertextuality in the
Works of William Faulkner, Faulkner and History,
Faulkner After the Nobel Prize,* and *The French Face of
Faulkner.* He has translated most of Faulkner's
posthumous works for the French publisher Gallimard and
has published many articles on Faulkner in French and
American literary magazines.

Library of Congress Cataloging-in-Publication Data
Gresset, Michel.
[Faulkner. English]
Fascination : Faulkner's fiction, 1919–1936 / Michel
Gresset ; adapted from the French by Thomas West.
p. cm.
Translation of: Faulkner.
Bibliography: p.
Includes index.
ISBN 0-8223-0811-8
1. Faulkner William, 1897–1962—Criticism and
interpretation. I. Title.
PS3511.A86Z7841413 1989
813'.52—dc19   88-16955